Contributions to Economics

More information about this series at http://www.springer.com/series/1262

Hanna Makhavikova

Determinants of FDI in Central and Eastern Europe

The Effects of Integration into the European Union

Springer

Hanna Makhavikova
Faculty of Economics and Management
Otto-von-Guericke University Magdeburg
Magdeburg, Germany

ISSN 1431-1933 ISSN 2197-7178 (electronic)
Contributions to Economics
ISBN 978-3-030-06318-4 ISBN 978-3-319-91878-5 (eBook)
https://doi.org/10.1007/978-3-319-91878-5

Printed on acid-free paper

This Springer imprint is published by the registered company Springer International Publishing AG part of Springer Nature.
The registered company address is: Gewerbestrasse 11, 6330 Cham, Switzerland

Preface

Since the dissolution of the Soviet Union, the transitional economies of Central and Eastern Europe (CEE) have experienced a unique type of political and economic change in modern times. While the transition process of CEE has been characterised by both success and disappointment, continuously increasing foreign direct investment (FDI) inflows have been seen as a potential catalyst for the economic changes evident within these countries over the last 25 years. Therefore, the question on FDI has been chosen deliberately as a key aspect of this research.

In this regard, analysing the experiences of the leading CEE economies is a worthwhile pursuit for other countries looking to correct their key economic measures.

However, more than two decades on from the beginning of the transition of former centrally planned economies in Europe, it is still difficult to identify the key factors attracting foreign investors. This is because these countries' respective transitional courses began with a different economic potential, disparate policies and resource endowments.

Moreover, in the early 1990s, parallel to the transition process, post-soviet countries started integrating dynamically into the world economy and the EU in particular. An important facet of European economic integration was the development of a free-trade area in Central and Eastern Europe that improved market accessibility. These forces significantly affected the strategies firms chose in order to supply markets in CEE.

As integration with the EU can be viewed as a determining element of the operating business environment, and may directly influence the level of FDI flow, the role of integration in encouraging FDI is emphasised within this book.

This book, *Determinants of FDI in Central and Eastern Europe: The Effects of Integration with the European Union*, aims to provide the reader with theoretical and empirical analysis of FDI inflows in CEE after closer integration in the European Union.

It covers a range of subject matter, from the analysis of trends and patterns of FDI inflows in CEE and in-depth study of EU accession process to analytical modelling, empirical estimations and robustness tests of the results. We sincerely hope that students, academicians and policymakers with an interest in the eastern EU enlargement and its influence on FDI will find the analysis in the book valuable and illuminating.

This book is the author's dissertation project. The author would like to express her sincere gratitude to Prof. Dr. Dr. h c. Karl-Heinz Paqué and Prof. Dr. Dr. h. c. em. Gerhard Schwödiauer for their professional advice, constructive critiques, patient guidance and willingness to generously invest their time towards this research.

The author would like also to express her special thanks to her husband and parents for their valuable support and encouragement.

Nuremberg, Germany Hanna Makhavikova

A Note on Terminology

The acronym CEEC (which stands for Central and East European countries) includes here 19 countries: Albania, Bosnia and Herzegovina, Bulgaria, Croatia, the Czech Republic, Estonia, Georgia, Hungary, Latvia, Lithuania, Moldova, Montenegro, Poland, Romania, Serbia, Slovakia, Slovenia, TFYR Macedonia and Ukraine. The number of countries may differ from the definitions of international organisations which include some extra countries or do not include some countries mentioned above.

Central Europe (CE) refers to the first-wave integration round countries as the Czech Republic, Estonia, Hungary, Latvia, Lithuania, Poland, Slovakia and Slovenia. Southeast Europe (SEE) includes the second-wave countries as Bulgaria, Romania and Croatia, which joined the EU in the sixth round.

WB stands for the Western Balkans (Albania, Bosnia and Herzegovina, Montenegro, Serbia and TFYR Macedonia). GMU is for Georgia, Moldova and Ukraine (the former members of the USSR).

Contents

Chapter 1
Introduction

1.1 Problem Statement

After the dissolution of the Soviet Union, the post-Soviet countries in Central and Eastern Europe experienced a unique type of political and economic change in modern times—a transition from socialism to capitalism, which was both a political and an economic process.

All CEE countries had similar goals: adoption of the market economic system, acceleration of economic growth and integration into the world economy. The most important transition actions were implemented in the 1990s. However, not all countries have followed the same development trajectory. Whereas, Central European countries quickly recovered from the decline in output and prepared for accession to the European Union, the Western Balkans and former Soviet republics, excluding the Baltic, suffered a prolonged drop in output that lasted throughout most of the 1990s and early 2000s (Roland and Verdier 2003).

One of the primary factors in CEE economic development over the last two decades has been the continuously increasing amount of foreign direct investment (FDI). The inflow of foreign investment is widely considered to be an important channel for restructuring state-owned enterprises, creating competition in the markets, and providing important inflows of capital, technology, and business skills across national borders. For transitional economies, without adequate sources of domestic savings, attracting foreign direct investment became the only precondition for future economic growth. This implies that foreign direct investment (FDI) may be one of the keys in the transformation of former centrally-planned economies.

Some transitional economies have attracted significant amounts of FDI in the brief period of time since the collapse of the centralised systems. However, as shown in Fig. 1.1, the inflows to most countries in the region were unstable during this timespan. Moreover, some countries were much more successful than others.

H. Makhavikova, *Determinants of FDI in Central and Eastern Europe*, Contributions to Economics, https://doi.org/10.1007/978-3-319-91878-5_1

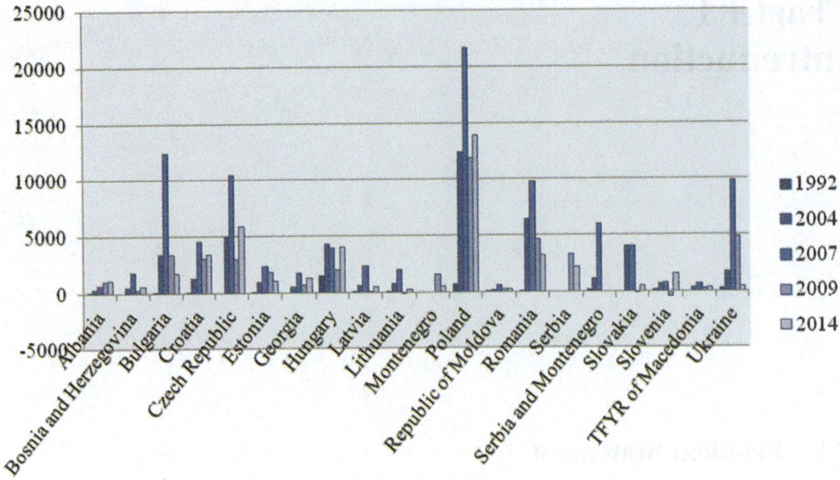

Fig. 1.1 FDI inflows in CEE in 1992, 2004, 2007, 2009, 2014 (in millions US dollars). *Source*: Author's illustration based on the data from UNCTAD (2016)

Matching the real-world developments, an extensive economic literature has been developed in recent years that attempts to explain the nature, causes and consequences of FDI.

However, more than two decades after the beginning of the transition of former centrally-planned economies in Europe, it is still difficult to identify the most important factors that attracted foreign investors, because each country had its own transition course with different economic potential, policies, and resource endowments. Moreover, parallel with the transition process, the post-Soviet countries started dynamically integrating into the world economy and in particular into the EU. EU membership was the strongest guarantee for these countries to achieve recovery of their economies, higher growth rates, and a stable business environment.

With the integration of the CEECs into the EU and the resulting gradual reduction of intraregional trade barriers, the CEECs began to attract foreign investors interested in installing low-cost production facilities and in serving not only local CEE markets, but also neighbouring countries, thus becoming export-platforms (See Neary 2002; Ekholm et al. 2007).

As integration with the EU can be viewed as a determining element of the operating business environment, which may directly influence the rate of FDI flows, the question of the role of integration in encouraging FDI has been deliberately chosen as a key aspect of this research. This is the subject that we explore in this book.

1.2 Literature Survey

On the growing importance of FDI in the world economy, especially in transitional countries, a vast empirical literature has been developed on FDI determinants. This is not surprising, since foreign capital has played an important role in most countries during the 23-year transition to market economies.

Many studies have sought to identify the determinants of FDI inflows and investigate the experience of successful CEE countries. Some have focused on the key features of FDI in Eastern Europe—its volume, forms, origins, destination by economic activity, and case studies (Meyer 1998; Lankes and Venables 1996; Tondel 2001; Shiells 2003). Others have been based on econometric research (Gelb et al. 1999; Resmini 2000; Kalotay and Hunya 2000; Janicki and Wunnava 2004; Botrić and Škuflić 2006). Still, after more than two decades of "transition" of former centrally planned economies, it remains difficult to identify the most important attractors of foreign investment, since each country started with different economic potential, policies, and resource endowments.

On the whole, the effects of regional economic integration on FDI inflows have received more empirical attention than theoretical analysis. That is why in this book we present a theoretical model that helps us organise our thinking about the FDI determinants in CEE after closer integration into the EU.

1.3 Scope and Constraints

This book contributes to the literature by: (1) covering all Central and East European members and candidate countries where there exists a large discrepancy between economic development levels in attracting FDI; (2) investigating a period over 20 years where FDI inflows reached their peak and bottom level during the financial crisis; (3) developing a theoretical model that explains the FDI patterns in a simplified world; (4) taking into a consideration a broader set of integration variables.

An overview of the existing literature shows that the most of the studies aimed at an estimation of the effects of the EU accession on FDI inflows consider almost the same group of countries—the ten EU-accession countries from CEE (Bulgaria, Czech Republic, Hungary, Latvia, Lithuania, Poland, Romania, Slovak Republic, Slovenia, Estonia). These findings are now questionable, because any current integration of the CEE countries within the EU includes an additional nine countries, which differ in many macroeconomic characteristics and liberalisation progress from those original accession countries.

In our book we include both the new members of the EU—Bulgaria, Croatia, Czech Republic, Hungary, Latvia, Lithuania, Poland, Romania, Slovak Republic, Slovenia, and Estonia—and EU candidate countries—Albania, Bosnia and Herzegovina, Macedonia, Montenegro, Serbia, Ukraine, Moldova and Georgia.

Another limitation of previous econometric studies is the limited timespan used in their analyses, ranging from only 3 to 10 years. This can be partly justified by both the limited time period since the start of the transition, the opening up of the CEECs to FDI, and data availability constraints. This limitation, however, makes it difficult to determine conclusions. Our studied time period spans 23 years, 1992–2015, and includes the entire period of EU accession, the financial crisis, and the recovery.

The most important limitation of the previous research is the absence of a complex study that includes all steps and types of integration with the EU. Previous studies investigated either the FTA or accession to the EU. In our book, we indicate three types of collaboration according to the tightness of relations: the free-trade agreements (trade liberalisation), Association Agreements (regulate economic, political, social and cultural aspects), and the EU accessions.

As we will further observe, there is considerable empirical evidence that economic integration has dramatically changed the patterns of foreign direct investments (FDI). However, so far these relations have scarcely been theoretically explored. Moreover, the existing theoretical models, for the most part, have been not been tested empirically. In our book, we develop a theoretical model based on the findings of Neary (2002). It explains the change of the choice of location for foreign investors connected with the removal of intra-regional trade barriers. We empirically confirm our theoretical assumptions by an empirical analysis based on the panel dataset of FDI in 19 Central and Eastern European countries (CEECs) from 1992 to 2015.

1.4 Methodology

As far as the role of the European Union in the mobilisation of FDI is still uncertain, in our book we will examine the ability of 19 CEE transition countries to attract foreign direct investment. In such a context, we adopt a modified version of the Neary (2002) model. We construct a model where firms are making strategic location decisions in choosing how to serve their target markets: in other words, making strategic choices between export and FDI.

We begin with the examination of three scenarios: (1) a symmetric situation where external and internal trade barriers are the same, (2) forming of the region with preferential trade costs, (3) abolition of internal trade barriers. Finally, we provide a model of FDI locations in all three situations.

Our theoretical model aims to provide theoretical evidence concerning the hypothesis that FDI may be sensible not only for traditional FDI location determinants but also for the integration of specific factors.

In our model, FDI appears in two cases: to supply each country separately from local plants, and to establish an export platform to supply all members of the integration union. In the second case, multinational corporations move their production to countries that have lower production costs and better access to larger markets.

In the final analysis, we want to have an empirical model that explains FDI location in CEE. To measure the effect of EU integration we include market access variables that measure the market size of the neighbouring countries for different integration agreements.

We also include nine integration variables, namely membership in the FTAs, the signing and entering into force of the Association Agreements, the application for EU membership, the granting of candidate status, the start of negotiations, the signing of the Accession Treaty with the EU, membership in the EU, and Euro area membership, to measure the institutional improvement associated with EU integration.

The empirical data is taken from various sources, mostly the World Bank, European Bank for Reconstruction and Development, International Monetary Fund, the United Nations Economic Commission for Europe (UNECE), the United Nations Conference on Trade and Development (UNCTAD 2016), as well as publications on the subject.

Given the high quality of data that is used, both fixed effects (FE) and random effects (RE) models are employed in order to compare the results of various estimation methods. Relying on the Hausman test, a FE model is used to test various variable combinations. The factors are calculated both for the whole region and for sub-regions (Central European countries, South-East Europe, the Western Balkans and a group of countries that in 2014 signed the Association Agreements).

However, it is difficult to make precise forecasts and policy suggestions. Still, it is concluded that besides the importance of traditional factors, the impact of integration variables in the region should not be neglected.

1.5 Aims and Objectives

The aim of the book is to explain the determinants of FDI inflows that enabled leading CEE countries to succeed in the mobilisation and placement of FDI. We also want to assess the impact of broad regional integration, membership in FTA and the EU, and the signing of Association Agreements on countries' ability to generate higher FDI inflows.

Hence, the main motivation for this study is to provide empirical evidence for the identification of determinants in attracting FDI for EU members and potential candidate members. The inclusion of candidate countries in the sample is an important feature of this study for the reason that these countries have strategic, economic, and geopolitical importance for foreign investors.

The objectives of the research are: (1) to measure the amount and characteristics of FDI inflows in the CEE countries; (2) to summarise the theory on the determinants of FDI; (3) to outline a conceptual theoretical model; (4) to investigate empirically the key factors of investment attractiveness that determine the location of FDI in CEE; (5) to explore the effect of integration with the European Union on FDI inflows; (6) to identify how the experience of FDI mobilisation in leading CEE countries can be effectively applied in other countries in the region.

1.6 Structure of the Book

The book is organised as follows.

The second chapter provides basic information on the subject. After providing the basic concepts of FDI in the first section of the second chapter, we analyse the key characteristics of FDI inflows to the region in the second section. Here we consider the FDI inflow trends in the region. We mostly explore the reports of international organisations, such as the United Nations Organisation, the World Bank, OECD, the International Monetary Fund etc. In the third part we provide an overview of the main empirical literature on FDI in CEE and its main limitations. In the fourth part we examine the gradual integration of CEE countries into the European Union, changes that occurred in the political and economic domain that stimulated an increase in FDI inflows.

The third chapter considers the theoretical framework. We begin with an examination of the related literature in the first section. In the second section we consider three scenarios in similar countries. In the third section of the chapter, we investigate heterogeneous countries with different market sizes, external tariffs, labour and installation costs. And in the fourth section, we derive a FDI model.

In the fourth chapter we go on to test the hypotheses about FDI in the CEECs empirically. The first empirical part of the chapter describes the factors of the empirical model. In the second part, its robustness is checked, and in the third results are discussed. In the fourth section, we made an attempt to identify the main differences of FDI's impact on different sub-regions and time periods.

The conclusions in the fifth chapter point to the main results and contributions. We also discuss the book's limitations and areas for further research.

References

Botrić V, Škuflić L (2006) Main determinants of foreign direct investment in the southeast European countries. Transit Stud Rev 13(2):359–377

Ekholm K, Forslid R, Markusen J (2007) Export-platform foreign direct investment. J Eur Econ Assoc 5(4):776–795 http://EconPapers.repec.org/RePEc:tpr:jeurec:v:5:y:2007:i:4:p:776-795

Gelb A, Melo M, Denizer C, Tenev S (1999) Circumstance and choice: the role of initial conditions and policies in transition economies. The World Bank

Janicki HP, Wunnava PV (2004) Determinants of foreign direct investment: empirical evidence from EU accession candidates. Appl Econ 36(5):505–509

Kalotay K, Hunya G (2000) Privatization and FDI in Central and Eastern Europe. Transl Corp 9 (1):39–66

Lankes H-P, Venables AJ (1996) Foreign direct investment in economic transition: the changing pattern of investments. Econ Transit 4(2):331–347

Meyer K (1998) Direct investment in economies in transition. University, Dissertation – London. Elgar, Cheltenham. ISBN: 978 1 85898 736 1

Neary JP (2002) Foreign direct investment and the single market. Manchester School 70 (3):291–314 https://ideas.repec.org/a/bla/manchs/v70y2002i3p291-314.html

Resmini L (2000) The Determinants of foreign direct investment in the CEECs: new evidence from sectoral patterns. Econ Transit 8(3):665–689

Roland G, Verdier T (2003) Law enforcement and transition. Eur Econ Rev 47(4):669–685

Shiells CR (2003) FDI and the investment climate in the CIS countries. http://www.imf.org/external/pubs/cat/longres.aspx?sk=16950

Tondel L (2001) Foreign direct investment during transition: determinants and patterns in Central and Eastern Europe and the former Soviet Union. Chr. Michelsen Institute, Development Studies and Human Rights, Bergen. ISBN: 9788290584936

Chapter 2
Theoretical Foundations

2.1 Concepts of FDI

2.1.1 Forms of Foreign Investment

The definition of a certain capital flow or asset as "foreign direct investment" bestows certain rights on foreign investors and thus facilitates foreign investment. The definition also raises concerns. Therefore, a detailed examination of the types, forms, functions and components of FDI investment is required. We start from the investigation of international investments in general.

International investments are a type of international activity that implies the purchase of a financial product or other item of value with an expectation of favourable future returns. There are three main types of international investment, depending on the functions and aims of investing: direct, portfolio and credit.

Foreign direct investment (FDI) is the main form of export of private entrepreneurial capital that allows for the establishment of efficient controls and permits direct control for the investor. There are many definitions of FDI, but all aim to encompass a home country's desire to obtain and manage an asset in a host country. FDI occurs when a firm invests directly in production or other facilities in a foreign country. At the same time, the share of an investor in the equity or share capital should be at least 10%.

The International Monetary Fund defines foreign direct investment as follows:

> [. . .] the category of international investment that reflects the objective of a resident entity in one economy obtaining a lasting interest in an enterprise resident in another economy. (The resident entity is the direct investor and the enterprise is the direct investment enterprise.) The lasting interest implies the existence of a long-term relationship between the direct investor and the enterprise and a significant degree of influence by the investor on the management of the enterprise (International Monetary Fund 2005, p.86, art. 359)

> [. . .] Although the 10 per cent criterion is specified in the Manual, some countries may choose to allow for two qualifications that involve a degree of subjective judgment. First, if the direct investor owns less than 10 percent (or none) of the ordinary shares or voting power

H. Makhavikova, *Determinants of FDI in Central and Eastern Europe*,
Contributions to Economics, https://doi.org/10.1007/978-3-319-91878-5_2

> of the enterprise but has an effective voice in management, the enterprise may be included. Second, if the investor owns 10 per cent or more but does not have an effective voice in management, the enterprise may be excluded. Although the application of these two qualifications is not recommended in this Manual, countries that apply such qualifications should identify the aggregate value of transactions in order to facilitate international comparability (International Monetary Fund 2005, p.86, art. 363).

This definition is also consistent with the OECD Benchmark Definition (OECD 2009) as well as the UNCTAD definition of FDI (UNCTAD 2003).

> [...]a category of cross-border investment made by a resident in one economy (the direct investor) with the objective of establishing a lasting interest in an enterprise (the direct investment enterprise) that is resident in an economy other than that of the direct investor. The motivation of the direct investor is a strategic long-term relationship with the direct investment enterprise to ensure a significant degree of influence by the direct investor in the management of the direct investment enterprise. The "lasting interest" is evidenced when the direct investor owns at least 10% of the voting power of the direct investment enterprise. Direct investment may also allow the direct investor to gain access to the economy of the direct investment enterprise which it might otherwise be unable to do (OECD 2009).

Thus, according to OECD and the IMF, a direct investor acquires 10% or more of the ordinary shares or voting power of the enterprise; they therefore play a significant role in influencing the management of the enterprise. Although the 10% criterion is specified, subjective involvement is implied in some countries. For example, Turkey does not use the 10% threshold rule. All enterprises with foreign ownership are treated as FDI, regardless of the %age of ownership of non-residents. Israel applies a 10% criteria for traded enterprises only, whereas all non-traded enterprises with foreign ownership are treated as FDI, regardless of the percentage of ownership by non-residents (International Monetary Fund and Organisation for Economic Co-operation and Development 2010).

If the direct investor owns less than 10% of the ordinary shares of the voting power of the enterprise, but has an effective voice in management, the investment might be included as FDI. On the contrary, if the investor owns 10% or more of the ordinary shares or voting power, but does not have an effective voice in management, the investment might not be included as FDI.

Thus, FDI is not just a transfer of ownership, as it usually involves the transfer of factors complementary to capital, including management, technology and organisational skills.

The second form of international investment is **portfolio investments**. There are several characteristics that tend to define the nature of foreign portfolio investment. Typically, portfolio investments are defined as transactions involving debt or equity securities, other than those included in direct investment. They usually do not imply the management of the asset, but purely financial reasons, often on a short-term basis. According to OECD (2009) "*[...]The objectives of direct investment are different from those of portfolio investment whereby investors do not generally expect to influence the management of the enterprise*". Moreover, control of technology, management, and even crucial inputs can confer *de facto* control. Despite the fact that portfolio investments do not provide investors with a controlling interest in the issuing company, investors have two channels of possible income: changes in the market price of the asset and share of profits (dividends).

The third form of international investment is **credit investments** that represent loans from foreign banks, international corporations, individual governments, international financial institutions, as well as individuals and companies to finance investment projects in the recipient country. Long-term investments and their exploitation in real assets are distinctive features of this form of international crediting (OECD 2009).

In practice, the line between different types of investment is sometimes difficult to draw. In some circumstances, foreign investors may use their assets as collateral to borrow from local capital markets and use the proceeds for hedging or speculation. Conversely, venture capitalists can take a significant management interest in a venture without a large shareholding—and their activity, conventionally defined as portfolio investment, is similar to direct investment. But for the bulk of investment flows, a distinction between FDI and non-FDI is possible (Wacker 2013).

Foreign direct investments are a more preferable form of international investment for importing countries, but their implementation is riskier than credit and portfolio investments. The risks occur because investors tend to lose the opportunity for rapid withdrawal from the host country due to the low liquidity of the invested capital. In addition, foreign direct investment presupposes longer investment launching.

2.1.2 Functions and Types of FDI

FDI plays a significant role in the modern global economy, realising its functions through a variety of forms and types. Taking a more practical view of FDI, it is possible to distinguish various types of **investments** based on such issues as the direction of flows, strategic motives, economic categories, time periods and launching times, components, and modes of entry and ownership, among others.

We should differentiate between FDI **flows** and **stocks**. The flow of FDI refers to the amount of FDI undertaken over a given time period (e.g. a year). Whereas the stock of FDI refers to the total accumulated value of foreign-owned assets at a given time (which takes into account possible divestment along the way).

Investors are the **subjects of investment activity** that decide to invest and realise their decisions. According to the OECD, a direct investor could be classified to any sector of the economy and could be any of the following: an individual, a group of related individuals, an incorporated or unincorporated enterprise, a public or private enterprise, a group of related enterprises, a government body, an estate, trust or other societal organisation, or any combination of the above (OECD 2009).

In principle, all FDI can be made by private or public institutions and by individual or corporate actors. Individual investors may engage in the acquisition of controlling shares in foreign companies, though it is not a common occurrence, but, in practice, most FDI is made by the corporate sector. Therefore TNCs are responsible for most investments worldwide.

The major distinction between the different types of foreign investment is between **outward FDI** and **inward FDI**. Investing abroad, a foreign investor makes an investment, which in relation to the national economy is called "outflows". In the host country, the recipient country, these investments are considered foreign (or "inflows"). Negative flows generally indicate disinvestments or the impact of substantial reimbursements of inter-company loans (OECD 2009).

Each country's central statistical office collects data for both FDI inflows and outflows. The destination country of the investment is referred to as the host country. Information on FDI flows comes from the balance of payment statistics of the various countries. The data records the year-to-year value of investments on the basis of the balance of payments statistics, therefore on the basis of records of currency movements for investment purposes. This means that the records are made on the basis of how the investment is funded. At a global level, the total value of inward and outward data should coincide. They usually do not for statistical reasons related to a lack of consistency in the methods of measurement and data collection in various countries (UNCTAD 2009a).

Strategically FDI comes in three types: horizontal (where the company carries out the same activities abroad as at home), vertical (when different stages of activities are added abroad, they can be either suppliers or consumers of an investing company), and conglomerate (where an unrelated business is added abroad). The last type of FDI leads to the internationalisation and diversification of economic activity (Shenkar and Luo 2004).

International investments as an **economic category** represent capital placement by economic agents in some foreign tangible, intangible and financial assets with the aim to generate some benefits. FDI as well may consist of the different **components.** They are equity capital, reinvested earnings and other capital (mainly intra-company loans) (UNCTAD 2016a, Methodological Note).

Equity capital is the foreign direct investor's purchase of a foreign company's shares. Equity capital comprises of equity in branches, all shares in subsidiaries and associates, and other contributions of equity. Shares, stocks, participations, depositary receipts or similar documents usually evidence ownership of equity (Wacker 2013).

Reinvested earnings comprise the investor's share of earnings (dividends) reinvested in additional shares. This type of investment refers to direct investment because the earnings of the direct investment enterprise are deemed to be the income of the direct investor, whether they are reinvested in the enterprise or remitted to the direct investor.

The short-term and long-term credits between incorporated or unincorporated enterprises (parent enterprises, and subsidiaries, branches and associates) refer to intra-company loans. The intra-company debt transactions are also a part of FDI.

As countries do not always collect data for each of those components, the data on FDI is not fully comparable across countries. In particular, data on reinvested earnings, the collection of which depends on company surveys, is often unreported by many countries. Overall, equity investments dominate among these three main forms of FDI.

Foreign direct investors may also obtain an effective voice in the management of another business entity through means other than acquiring an equity stake or an effective voice. These are **non-equity forms of investment**, and they include subcontracting, management contracts, turnkey arrangements, franchising, licensing, leasing and product sharing (Shenkar and Luo 2004).

The manner in which a firm chooses to enter a foreign market through FDI is referred to as **entry mode**. Entry mode examples include greenfield investment, cross-border mergers and acquisitions (Chaudhuri and Mukhopadhyay 2014).

A Greenfield investment is the setting up of a brand-new company in another country. Mergers and acquisitions are also called "Brownfield" investments. They occur when a foreign firm buys out a share or the entire company in a host country.

When a foreign firm decides the entry mode, its choice is usually influenced by the host country and industry-specific factors. Thus, Greenfield investments appear in high-technology industries and in countries that usually had no such production facilities before foreign investors arrived.

The choice mergers and acquisitions may be influenced by attitudes toward takeovers, conditions in capital markets, policies, privatisation, regional integration, currency risks, and the role played by intermediaries (e.g. investment banks) actively seeking acquisition opportunities and taking the initiative in making deals.

FDI—whether by Greenfield or mergers and acquisitions—leads to international production. The official statistics on FDI do not usually distinguish between Greenfield and mergers and acquisitions' FDI. Databases on mergers and acquisitions are usually supplied by private research businesses that collect the data on the basis of stock exchange selling and purchasing deals. They are not directly comparable with overall FDI data; this is a source of difficulty for researchers in the field.

In accordance with the **period and launching time** of international investments, long-term, permanent, medium-term and short-term investments can be distinguished. According to the **risk involved**, international investments are classified into low-risk and high-risk (speculative) investments.

FDI can also be classified by the **functions** they possess. The main functions of FDI indicate their role in the global economy (Estrin and Meyer 2011):

(1) capital building—is shown in the creation of the global capital stocks, i.e. international investments favour the increase of savings in the world;
(2) stimulating economic growth—means that investment has a direct influence on production, GDP, R&D and employment growth, both in the home and host countries;
(3) sanitising—implies that international investments contribute to the ousting of less efficient national and international companies, which leads to a more efficient reallocation of resources in the global economy;
(4) innovation—is shown in new technologies and improved management practices both in international companies and national firms, as a result of the demonstration effect and the use of vertically integrated communications;
(5) structure-building—means the sectoral and regional structure of economic changes by the international investment market;

(6) benchmarking—shows that international investment flows and stocks signal the effectiveness of economic policy in a country;
(7) integration—implies that international investment creates prerequisites for the integration of different economic systems.

Thereby, FDI have the following positive effects:

(1) Foreign investors **bring in new technologies** at a lower costs, experience and training of employees. In addition, advanced the technologies and skills embodied in FDI are transmitted to local firms, inducing them to improve their efficiency through learning by watching; i.e. by learning and interacting with foreign firms (Bengoa and Sanchez-Robles 2003). After observing an innovation adapted to local conditions, local entrepreneurs may recognise their feasibility, and thus strive to imitate them. As local businesses observe existing users, information about new technologies and business practices is diffused, uncertainty is reduced, and imitation increases.
(2) They possess a world-reputed brand name, which can **promote exports**, and get export credits from the cheapest source in the international financial market. Investors have links with foreign suppliers, distributors and consumers, that results in an increase of exports (Altenburg 2000; UNCTAD 1999, Chap. 8).
(3) They **employ a labour force**, which helps to raise the income of employed people, which in turn raises demand and industrial production in the country. It is called "crowding-in effect" of FDI (Dunning 1993, Chap. 13; UNCTAD 1999, Chap. 9).
(4) FDI contributes to **human capital formation**. Multinationals often offer additional training and professional development opportunities for local employees. Moreover, in a TNC workers collaborate with foreign headquarters and subsidiaries, thus, obtaining higher qualifications and a better experience. Trained local employees may further move to locally owned firms or set-up own businesses. Even if only a few employees move, those who do make a substantive contribution to local business (Altenburg 2000).
(5) FDI helps either **import substitution or export promotion**. The host country is able to produce items that were being imported earlier. FDI is able to augment exports because foreign investors bring in knowledge of export mechanics and of foreign markets.
(6) They **strengthen the national currency and cause the growth of national reserves**. Since FDI is not a financial liability, it does not contribute to an increase in external debt. In addition, it is steadier than portfolio investment (UNCTAD 1999, Chap. 6).
(7) Foreign investors **improve the infrastructure of a country** by investing in sectors such as basic economic infrastructure, social infrastructure, financial markets, and marketing.

Thus, FDI in Central and Eastern Europe has become a policy target and an instrument of macroeconomic development. With the accession of lower-income members to the EU, FDI has become perhaps the leading means of effecting economic development and European integration.

2.1.3 The Factors of FDI

There are two groups of **factors** that influence the intensity of FDI: microeconomic and macroeconomic factors.

Microeconomic factors push a company to enter a foreign market in the form of FDI. These factors are quite diverse and include:

(1) disposal financial resources;
(2) access to cheap capital sources;
(3) company's business strategy;
(4) Global market position goal.

These factors are often a part of a corporate strategy of a company and as such are often not observable.

Macroeconomic factors attract foreign investors to a particular country. They include government policy (tax, trade, monetary policies, etc.) and business cycle factors (GDP growth, the dynamics of exports).

Dunning (1993) classified FDI macro determinants according to the four types of FDI motivation.

First, market-seeking investment is undertaken to sustain existing markets or to exploit new markets. Because the reason for this type of investment is to better serve a local market by local production, the market size and market growth of the host economy are the main factors that encourage market-seeking FDI. The impediments in serving the market, such as tariffs and transport costs, also encourage this type of FDI. Apart from market size and trade restrictions, companies may engage in market-seeking investment when their main suppliers or customers have set up foreign production facilities and, in order to maintain their business, they must follow them overseas (Dunning 1993).

Second, when firms invest abroad to acquire resources not available in the home country, the investment is called resource seeking. Unlike market-seeking FDI, this type of FDI is intended to serve not only the local market but also the home and third country markets. Availability of natural resources, cheap and skilled labour, and physical infrastructure are the main attractors of resource-seeking FDI (Dunning 1993).

Third, the investment is rationalised or efficiency seeking when the firm can gain from the common governance of geographically-dispersed activities in the presence of economies of scale and scope. Efficiency-seeking investors aim to take advantage of different factor endowments, cultures, institutional arrangements, economic systems and policies, and market structures by concentrating production in a limited number of locations to supply multiple markets (Dunning 1993).

Finally, firms may increasingly use FDI to obtain strategic assets, both tangible and intangible, which may be critical to their long-term strategy. Strategic asset-seeking investments may include the brands, human capital, distribution networks, etc. that enable a firm to compete in a host and foreign markets. Alternatively, strategic asset-seeking investments may not involve strengthening the firm's position, but rather weakening the competitive position of its competitors (Dunning 1993).

More general factors may also affect FDI inflows: political stability, a sound macroeconomic framework, welcoming attitudes to foreign investment, adequate skills, low business transaction costs, good infrastructure and the like.

TNCs decide to invest abroad by looking at both push (microeconomic) and pull (macroeconomic) factors. But pull and push factors are not sufficient to explain the final choice of host locations: an understanding of TNCs' motives, strategies and context is required. Moreover, to understand FDI one must first understand the causes for preference of FDI as a mode of entry and the location of the investments. That is why it is important to identify the main trends in FDI theory and highlight how these theories were developed, the motivations that led to the need for new approaches to enrich economic theory of FDI.

2.2 Patterns of FDI in Central and Eastern Europe

In the 1990s, the fall of the Soviet Union and the opening up of the Central and Eastern European countries (CEECs), as well as their transition to market economies, created a particularly favourable area for the international expansion of multinational corporations and the rise of FDI in these economies.

In this chapter, we describe the patterns of FDI over a 23 year period, 1992–2015. For convenience, we divide the studied time period into four shorter periods: 1992–1998, 1999–2004, 2005–2008, 2008–2015,—in accordance with the EU announcements and waves of integration.

2.2.1 1992–1998

The economic transition process began in the late 1980s with the Balcerowicz reforms in Poland and structural reforms in Hungary. The end of the Soviet bloc as an integration union was in January 1990 on the meeting of COMECON in Sofia, the Soviet Union itself collapsed after the signing of the declaration of the Soviet of the Republics of the Supreme Soviet of the Soviet Union (Declaration № 142-H 1991; Stern 1997).

In the early 1990s, policy changes in the Central and Eastern Europe countries were very dramatic. The openness of the economies made the countries in the region quite attractive for foreign investors because of their large domestic markets with relatively high purchasing power and consumer demand, as well as considerable business opportunities, high skill levels, low wages, low production costs, and proximity to the EU market.

During the 1990s, virtually all countries in Central and Eastern Europe had passed legislation encouraging FDI, and several countries had passed privatisation laws. An important step in 1990 was the allowing of 100% foreign ownership of enterprises in the USSR and permission of profit repatriation. Policies involving privatisation and deregulation opened to all competitors markets that had previously been restricted to government-owned or regulated domestic enterprises. The Visegrad Countries adopted separate commercial legislation dealing with monopolies, bankruptcies, securities, stock exchanges etc. Meanwhile, the evolution of the legislative framework was less advanced in SEE and CIS (UNCTAD 1994).

In the 1990s, inflows of FDI into CEE was unevenly distributed (See Fig. 2.1). Some of the countries in the region became relatively large recipients of FDI, while others were not yet significant host countries. Moreover, inflows were unstable and fluctuating (see Fig. 2.2) due to the continuous disintegration of the region (the dissolution of Czechoslovakia in 1993), wars (Kosovo conflict) and economic crises, such as the financial crisis in Russia in 1998.

FDI strongly favoured the Czech and Slovak republics, and Hungary and Poland, because they made progress with economic reforms, and were close to the EC, with which they concluded association agreements. It was also a reflection of the different speed and success of these countries in approaching stable, market-oriented, investment-conducive environments through privatisation and the establishment of the market system.

Foreign investors were mainly attracted to Poland, the leading recipient in the region, by its large domestic market. Hungary was the second largest FDI recipient and during this time attracted $20,7 billion (UNCTAD 2016b). Only in Slovakia was good economic performance not coupled with a significant increase in FDI inflows.

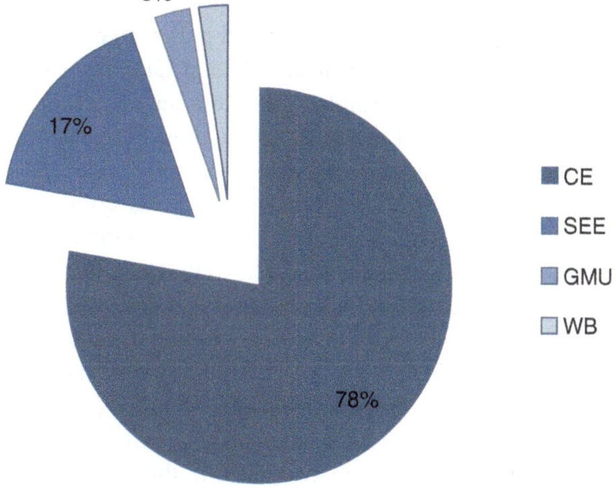

Fig. 2.1 Inward FDI stock, by sub-regions (1998), %. *Source*: Estimated by the author based on UNCTAD (2014a). *Note*: CE includes the Czech Republic, Estonia, Hungary, Lithuania, Latvia, Slovenia and Slovakia, SEE includes Bulgaria, Romania and Croatia, GMU covers Georgia, Moldova and Ukraine, WB is for Albania, Bosnia and Herzegovina, Macedonia, Serbia and Montenegro. Serbia and Montenegro is represented as one single state

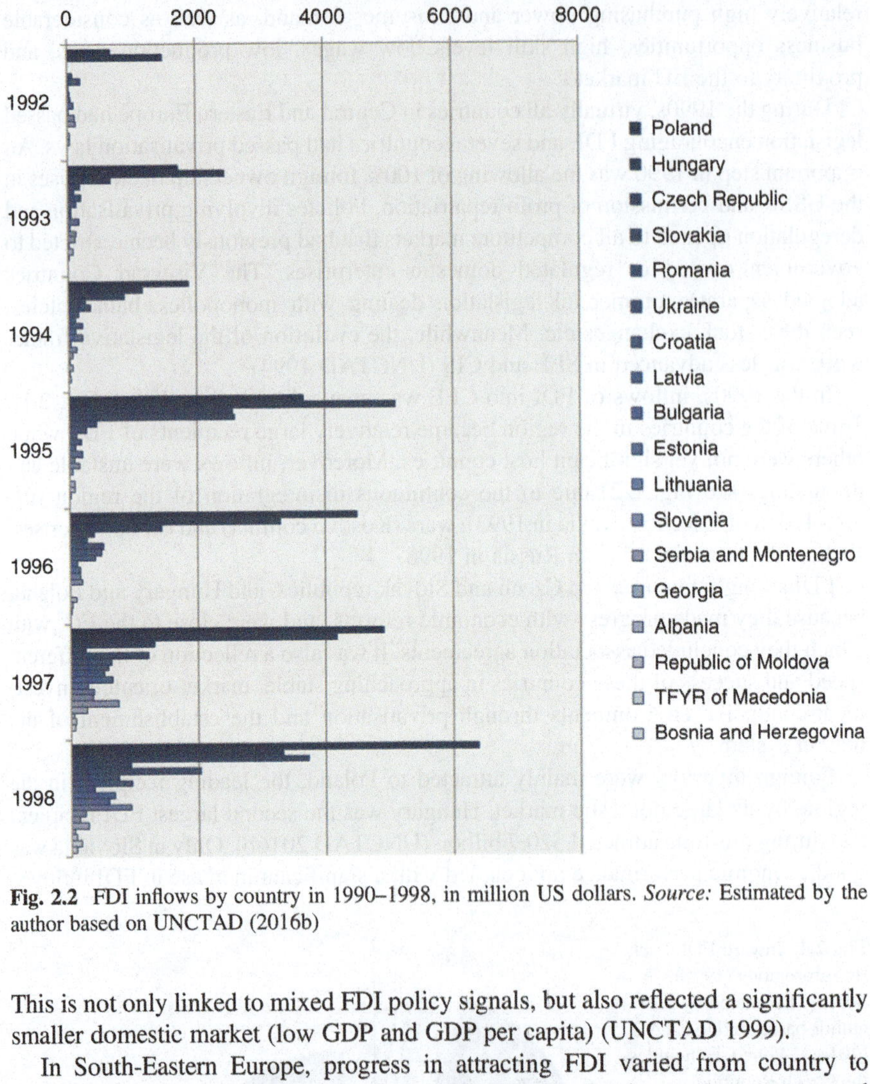

Fig. 2.2 FDI inflows by country in 1990–1998, in million US dollars. *Source:* Estimated by the author based on UNCTAD (2016b)

This is not only linked to mixed FDI policy signals, but also reflected a significantly smaller domestic market (low GDP and GDP per capita) (UNCTAD 1999).

In South-Eastern Europe, progress in attracting FDI varied from country to country. Romania attracted by far the most FDI. The foreign investors were attracted by the huge size of Romania's economy, with its population of 21,4 million (UNCTAD 2016d). The impact of war was obvious in the case of Croatia where significant foreign investment activity only started in 1996 (Estrin and Uvalic 2013).

The former Yugoslav Republics attracted little FDI during the first half of the 1990s. The reason for this was political risk and economic instability, as well as competition from more promising, effective, and stable transition economies. By 1998, inward FDI stock in Albania, Bosnia and Herzegovina (was at war in 1992–1995), Macedonia, Serbia and Montenegro amounted to only US$5,1 billion or 6,5% of total inward FDI stock in all 19 CEE economies (UNCTAD 2016b). This is rather less than their share (9,2%) in the total population of the transition region

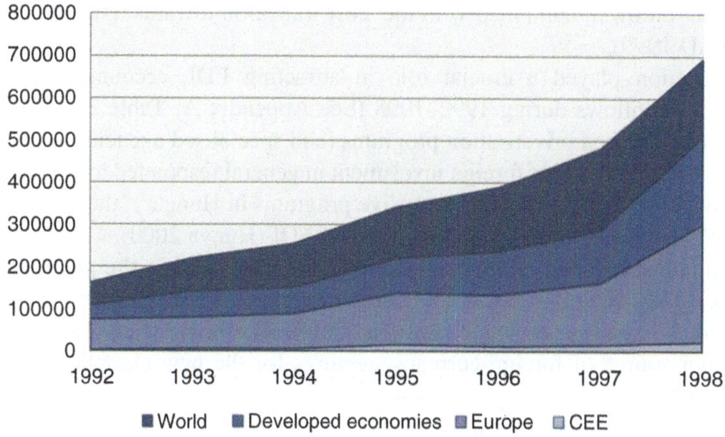

Fig. 2.3 Total World FDI inflows, in million US dollars. *Source*: Estimated by the author based on UNCTAD (2016b)

(UNCTAD 2016d). Without a basic level of political stability, no investor went into the region. The situation improved after the signing of the Dayton Peace Accords in 1995, although many SEE countries continued to lag behind the CEE as FDI recipients (Estrin and Uvalic 2013).

Despite the continuing growth of FDI in Central and Eastern Europe, inflows into this region remained small by world standards. They accounted for only 3% of total World FDI inflows (see Fig. 2.3) (UNCTAD 2016b).

The transition from administrative to market economies created major economic and political uncertainties. Moreover, post-Soviet countries didn't have the pure business, regulatory and administrative infrastructure required for the effective functioning of a market economy, with underdeveloped services, business support, and administrative foundations.

The inward FDI flows in the CEE countries were dominated by investors from the European Union. In this respect, the possible accession of some countries in the region to the European Union partly explained the relative importance of EU investment in Eastern Europe. In 1992–1998, the Netherlands, Germany and the United States were the main source countries for FDI inflows in this region (see Appendix A, Table 2.4). Furthermore, TNCs from Western Europe especially helped establish new trade linkages between Central and Eastern Europe on the one hand, and the European Union and European Free Trade Association on the other, sometimes in the framework of the regional core network strategies.

Former USSR countries were also important investors in the Baltic States and the other republics of the former USSR, usually through joint-venture agreements that represent old supplier and customer links (UNCTAD 2014a).

The inflows in the region strongly depended on external sources. See, for example, the slump of the growth of inflows in 1994 (Fig. 2.2) due to the lingering economic recession in some Western Europe countries (the main source of investment inflows), combined with the slow transition towards a market economy (UNCTAD 1999).

Privatisation played a crucial role in attracting FDI, accounting for nearly two-thirds of inflows during 1992–1998 (See Appendix A, Table 2.5). Most CEE countries established privatisation programs (and specialised agencies to implement them), and the amounts of foreign investment in general responded to the measure of privatisation programs. Thereby, intensive programs in Hungary, the Czech Republic and Poland brought the largest amounts of FDI (Hunya 2000).

At an industrial level, in all countries the amount of FDI in **the primary sector** was negligible. Nevertheless, some foreign investors were interested in potential petroleum exploration and exploitation in the former USSR, which was expected to be a major source of foreign-currency earnings for the new republics (UNCTAD 1999, p. 435).

Manufacturing was the single largest sector of FDI in most CEE countries. Investment in high-technology industries involving computer and computer-related technologies and telecommunication was particularly imperative. Manufacturing was the lead sector in six countries (Bulgaria, Croatia, Czech Republic, Poland, Romania and Ukraine), although in three of them (Czech Republic, Poland and Ukraine) it was closely followed by the services sector. Services were dominant in seven countries (Estonia, Hungary, Latvia, Lithuania, Republic of Moldova, Slovakia and Slovenia) (UNCTAD 1999, p. 435).

Services were traditionally neglected in former planned economies, but in the 1990s it was considered to be vital to the success in the transition process. The majority of foreign capital in services was in hotels and restaurants and in wholesale and retail trade, which may be explained by the small size of initial capital required for investment, and by the increasing demand for such services by both domestic and foreign enterprises (UNCTAD 1999, p. 435).

In summary, the period 1992–1998 is characterised by dramatic changes in the policies of CEE countries. The opening of those economies allowed foreign participation to lead to a heavy increase in inflows of FDI. The political changes also implied the creation of financial markets, new legislature and business infrastructure. Such policy changes undoubtedly resulted in the increase of the attractiveness of the CEE countries.

2.2.2 1999–2003

The period 1999–2003 is characterised by stable inflows in CEE countries, while global FDI inflows declined by more than 40% (See Fig. 2.4). This suggests that CEE was viewed as a stable and promising region for FDI. As in the previous period, the distribution of inflows in the region was also uneven (see Fig. 2.5).

By the end of 2003, the inward FDI stock of Central and Eastern Europe reached $235,3 billion. This stock was mainly concentrated in three countries: Poland ($56 billion), Hungary ($48 billion), and the Czech Republic ($45 billion), together

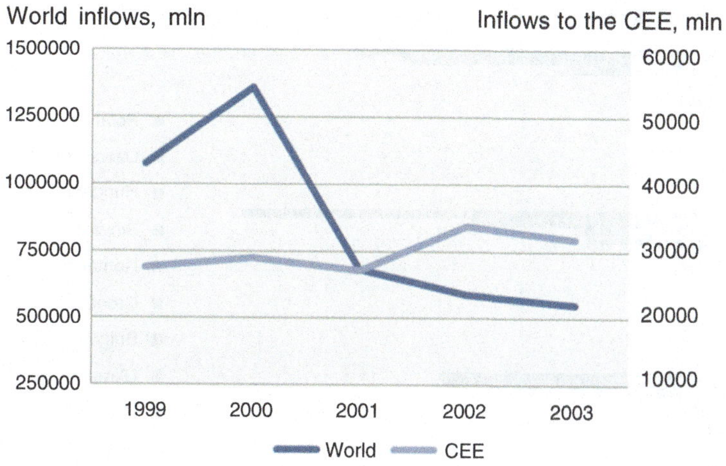

Fig. 2.4 FDI inflows to CEE and World inflows in 1999–2003, in million US dollars. *Source*: Estimated by the author based on (UNCTAD 2016b). *Note*: The left scale is for the World inflows, the right scale is for the inflows into CEE

accounting for almost two-thirds of total inward FDI stock in Central and Eastern Europe (UNCTAD 2016b). However, some leading countries—the Czech Republic, Hungary, Lithuania, Poland, Slovenia, Slovakia—showed cuts in FDI inflows in 2003 (UNCTAD 2016b). The reasons lie in the countries' economies: privatisation was coming to an end and macroeconomic problems surfaced. Uncertainties related to elections in some of the target countries like the Czech Republic and Hungary also made investors delay new investments and acquisitions (Sapienza 2009). The governments, however, tried to stimulate inflows of FDI by introducing special programs to attract foreign investors. Increasing volumes of investment in new projects indicated that such projects at least in part compensated for the end of privatisation-related FDI inflows.

Among the top investors to CEE countries were developed countries such as Germany, USA, the Netherlands, Austria and Italy (UNCTAD 2003).

In 2004, eight countries planned to join the EU, with full membership in the Union meaning that they needed to adopt EU law. In 2003, a number of CEE countries introduced policy measures aimed at liberalising, promoting and protecting FDI. Accession countries had to learn how to make the best use of facilities available to them for promoting investment, such as EU regional development funds. The accession countries also had to develop an institutional framework to administer and properly channel the variety of funds available from European Community sources for assisting economic development. In their search for international competitiveness under EU membership, some accession countries also lowered their corporate taxes. The combination of factors, combined with a favourable business climate, a highly skilled workforce and free access to the rest of the EU market through the Association Agreements, made the eight accession countries attractive locations for FDI. That applied especially to efficiency-seeking FDI both from other EU countries

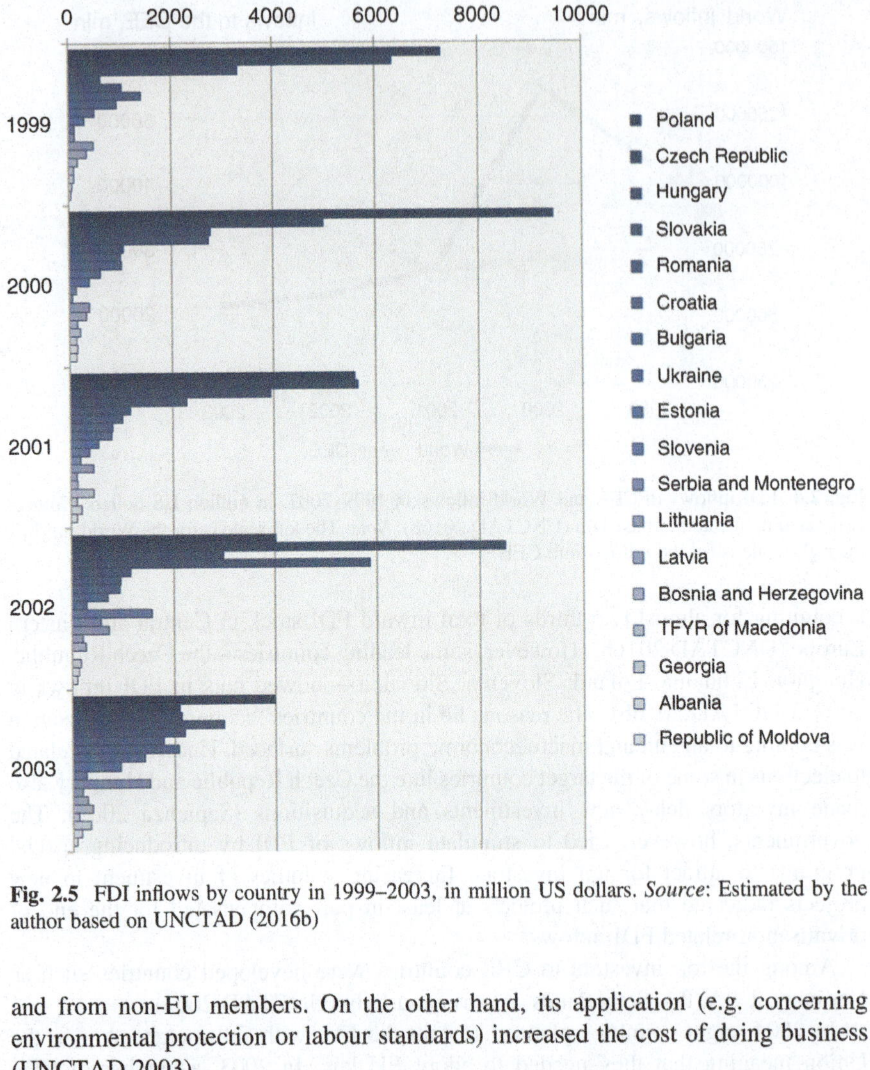

Fig. 2.5 FDI inflows by country in 1999–2003, in million US dollars. *Source*: Estimated by the author based on UNCTAD (2016b)

and from non-EU members. On the other hand, its application (e.g. concerning environmental protection or labour standards) increased the cost of doing business (UNCTAD 2003).

There was a considerable increase in FDI inflows to the SEE region in the early 2000s. FDI inflow to SEECs developed in line with improvements in political stability and progress in transformation. Since 2000, the SEE countries have implemented trade liberalisation with the EU and with the Western Balkans region, gradually improved the business environment, and privatised many enterprises and almost the entire banking sector. They also had growing economies and a local market that attracted Greenfield investments in the consumer goods sector. The relatively low-cost labour force attracted export-oriented investments primarily in Romania but also in Bulgaria. During this time, privatisation deals in Bulgaria and Croatia, and Romania were also accelerated (Estrin and Uvalic 2013).

Liberalisation in the SEE countries and the Western Balkans were more limited. But the trade agreements with the EU (FTAs or Association agreements) affected market size, which one of the key determinants of FDI. There was, thus, improvement in FDI inflows across the region, albeit it was very slow. Still the overall amount of FDI stock of $5,1 billion by 2003 could not be compared to the size of the countries not to speak about their investment needs (UNCTAD 2016b). Western Balkan countries became more stable but the transformation to market economies was still incomplete and investors rarely risked coming to these countries. The international community also changed its policies towards the region at the end of the Kosovo conflict in 1999. Investments coming in through privatisation or Greenfield only served the local market.

Among the countries investing in SEECs, EU members have increased their share over the last few years. But the EU share in the rest of the region is smaller than in case of the CEECs. The exception is Albania where Italy and Greece were responsible for almost all the investments. Banking and manufacturing took the most prominent places among the most preferred sectors for investment. There was a huge amount of FDI within the region, such as Slovenian investment in Croatia and Croatian investment in Bosnia and Herzegovina—but some of these investments resulted from the disintegration of Yugoslavia and did not represent new investments (UNCTAD 2004).

The distribution of FDI by economic activity is not very well documented. Based on the information available, FDI stocks in manufacturing were not the most important activity for investment, accounting for only 39% of the capital invested by 2002. Service-related FDI inflows into CEE followed the trend of growth in services. In the largest host countries of the region (the Czech Republic, Hungary, Poland), the industrial composition of inward FDI gradually shifted from manufacturing towards services (UNCTAD 2004, p.30).

In conclusion, the enlargement of the EU offered attractive locations for FDI in candidate countries. Access to the rest of the EU market made these eight countries attractive locations for FDI, both from other EU countries and from non-EU members. That applied especially to efficiency-seeking FDI. Other members of the region also experienced considerable changes in their political and economic environment. As a result, they attracted greater amounts of FDI.

2.2.3 2004–2008

During 2004–2008, FDI flows into the area grew (Fig. 2.6). Inward FDI inflows in the Central European countries increased significantly in 2004 once they joined the EU. Moreover, the Czech Republic, Hungary and Latvia showed an increase in two times in FDI inflows. In Poland, FDI inflows trebled and quadrupled in Lithuania. By 2005, the Czech Republic, Estonia and Hungary reached their historical maximum. After that, inflows started to fall down. This decline was mostly associated with the termination of privatisation programs. Latvia, Lithuania and Poland reached

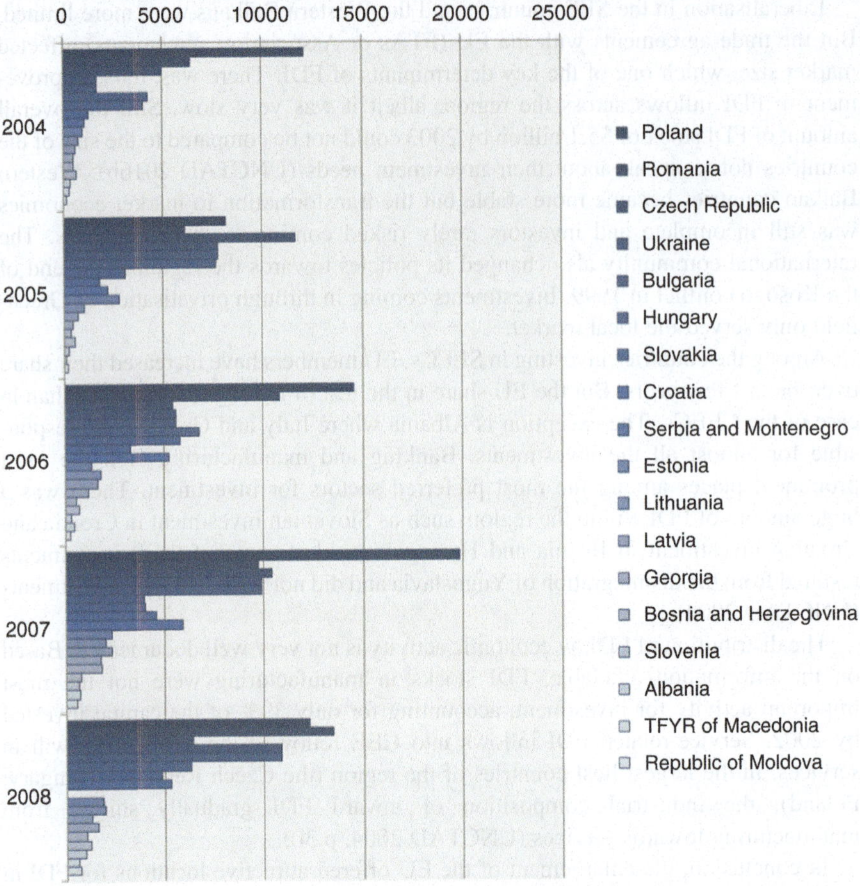

Fig. 2.6 FDI inflows by country in 2004–2008, in million US dollars. *Source*: Estimated by the author based on UNCTAD (2016b)

their peaks only in 2007. Poland attracted $21,6 billion in 2007 and was the top recipient of FDI inflows among the CEECs, as a result of increased investments not only from European investors, but also from Japanese companies (UNCTAD 2016b).

All SEE countries have significantly attracted more FDI with respect to the 1990s, but the increase has been uneven. The inflows to Romania and Bulgaria grew substantially during 2004–2007, as a result of their joining the EU on 1 January 2007, and in this regard they harmonised their legislation with the EU's. They also undertook reforms related to judicial independence, accountability, fighting corruption, and the tackling of organised crime. All these measures improved the business climate for all investments (UNCTAD 2009b). Moreover, Romania became the second largest host-country in 2004–2008, with an average inflow of $13,5 billion, with most of its flows coming from privatisation. Croatia had insignificant levels of

FDI inflows, because of a post-conflict situation that increased uncertainty in the country and slowed down the development of infrastructure (UNCTAD 2014b).

During this period, inward FDI flows in Ukraine, Georgia and Moldova reached a new record high. The growth rate of inflows was high, especially in the first half of 2008. However, with the crisis deeply affecting several countries by late 2008, initial hopes that the region would prove relatively immune to the global turmoil evaporated. Moreover, in the second half of 2008, conflict in Georgia reduced inflows in this country.

In 2008, Ukraine had the luck to attract $10,8 billion of FDI inflow, the greatest amount of FDI in Ukraine ever, despite uncertainties caused by domestic politics (UNCTAD 2016b). The most inflows were caused by the opening of its banking industry to FDI as a consequence of the accession to the WTO.

In the Western Balkans, the eastward expansion of the EU in 2004 and 2007 created major transportation and logistical advantages, as these countries became immediate neighbours of the EU.

The Western Balkans went through substantial changes during this period. Thus, Serbia and Montenegro, which used to be the one state, became two independent states in June 2006. Serbia's southern province, Kosovo, officially remained part of Serbia after the 1999 conflict (according to the UN resolution), however, it proclaimed its independence in February 2008 (Estrin and Uvalic 2013).

The Western Balkans signed Stabilisation and Association Agreements with the EU that offered trade liberalisation, new financial assistance programs, contractual relations, and even prospects of EU membership. That is why these agreements shaped the FDI inflows in the region.

The relative success of the Western Balkan countries in attracting FDI during the 2000s was probably more related to the fact that large privatisation processes in the new EU member states had already been completed, and, based on the positive experience foreign investors had with those countries, they turned their focus to the new markets that were being privatised.

In contrast to previous periods, the countries with large market sizes dominated in attracting FDI during 2004–2008. This also confirms the fact that traditional determinants became more important rather than transition progress and stability.

As in the previous periods, the EU member countries were the major investors in the CEE countries. They accounted for 77% of FDI in the region (See Fig. 2.7). The largest investors in these countries were Austria, Germany, the Netherlands, Luxembourg and France. A significant share of inflows contained round-tripped capital, which made Cyprus and Luxembourg important investors in the region. The EU was a more important source of FDI inflows in the CE and SEE countries (79%) than in the Western Balkans (49%). In the Western Balkans, a high share of FDI came from Russia and neighbouring countries (the WB and SEE). This confirmed the hypothesis that this region remained risky from the point of view of investors from developed countries (UNCTAD 2016b).

During 2004–2008 the primary and tertiary sectors in CEE received higher inflows, while flows into manufacturing declined. The primary sector continued to attract investors, despite new restrictions and existing uncertainties in this sector.

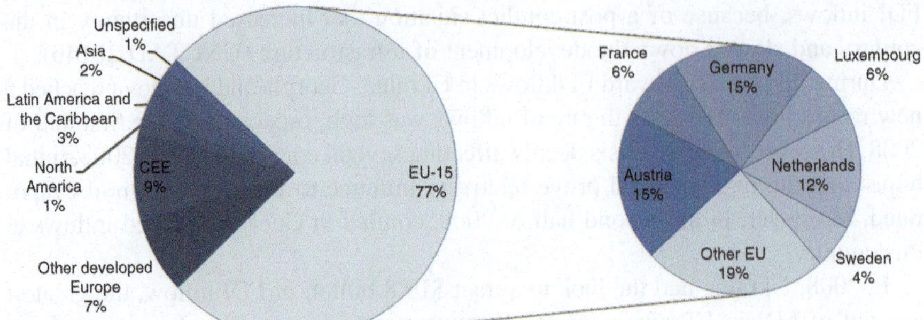

Fig. 2.7 Geographical sources of inward FDI inflows accumulated between 2004 and 2008, in %. *Source*: Estimated by the authors based on UNCTAD (2014a)

FDI inflows to the manufacturing sector decreased during the research period. However, within manufacturing there was a significant increase of flows to the chemical industry due to substantial cross-border acquisitions in the pharmaceutical industry in Croatia and Romania (UNCTAD 2009b).

FDI in services was upward notably in the banking industry, energy generation, telecommunications, transportation, real estate and business activities. Investment in industries such as information technology and business services was particularly significant because of the region's skilled labour force (UNCTAD 2009b).

This period showed that the average inflow to the CEE countries was $5 billion. In seven countries the inflows exceeded this amount—Ukraine, Bulgaria, Romania, Hungary, Czech Republic, Poland—in four of them, inflow was even more than $10 billion per year (Poland, Romania, Ukraine and Bulgaria). In 12 countries in the region, FDI flows remained below $1 billion. But in certain economies such as Montenegro, they were still considerable in relation to the size of the economy (UNCTAD 2016b).

Thus, despite entry into the EU and the expected burst of investor interest, risks persisted in the new EU member countries. EU reforms are expected to bring infrastructure investments and give regulatory stability to the EU single market, but the economic and social costs of adjustment were high. EU law likely added a new layer of regulations and may have undermined new members' relative FDI advantages in areas such as taxes and labour costs. These factors also pushed investors further East and South outside the new EU.

Countries on the western side of the region had a more advantageous geographical location: close to the EU, which is one of the largest markets in the world. Thus, the benefits for the "new neighbours" were big. In addition, some of the countries in the region possess significant natural resources, which attracted large projects from major investors. Other countries offer relatively skilled labour at competitive wages. As for market-seeking investment, the main pull factor was a prospective increase in local purchasing power, which has been low so far.

2.2.4 2009–2015

The period 2009–2015 stands out because of the financial crisis. The upward trend for the region had continued by 2008 for 6 consecutive years, during which time FDI inflows increased fivefold. During 2009 the CEE region experienced a collapse in inward flows of FDI (See Fig. 2.8). The intensity of the recession was not uniform across the region. In 2009 the inflows in the Czech Republic, Hungary, Croatia and Ukraine dropped twice, and three times in Bulgaria and Romania. The FDI inflows in three countries in the region—Lithuania, Slovakia and Slovenia—were even negative. In spite of this slump in 2009, by 2011 FDI inflows had recovered and were the fourth largest in the history of the region. However, by 2015 they had not reached pre-crisis levels (UNCTAD 2016b).

During the economic and financial crisis, investment flows all over the world dropped due to a reduction in economic activity and loss confidence in the existing economic and financial system; as the result, many investment plans were cancelled or postponed. The decline of FDI flows to CEE was principally due to the cutback of flows from EU countries, the dominant source of FDI in the region.

The question remains of whether the countries analysed experienced a larger decrease in FDI than other developing and developed countries. According to data from UNCTAD (2016b), global FDI decreased in 2009 by 20%, whereas the decline of inflows in the Western Balkans was only 21%. FDI inflows to first and second integration wave countries fell by 51% and 61% correspondingly. The decline of FDI inflows in Georgia, Moldova and Ukraine averaged 56% (UNCTAD 2016c).

The global slowdown of economic activity, limited access to finance and collapsing export markets resulted in the retirement of FDI, and has put the vulnerable economies of CEE under severe strain, whose impressive growth in the 2000s was increasingly dependent on the external markets of Western Europe and the large inflows of foreign capital.

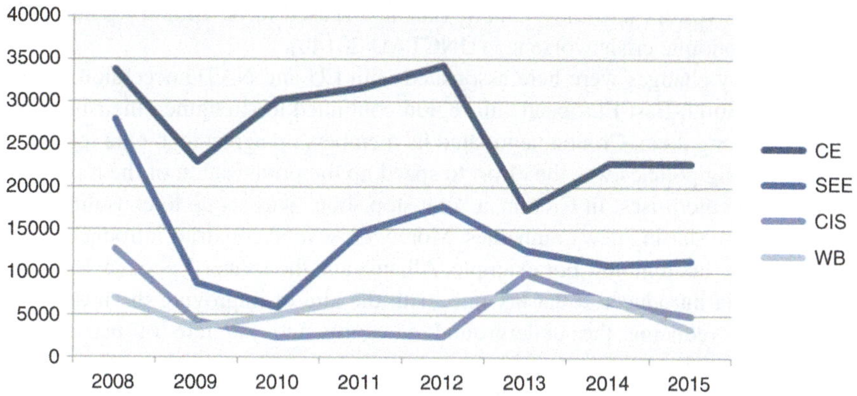

Fig. 2.8 Inflows to CEE, in million US dollars. *Source*: Authors' elaboration based on UNCTAD (2016b) data

By 2015, Poland had attracted the highest FDI stock ($213 billion) among all Central and Eastern European countries (UNCTAD 2016b). Its FDI inflows increased considerably after the country's accession to the EU. They fell during the crisis, but it experienced a much smaller 2009 decline than the region overall, remaining at higher levels than in other countries of the region.

The rapid growth of FDI flows to CEE partly reflected steps taken by countries in the region to open up their economies to foreign investment. Thus, Poland as well as Latvia privatised companies in the aerospace and telecommunications fields (UNCTAD 2009b).

Some CEE countries, however, introduced more restrictive policies, particularly regarding FDI in the extractive industries and other "strategic sectors", with the aim of protecting sensitive industries for national security or strategic reasons. This restriction trend reflected tendencies in other parts of the world. Some countries stopped further privatisations and even announced re-nationalisation plans in some strategic industries, as was the case in Slovakia and Estonia (UNCTAD 2014b). In Lithuania and Poland, the governments prevented the privatisation of firms that were deemed to be of national strategic importance.

The tax policy of several developed countries was also favourable for foreign investors. In Poland, a lot of tax cuts and tax incentives were introduced. In Hungary measures to reduce bureaucracy and administrative barriers eased the process of starting and doing business in the country (UNCTAD 2015).

The data for FDI inflows showed a reduction of FDI both into Romania and Bulgaria by 65% in 2009 (UNCTAD 2016b). In South-East Europe, privatisation still dominated the remaining State-owned enterprises.

Among the Balkan countries, the largest decline was in FYR Macedonia reaching 65%, following by Bosnia and Herzegovina (57%) and Serbia (26%). The remaining countries in the sample, Albania and Montenegro, actually recorded increases in FDI in 2009 (UNCTAD 2016b). The falls in the region were partly as a result of the sluggishness of investment from EU countries (traditionally the dominant source of FDI in this sub-region). In particular, Greece, which used to be a gateway or conduit for foreign investors into the Western Balkans, ceased to be an entry point as its domestic economic crisis worsened (UNCTAD 2014b).

The policy changes were here associated with EU and NATO accession. Countries in the South-East European sub-region continued to strengthen their ties with the EU. Among them, Croatia negotiated its membership agreement. One feature of these changing policies was the effort to speed up the privatisation of the remaining state owned enterprises. In Croatia, a "one-stop shop" was set up to consolidate the procedures for starting new companies. Moreover, several countries introduced new, low corporate tax regimes. For example, Albania and the former Yugoslav Republic of Macedonia introduced a flat tax rate, with the aim of improving the investment climate and reducing the underground economy and the rate of tax evasion (UNCTAD 2015).

As in the other countries in the region, FDI flows to Ukraine, Moldova and Georgia fell. In these countries, inward FDI was motivated by a desire to gain access to large and growing local consumer markets and to benefit from business opportunities arising from the liberalisation of selected industries. Thus, Ukraine introduced a new law on joint stock companies. Ukraine's accession to the WTO in 2008 stimulated inward FDI in certain industries, such as banking and steel (UNCTAD 2009b).

In three countries in the region, the average FDI inflows did not exceed $1 billion, namely in Slovenia, Georgia, Montenegro, Latvia, Lithuania, Bosnia and Herzegovina, TFYR of Macedonia and the Republic of Moldova.

We see that in 2009–2015 larger countries continued attracting significantly more FDI (Fig. 2.9).

In 2009–2015, FDI in the primary sector FDI varied by industry. The decline in some industries was due to the restrictions implemented. However, strategic investors still saw advantages in investing in the primary sector, mainly in the petroleum and gas industry. Foreign investors were motivated by the continued strong growth

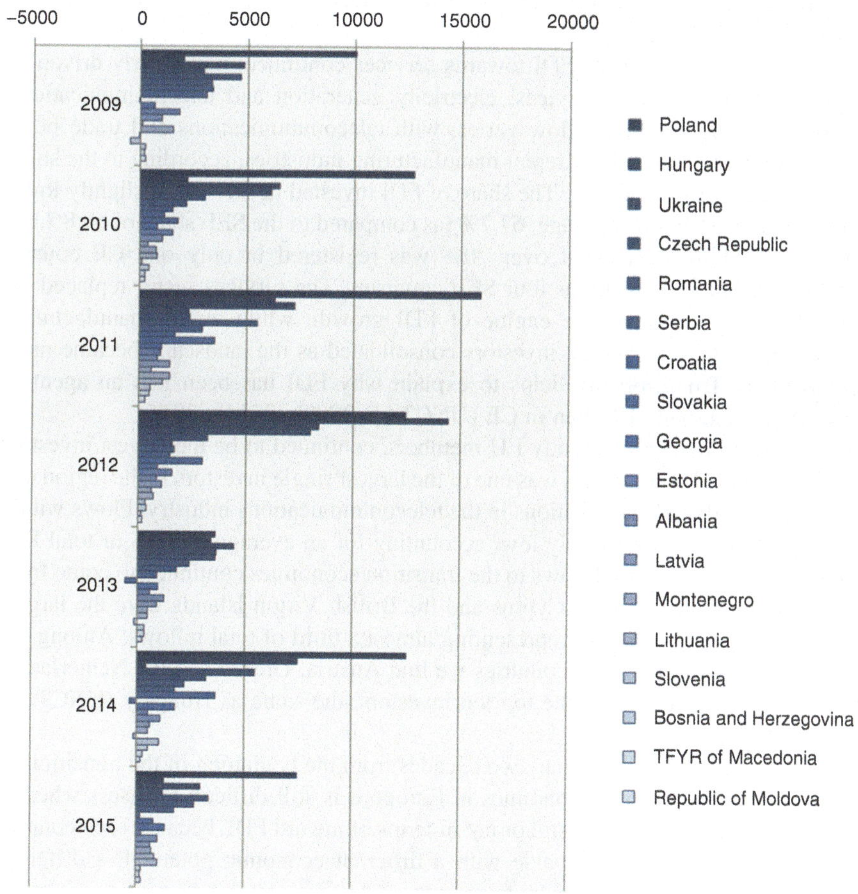

Fig. 2.9 FDI inflows by country in 2009–2015, in million US dollars. *Source*: Authors' elaboration based on UNCTAD (2016b) data (World Investment Report)

of the domestic market and low labour costs, and high returns in energy (UNCTAD 2015).

FDI in the manufacturing sector in CEE increased, because of increased market opportunities and improvement of the business environment. There was increased activity in the automotive industry. The food and beverages industries also benefited from a high growth of FDI in the studied period. This was fuelled by foreign manufacturers' search for low-cost, highly skilled labour and access to a growing market. There were substantial differences across countries in attracting FDI in manufacturing sector. In the CE countries manufacturing accounts, on average, for 30% of inward FDI stock, compared to about 25% in the SEE countries and the Western Balkans, again with substantial variations between countries. Thus, the Czech Republic, Poland and Slovakia have attracted substantial amounts of FDI in manufacturing—well over 30%. Bosnia and Herzegovina have attracted 35% of their total inflows in manufacturing, Macedonia 31% and Romania 32%. Whereas Croatia attracted only 21%, Serbia 19%, Bulgaria 17%, and 16% in Albania (UNCTAD 2014b, 2015).

The widespread shift of FDI towards services continued, particularly driven by investments in financial services, electricity generation and telecommunications. The second biggest FDI inflow varies, with telecommunications and trade being very important, alongside different manufacturing industries, according to the structure of the specific economy. The share of FDI invested in services is slightly lower in CE than in SEE—on average, 67,7% (as compared to the SEE share of 69,8%). A share of FDI in services of over 70% was registered in only one CE country (Slovenia), but in as many as four SEE countries. The services sector replaced the manufacturing sector as the engine of FDI growth, while in the manufacturing sector, domestic and foreign investors consolidated as the landscape became more competitive. This probably helps to explain why FDI has been less an agent of structural change in SEE than in CE (UNCTAD 2009b, 2014b, 2015).

Developed countries, mainly EU members, continued to be the largest investors in CEE, but the United States was one of the largest single investors in the region due to some considerable acquisitions in the telecommunications industry. Flows within the region remained relatively low, accounting for an average of 10% of total FDI flows. A large part of FDI flows to the transition economies continued to come from round-tripping. As a result, Cyprus and the British Virgin Islands were the largest two investors in the region, representing almost a third of total inflows. Among the major investors in the CEE countries we find Austria, Greece and the Netherlands. Germany has been among the top ten investors, the same as Hungary (UNCTAD 2014b, 2015).

In summary, after more than two decades from the beginning of the transition of former centrally-planned economies in Europe it is still difficult to assess whether the process itself was successful or not in terms of inward FDI, because each country started its own transition course with a different economic potential, a different history and different resource endowments.

According to the data it is also still difficult to identify the most important factors that influence the decision to invest in a particular country. We can see that on different stages of transformation and integration and for different countries some factors such as accession to the EU, privatisation, labour costs, natural resource endowments and market size were more or less significant.

2.3 Empirical Literature on the FDI Determinants

On the score of the growing importance of FDI in the world economy, especially in transitional countries, a vast empirical literature on FDI determinants has been developed. The classical model of the determinants of FDI begins from the earlier research work of Dunning (1973) and Dunning and McQueen (1981) which provides a comprehensive analysis based on ownership, location and the internationalisation (OLI) paradigm. Dunning's eclectic paradigm became the overall framework most often used in empirical studies of the determinants of FDI. In order to explain the motivation for foreign investment, the authors distinguish between three traditional types of FDI: market, resource and efficiency-seeking investments.

2.3.1 Market and Resource-Seeking Motives

The size of the markets was demonstrated to be of high importance in many previous empirical works that studied the determinants of FDI in CEE. Thus, Meyer (1998) as well as Brenton (1999), Kinoshita and Campos (2003), and Faeth (2009) found that market size was the primary determinant of foreign direct investment in the CEE region. Benacek et al. (2000) suggested that national and regional market access was the primary factor that influenced potential investors, with market potential as a dominant factor. The reasoning behind the market-related factors' impact on FDI is that firms are seek new market opportunities for their products and are attracted by current demand and a relatively low competition in a country, the potential of economies of scale within large in absolute size markets and the expectation of sustained economic growth and further demand growth through a catching up of consumption.

There was some evidence that similarity and proximity to the EU were important factors in observed trade and investment decisions. This helps to explain why a large portion of FDI in early the 1990s was directed to Hungary and the Czech Republic (Holland and Pain 1998).

However, according to Botrić and Škuflić (2006), market seeking might not be the main reason why investors chose to invest in the CEE countries. Even though the GDP level turned out to be significant and positive, the coefficient value was relatively small. This confirmed the negative coefficient on population and the GDP growth rate.

Many authors have tried to assess the *resource-seeking* motives in the CEE countries. This type of investment motive is important for vertical investment and implies relocation rather than replication of production activities in order to lower production costs.

The influence of labour costs on FDI is found to be inconclusive: some studies find it relevant while others find it insignificant.

For instance, Lankes and Venables (1996), Lansbury et al. (1996), and Carstensen and Toubal (2004) stated that the wages of unskilled workers and the presence of skilled workers had a significant effect on the investors' decision to choose a certain location within Central and Eastern Europe. Lankes and Venables (1996) also suggested that productivity differences affect the location decision, except in the case of investors that intended to bring new technologies with them.

Bellak and Leibrecht (2007) empirical results supported these findings. They found that from a broader European perspective low labour costs attract more FDI into the CEECs and the fact that labour is still relatively immobile could provide an incentive for CEE governments to introduce policies to keep wages low. Merlevede and Schoors (2004) found that labour cost alone is insignificant, but when related to the time variable, it reveals a significant, negative impact on FDI. This indicates that the impact of the relative unit labour cost as a determinant becomes more important during a transition period.

Resource-seeking FDI also refers to specific locations with abundant natural resources and raw materials, such as natural gas or oil (Kinoshita and Campos 2003). Shiells (2003) showed that FDI inflows have generally been related to natural resource extraction or energy transportation infrastructure projects, large privatisation transactions, and debt/equity swaps to pay for energy supplies. According to Shiells, FDI into the CIS countries was mainly "resource seeking," whereas FDI into countries that were more advanced in the transition process was more often "efficiency seeking," i.e., oriented toward export-processing based on low (productivity–adjusted) labour costs (Shiells 2003). Tondel (2001) and Janicki and Wunnava (2004) also indicated a difference in the motive for investing in CIS and in CEE and Baltic states. The findings supported a hypothesis of market-seeking and resource-seeking investments prevailing in the CIS. Investments in the CEE and Baltic states, on the other hand, appeared more risk sensitive, suggesting a role for efficiency-seeking or vertical investments (Tondel 2001). As natural resources are widely available in post-communist CIS nations but rarely present in the countries of CEE, resource-seeking FDI is often left out of the models of FDI determinants in the Central and Eastern European countries.

In general, many results have confirmed that market access is considered the most important factor in the investment decision, with factor costs playing a lesser, although in many cases still significant role.

2.3.2 Efficiency-Seeking Motives

Many authors tried to estimate the factors that refer to the overall quality of the host countries' investment climate in terms of political, economic and cultural factors (efficiency-seeking factors). And they very often refer to transition-specific factors.

Thus, for instance, Melo et al. (1996) took an integrated approach to evaluating the interaction of initial conditions, e.g. level of development, macroeconomic distortions, membership of the former Soviet Union, urbanisation, trade dependence, political change, reforms and economic performance. According to the study of Melo et al., initial conditions were the determining factors for economic performance among the transition economies, but economic liberalisation was the most important factor determining differences in growth (Melo et al. 1996).

These findings were supported by many other researchers. Thus, Janicki and Wunnava (2004), as well as Demekas et al. (2005), revealed that countries which had succeeded in creating a strong economic and political environment, characterised by financial market stability, with smaller risks of a financial crisis or default, were likely to gain foreign investment. They also found that openness to trade was the most significant of all variables, and it was explained by the fact that trade and investments complement each other (Janicki and Wunnava 2004; Demekas et al. 2005).

Kinoshita and Campos (2003) compared the strength of efficiency-seeking motives in CIS and non-CIS countries. They found that the infrastructure and the openness of the economy have a statistically significant effect on FDI only in the CIS countries. However, in non-CIS countries the agglomeration and the distance from the core of the EU had a stronger effect. The extent of external liberalisation, the removal of FDI restrictions, and the quality of the legal and bureaucratic environment are found to affect FDI in all countries.

Brenton et al. (1998) employed the economic freedoms index of the Heritage Foundation as an additional independent variable to test whether a business-friendly environment matters for foreign investors. The results suggested that policy makers in the CEEC should stimulate the ease of doing business to boost FDI inflows (Brenton et al. 1998). D. P. Woodward (2000) found that a flexible taxation system might encourage investors and remove existent barriers towards productivity growth process (Woodward 2000).

Similarly, Albulescu et al. (2010) pointed out an uncommon FDI determinant: financial stability. The results showed that a lower lending rate seemed to attract more FDI inflows into CEECs, with the stability of the financial and banking systems in the CEECs also proving to play a significant role in attracting FDI inflows (Albulescu et al. 2010).

Tintin (2011) found economically significant effect of institutions (especially economic freedoms) on FDI inflows in the CEEC. He found the state fragility index, political rights, civil liberties and other institutional variables to be empirically significant. Moreover, he proved that institutional indicators have different impacts across sectors (Tintin 2011). On the contrary, Bevan and Estrin (2011) did not find any significant impact of country risk, domestic price liberalisation and the development of competition policy, however, institutional development and the policy framework was relevant. Moreover, they did not find strong evidence for the importance of informal institutions, once formal institutions were controlled for. In other words, the development of formal institutions appeared to be closely associated with informal institutions (Estrin and Meyer 2011).

Altomonte (1998), Altomonte and Guagliano (2001), Resmini (2000) analysed the determinants of FDI inflows in the CEE countries by using sectoral FDI data. This approach is interesting because FDI is industry but not country specific. Moreover, in transition economies, the concentration of FDI in particular sectors may affect the path and the pace of the restructuring process, re-shaping the industrial specialisation of the host countries. Altomonte (1998) found that the relative cost of labour deters FDI only in sectors that have low or middle to low levels of sunk costs, while the level of risk affects all sub-sector specifications. Altomonte and Guagliano (2001) found that a healthy legal environment has a positive influence only on industries with high levels of sunk costs. The results of Resmini (2000) indicated that governments can play a role in attracting FDI since the most important variables, namely the stage of the transition process, the degree of openness of the economy and, even though to a lesser extent, the concentration of manufacturing.

As privatisation is the transfer of ownership rights of a state-owned enterprise to the private sector, representing the process through which the liberalisation of the market is made, a lot of studies are devoted to privatisation as a factor of FDI in the CEE countries.

The logic behind the importance of privatisation levels is well explained by Brada (1996) and Ash and Hare (1994). According to Brada (1996), "the main difference between socialism and capitalism lies in the ownership of property" (p.67). Therefore, only if transition countries are able to make successful changes in the ownership of productive assets will they succeed in attracting foreign capital. Ash and Hare (1994) complement these statements by stressing that privatisation contributes greatly towards the creation of a well-functioning and efficient market economy by lowering production costs, improving the quality of goods and services and encouraging innovation.

The advantages of privatisation were considered by Lansbury et al. (1996), Kalotay and Hunya (2000), Marinova and Marinov (2003), Carstensen and Toubal (2004), Johnson (2006) and Mateev (2009). All studies underlined the overall positive effects of privatisation-related FDI in Central and Eastern Europe. Estrin (1994), Kalotay and Hunya (2000), Carstensen and Toubal (2004) also found that the method of privatisation matters. In fact, restructuring and the establishment of strong corporate governance may be more important than the disposal of former State-owned assets (Kalotay and Hunya 2000). Notably, the privatisation methods: privatisation by vouchers, management and employee buy-outs (MEBO) and sales to outside owners (SOO)—were emphasised. SOO is considered to be the most beneficial method of privatisation. The arguments in favour of selling company's shares include direct financial revenues to the government, effective external capital inflows to a company as well as the transfer of technology and know-how (Estrin 1994). Carstensen and Toubal (2004) found that countries with SOO as a primary approach to privatisation had substantially higher foreign capital inflows. Distribution of shares to management and employees represents a less profitable method, as an insider approach does not directly bring new funds to a company or government and faces major problems of employees' motivation and company's performance as workers are often linked to consumption through higher wages. The least favourable method refers to privatisation by vouchers which fails to accumulate the government revenues desired and, even more importantly, does not ensure the emergence of adequate corporate governance (Estrin 1994). The results of Holland and Pain (1998) confirm the proposition by finding that privatisation by vouchers indeed tends to attract lower levels of FDI.

Johnson (2006), as well as Mateev (2009), did not find strong evidence that the method of privatisation had a significant effect on FDI receipts, contradicting previous results. One possible explanation was the study period of 2000–2006, in which most transition economies in the sample had completed their privatisation programs.

Brada et al. (2003) and Grcic and Babic (2003) studied the transition-specific factors, such as the advancement of privatisation, price and trade liberalisation, banking sector reform and the eradication of corruption. They found that compared with Central-eastern European and Baltic states, the South-eastern European countries were less successful in attracting FDI, reflecting a slower pace of reform, late commencement of privatisation and lower market confidence about EU accession prospects (Grcic and Babic 2003). Brada et al. (2003) also confirmed the importance of the political stability in the region for the Balkans.

In general, empirical findings suggest that determinants such as privatisation, trade regimes, and the level of infrastructure as well as proximity to the European Union appear to be important determinants.

2.3.3 Integration-Specific Factors

The degree of integration into the world economy is another factor that has been argued to affect the level of FDI. The political and economic integration of CEE with the EU gave a signal to foreign investors that these countries were better regulated and politically more stable. Thus, some studies were focused on the effects of integration with the EU.

Holland and Pain (1998) suggested that the effect of prospective EU membership on an investor's motivation to invest in a candidate country is twofold. First, the prospect of EU membership served as an external validation of the progress in transition, i.e. the extent of the success of each country's reform policies. Second, EU membership implied guarantees in terms of legal environment, and macroeconomic, institutional and political stability. Both effects served to reduce investors' perceived level of risk within the CEE. That is why the accession announcements made by the European Council measured the transition progress of the candidate countries.

Witkowska (2007) also showed in her study that all the adjustments to the EU requirements reshaped conditions for doing business in the new Member States and led to the improvement of their economic fundamentals (Witkowska 2007).

A considerable number of studies included an empirical model to study the effects of integration. They allow studying the international location choice in a context of regional economic integration when countries conclude multilateral free-trade agreements with the EU.

Seric (2011) presented an attempt to determine how the establishment of the Central European Free Trade Agreement (CEFTA) and the Baltic Free Trade Area (BAFTA) influenced the location decisions. He found that FTAs created formal intra-regional trade platforms. At the same time, they provided a training ground where CEE countries could become accustomed to the rules of free trade on their way towards full European Union (EU) membership. The positive and significant coefficients on two regional integration variables such as openness and FTA agreements suggested that deeper regional integration and membership in an FTA has tangible effects on attracting FDI (Seric 2011). The findings of Hengel (2011) can be viewed as a complement to the work of Seric (2011), by extending the analysis to SEE countries. He found that FDI in SEE was attracted to markets with higher incomes, greater trade openness and a higher degree of investment climate reforms. The coefficient on CEFTA was positive, but not significant.

Their analysis offered additional support for the claim that investment climate reforms were important for foreign investors. They offered evidence that reforms in infrastructure, competition policy, privatisation and enterprise restructuring could lead to noteworthy increases in FDI.

Some studies studied the threshold effect of EU membership by introducing structural shift dummy variables for key announcements of in EU accession. Bevan and Estrin (2000, 2004) investigated the effect of the European Union's enlargement process on foreign direct investment in CEE countries and showed that announcements impacted directly upon FDI receipts. They found that the Essen Council had no effect on FDI inflows, however, the promulgation of the Agenda 2000 had positive and statistically significant result on at least five of the ten accession countries (Bevan and Estrin 2000, 2004).

Altomonte and Guagliano (2003) found that Central and Eastern Europe displayed a greater potential in the attraction of FDI flows when compared to the Mediterranean region, in terms of both market and efficiency-seeking TNCs strategies. They found, that this was likely due to the higher degree of integration achieved among the CEECs (Altomonte and Guagliano 2003).

Clausing and Dorobantu (2005) also found that the release of the *Agenda 2000* in July 1997 affected foreign direct investment in first wave countries (Hungary, Poland, Czech Republic, Estonia, Slovenia) less than the second wave (Lithuania, Latvia, Slovakia, Bulgaria and Romania). The difference in the magnitude and statistical significance of the first and second wave dummy variables might be explained by the fact that the reforms in the first wave countries were more successful, and there were no doubts that these countries would join the EU. However, the second wave countries' transition processes were much slower, and their economies have not performed as well as those of the countries identified as the first wave. The release of the Agenda 2000 reduced the uncertainties surrounding these countries' prospects of joining the EU (Clausing and Dorobantu 2005).

Gungor and Binatli (2010) highlighted the impact of EU accession in CEE, Ukraine and Turkey. They considered three steps of the integration into the EU. Namely, candidate status, the start of the negotiations and membership in the EU. The empirical estimations suggest that the effect of the EU accession prospects is positive and significant. Thus, a large amount of FDI flows into the CEE countries is driven by the process of their integration to the EU (Gungor and Binatli 2010).

However, not all studies indicated positive effects of EU membership and FDI inflows. Thus, Brenton et al. (1998) indicated that FDI flows were positively affected by GDP size, whereas market size and EU membership did not appear to influence FDI flows in a statistically significant way (Brenton et al. 1998). Bos and van de Laar (2004) also found no evidence that an overall catch-up effect or announcement effect exists. Rather, economic fundamentals explain differences in inward investment in the region (Bos and van de Laar 2004).

2.3.4 Limitations of the Previous Researches

Despite the fact that many studies are devoted to identifying the determinants of FDI inflows and to studying the experience of successful CEE countries, the problem of the effective mobilisation of FDI in the leading countries of the region has not been fully investigated yet. Moreover, literature dealing in particular with the role of the European Union in the mobilisation of FDI is rather sparse. This scarcity is primarily due to the short period of the involvement into integration with the EU, which began only two decades ago.

The existing literature does not clearly indicate whether the integration with the European Union changes the amount of FDI received by the CEE countries. To find any evidence of the importance of integration with the EU, some authors included into their empirical models the proximity to the EU, the strength of trade linkages and openness of the economy (see Appendix B). Despite the fact that in some cases these determinants showed a positive and significant effect, they are not able to represent the full picture of the interaction with the EU because the relations between countries lie beyond the trade. In fact, the integration touches deeper fundamentals between countries as historic, cultural ties and, of course, economic and political relations.

The process of accession is very complicated and long, it includes many stages at which the accession countries are to harmonise its legislation with the EU one. However, the former research also did not investigate all the stages of the EU accession: either the FTA or accession to the EU.

Thus, the most important limitation of the previous research is the absence of a complex study that includes all steps and types of integration with the EU. For instance, Bevan and Estrin (2000, 2004) and Clausing and Dorobantu (2005) considered how the Agenda 2000 announcements affected FDI inflows into the CEE. Gungor and Binatli (2010) went further and included the accession steps as the becoming a "candidate country", the start of accession negotiation and, finally, membership of the EU. The full sequence of stages has been not still covered by the studies.

In our book, we indicate three types of collaboration according to the tightness of relations: the free trade agreements (trade liberalisation), Association Agreements (regulate economic, political, social and cultural aspects), and the EU-accession.

The overview of the existing literature (see Table 2.1) shows that the most of the studies that are aimed at the estimation of the effects of the EU accession on FDI inflows consider almost the same group of countries—the ten EU-accession countries from CEE (Bulgaria, Czech Republic, Hungary, Latvia, Lithuania, Poland, Romania, Slovak Republic, Slovenia, Estonia). These findings nowadays can be used with a great concern, because current integration of the CEE countries with the EU includes additional nine countries which differ a lot in many macroeconomic characteristics and liberalisation progress from those accession countries. Thus, the research foundation almost does not include the studies devoted to estimating the FDI determinants in the Western Balkans. Demekas et al. (2005) noted that SEE is a region not comprehensively covered in econometric studies on FDI in transition economies, in part due to the lack of comparable data. Of the more than 40 empirical studies reviewed in his paper, only four included any SEE countries and even that coverage is patchy and inconsistent (Demekas et al. 2005). Moreover, former researchers completely did not examine the effect of the accession process on FDI inflows in the former Soviet Countries in the context of the European integration. Few authors included, however, Ukraine as a control country (Bevan and Estrin 2004; Gungor and Binatli 2010). Nowadays, the CEFTA agreement is signed with Moldova and AAs were recently signed with Ukraine, Georgia, and Moldova. That is why these countries should also be included in the estimations.

In our book, we also include estimations for four different sub-regions: Eight Central European countries, South-East European countries, the Western Balkans, and three former members of the Soviet Union (Ukraine, Moldova, and Georgia). It is an important supplementary test, for instance, it was found by Estrin and Uvalic (2013) and Brada et al. (2006) that factors driving FDI to the Western Balkans differ from those that drive FDI to CEE: even when size of their economy, distance, institutional quality and prospects of EU membership are taken into account, Western Balkans countries receive less FDI (Estrin and Uvalic 2013). Similar conclusions were made by Campos and Kinoshita who studied initial conditions and agglomeration effects for FDI inflows in CIS and non-CIS (Kinoshita and Campos 2003).

Another limitation of previous econometric studies is the limited time span used in the analysis, ranging from only 3–10 years. This can be partly justified by both the limited time period since the start of the transition, the opening up of the CEECs to FDI, and data availability constraints. This limitation, however, makes it difficult to determinate conclusions. There are few studies that cover a period over 10 years: Bos and van de Laar (2004), Witkowska (2008), and Gungor and Binatli (2010). Our

Table 2.1 Studies of FDI determinants according to the year of publishing

Studies	Period studied	Countries studied	Proxies used	Results
Holland and Pain (1998)	1992–1996	Eight CEE countries	EU Trade Share, EU Proximity Dummy	Positive
Brenton (1999)	1992–1995	CEE and other regions	Preferential relations between countries	No effect
Bevan and Estrin (2000)	1994–1998	CEE accession countries and Ukraine	Announcement Dummy (the Essen European Council, The Agenda 2000 for two waves)	Positive but insignificant
Assenov (2003)	1991–2001	22 CEECs and former Soviet states	Ordinal EU membership dummy (2: 10 countries to become new EU members in 2004, 1: Bulgaria and Romania, 0: others)	Positive and significant
Altomonte and Guagliano (2003)	1990–1999	CEE	Regional economic agreements	Positive
Bos and van de Laar (2004)	1987–2001	207 countries (FDI from the Netherlands)	Regional dummy (CEE and Central Asia), historical and cultural ties	No effect
Bevan and Estrin (2004)	1994–2000	CEE accession countries and Ukraine	Announcement Dummy (Agenda 2000) from 1998 until time horizon	Positive
Egger and Pfaffermayr (2004)	1986–1998	55 countries (including 10 CEECs and Russia)	Comparison of bilateral effects of 15 EU member states and CEECs under the European Agreement obtained from the estimation of the gravity model to the bilateral effects of other countries.	Positive effect for FDI from EU-15 to 7 CEECs excluding Baltic states in 1995–1998
Clausing and Dorobantu (2005)	1992–2001	CEE, 15 members of the EU, Norway and Switzerland	EU announcement (1993 announcement and Agenda 2000) for two different accession waves; Membership in the EU	Positive
Witkowska (2008)	1991–2005	Poland, the Czech Republic, Hungary and Slovakia	EU policies (analysis)	Positive
Gungor and Binatli (2010)	1990–2009	CEE accession countries, Ukraine and Turkey	EU accession steps (0 = the EU does not approve a country as a candidate; 1 = a candidate country; 2 = accession negotiations have started; 3 = membership in the EU)	Positive

(continued)

Table 2.1 (continued)

Studies	Period studied	Countries studied	Proxies used	Results
Seric (2011)	1995–2000	CEE	Dummy variable for duration of membership in CEFTA	Positive
Hengel (2011)	1995–2000	SE	Dummy variable for duration of membership in BAFTA	No effect

Source: Author's generalisation of the above-mentioned works
Note: CEE here includes Bulgaria, the Czech Republic, Estonia, Hungary, Latvia, Lithuania, Poland, Romania, Slovakia, and Slovenia

studied time period spans over a 23 year period, 1992–2015, and includes the entire period of the EU accession, the financial crisis, and the recovery.

2.4 Accession Towards the EU

Understanding European integration is central to grasping the evolving link between FDI and the membership in the European Union.

CEE nations face three steps towards closer integration: FTAs, Association Agreements with the EU, and the third step—EU membership—is a composite of a number of steps and accession procedures (See Fig. 2.10).

2.4.1 Free Trade Agreements

From origin relations between the USSR and Western Europe were cool. The socialist republics refused to officially recognise the EC.

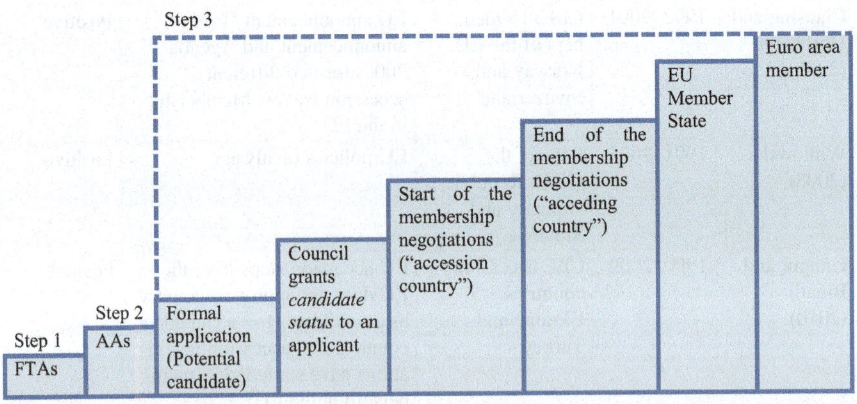

Fig. 2.10 Steps towards the EU membership. *Source*: Author's own work

However, during the 1970s the USSR adopted a slightly more constructive attitude to the EC and wished to develop trade links through COMERCON. Soviet exports to the EC averaged 1–2% of Soviet GDP and comprised mainly of oil, gas and other primary products, most of which were not produced within the EC. The EC negotiated some modest trade liberalisation with Yugoslavia, leading to a cooperation agreement in 1980 (Clark 1997).

Overall, EC-Eastern Europe relations were blocked by larger geopolitical disagreements, such as the Soviet invasion of Afghanistan and the imposition of martial law in Poland in 1981.

In 1986, negotiations between the EC and COMERCON were opened, though they proceeded slowly, in parallel with bilateral trade negotiations with the East European countries themselves. By December 1988, the EC's first trade and co-operation agreements with Hungary came into force. This was followed by similar agreements with Poland, the USSR, Czechoslovakia, Bulgaria and Romania (Clark 1997).

Just after the collapse of the Soviet Union, the relations between former Soviet republics and the EC had the potential for future development. Two FTAs (the Baltic Free Trade Area (BAFTA) and the Central European Free Trade Agreement (CEFTA)) were created in Central and Eastern Europe in order to favour international trade and competition in these countries.

The trade and co-operation agreements were an important stage in the development of EC assistance towards the transformational process. More than four decades of quasi-isolation of the CEECs from the world economy had serious detrimental consequences for their external economic relations. Artificial, non-market prices, rigidities due to the lack of convertible or at least transferable national currencies to settle intra-regional payments, and the overwhelming role of state institutions in virtually all aspects of intraregional trade led to distorted specialisation and enterprise-behaviour patterns that could not be determined once liberalisation had opened CEE economies up to western competition (Clark 1997).

Thus, the main motive of FTAs was to restore traditional relations with the developed Western world, above all with the Western Europe. These agreements aimed to expand trade in goods and services and foster investment by means of fair, stable and predictable rules, eliminate barriers to trade between members, provide appropriate protection of intellectual property rights in accordance with international standards and harmonise provisions on modern trade policy issues such as competition rules and state aid. FTAs in CEE covered almost all goods except coal, textile, agriculture etc.

At the same time intra-regional integration was not only seen as a final but as an intermediate stage of EU accession. It allowed the neutralisation of some problems. Indeed, the economies of the CEE were rather similar than supplemental. Their markets were poor in capital and raw (including energy) resources. In addition, CEECs had a large negative trade balance, which accounted for most the trade with the EU countries.

Steps were also taken on the approximation of the laws of the CEE to EU norms. It also includes clear and effective procedures for dispute settlement.

Table 2.2 FTAs in Central and Easter Europe, dates of entry and leaving

Countries	BAFTA		CEFTA		CEFTA 2006	
	Entry into force	Left	Entry into force	Left	Entry into force	Left
Estonia	01.04.1994	01.05.2004				
Latvia	01.04.1994	01.05.2004				
Lithuania	01.04.1994	01.05.2004				
Hungary			01.03.1993	01.05.2004		
Czech Republic			01.03.1993	01.05.2004		
Poland			01.03.1993	01.05.2004		
Slovak Republic			01.03.1993	01.05.2004		
Slovenia			01.03.1993	01.05.2004		
Romania			01.07.1998	01.01.2007		
Bulgaria			01.01.1999	01.01.2007		
Croatia					22.08.2007	01.07.2013
Republic of Moldova					26.07.2007	
FYR Makedonia					26.07.2007	
Albania					26.07.2007	
Bosnia and Herzegovina					22.11.2007	
Montenegro					26.07.2007	
Serbia					24.10.2007	

Source: Author's own work based on European Commission (2016a)

The CEFTA was signed on 21 December 1992 by the Czech Republic, Hungary, Poland and Slovakia. In the following years Slovenia, Romania, Bulgaria joined the agreement, and in 2003, immediately before the founder countries' accession to the EU, Croatia acceded as well. Nowadays CEFTA has expanded into southern Europe with members from the Western Balkans and Moldova. All of the new CEFTA countries are prospective members of the EU (see Table 2.2). There are three main requirements for membership in CEFTA:

(1) a trade agreement with the EU or an associated member of the European Union;
(2) membership in the WTO or GATT;
(3) bilateral free trade agreements with each of the participants of the agreement.

In 1994 Estonia, Latvia and Lithuania formed the BAFTA. In 1997 it was expanded on free trade in the agriculture sector. Like CEFTA, BAFTA was created to help prepare the countries for their accession to the EU by restructuring old trade relations. It provided access not only to the markets of the member-countries, but also to the rest of the European markets.

With the 2004–2007 enlargement of the EU, the original members of both these agreements left to join the EU.

2.4.2 *The European Stabilisation and Association Agreements*

As early as 1990, it was clear that the scale of the transition process required a more broadly-based response from the EC. In August 1990, the Commission proposed to the Council that association agreements should be negotiated with Czechoslovakia, Hungary and Poland, and eventually with other countries. The negotiations on the possible conclusion of association agreements with the CEECs were opened in December 1990.

The Europe Agreements with Hungary and Poland were signed in December 1991, with Bulgaria, the Czech Republic and Slovakia in 1993, Estonia, Latvia and Lithuania in 1995, and finally with Slovenia in 1996. The establishment of similar trade relations with Croatia was concluded only in 2001 and entered into force only in 2005. The entry into force of the European Agreements was substantially delayed by the slow action of EU member states' parliaments (European Parliament 1999; Clark 1997; European Commission 2016b).

Once these countries joined the EU, the AAs were transformed into the EU accession treaties. In 2014, three countries signed AAs with the EU: Georgia, Moldova and Ukraine.

All the European Agreements have the same structure. Though the agreements are concluded for an unlimited period, the achievement of their objectives is scheduled for a maximum of 10 years (subdivided into two steps, each lasting 5 years) (Grabbe 1999).

The agreements cover political and cultural cooperation, economic activities and favorable trade relations with the EU. More importantly, the agreements establish bilateral free trade areas between the EU and individual CEECs. The EU promises to remove tariffs and quantitative restrictions on most industrial products. The CEECs are allowed to remove tariffs more slowly. While much liberalisation occurs, a group of "sensitive" industrial products including some textiles, and some coal and steel products remain protected. Agricultural trade is mostly excluded from liberalisation. The AAs, however, do not imply a customs union for trade in industrial goods. Consequently, there is no Common Customs Tariff for the Community and the associated countries (Grabbe 1999).

The Association Agreements between the European Union, and Georgia, Moldova and Ukraine include an additional part of each country's agreement—The **Deep and Comprehensive Free Trade Areas (DCFTA)** Agreements. These agreements allow Georgia, Moldova and Ukraine access to the EU's internal market for goods and services on the mutually-opened trade rules. These agreements created new trade opportunities for businesses, investors, consumers and citizens from the EU on the one side and Georgia, Moldova and Ukraine on the other. The agreements with Moldova and Georgia were ratified and officially entered into force in July 2016, although parts of them have already provisionally been applied (COMM/PRESS/01 2015).

To this end, the AAs allow free movement of services, people and capital transfers concerning direct investment and payments for transfers of services and people.

However, capital transfers concerning direct investments and repatriated profits from such investments must be authorised. The movement of CEEC workers is to be governed by existing laws. The AAs also provide for bilateral national treatment of firms. One particularly noteworthy provision is the fact that the AAs open EU government procurement to CEECs firms under the same conditions as EU companies (Grabbe 1999).

The protection of intellectual, industrial and commercial property is provided for at the same standard as applies within the Union. Economic, financial and cultural cooperation is also foreseen in the AAs. A very important element of the Europe Agreements is the commitment of the CEECs to adopt laws on economic and related issues that approximate the EU laws, thus excluding one-time shocks. This includes competition rules and limits on state aid to industries. However, there is no provision for automatic accession of the associated States to the European Communities.

In the case of the Western Balkans, a special process, the **Stabilisation and Association Process** exists to deal with the special circumstances there. The Stabilisation and Accession Agreements are aimed at stabilising the countries politically and encouraging their swift transition to a market economy, promoting regional cooperation and eventual membership of the EU. However, while Association Agreements grant their signatories the status of EU candidates, the Stabilisation and Association agreements grant a status of "potential candidate" for EU membership (Rodin 2001).

Nowadays the Stabilisation and Association Agreement has been signed with Macedonia (2001), Albania (2006), Montenegro (2007) and Serbia (2008), Bosnia and Herzegovina (2008).

The trade provisions offered by the SAAs provide the Western Balkans with duty-free access to the Union's market for practically all goods, including agricultural products, with no quantitative restrictions, except for duty-free or preferential quotas for some fishery products, baby-beef and wine (Commission of the European Communities 2003).

Unlike the AAs, the Stabilisation and Association Agreements imply changes in the tariff structures and excises in many of the SEE countries. The SAA is a first step towards aligning the external tariffs towards EU levels. As most SEE countries have higher overall levels of protection than the EU, the resulting liberalisation boosted competition, but lower collection from trade taxes. The second challenge for tax policy is the adoption of the required EU levels of excises on alcoholic beverages, tobacco, energy, and electricity (FAD 2005).

Having previously been relatively closed economies, the accession countries became increasingly integrated with the EU markets through the AAs and SAAs. These agreements can impact FDI inflows in a number of channels. Indirectly, they signal to foreign investors the country's adherence to certain economic standards, as well as the adoption of regulations designed to harmonise its business and legal environment with the EU, and hence an increase of the probability of membership in the EU. A more direct impact of the association agreements was that they provided investors with duty-free access to EU markets. In combination with the geographical proximity to the EU and relatively low prices for production factors, the AAs and SAAs are argued to positively affect both investments from the EU and from third countries.

2.4.3 *The EU Accession*

The process of joining the EU consists of four preparatory stages. It starts with a formal application for EU membership. After that, a country becomes a **potential candidate**. When a country formally applies for a membership, the Commission analyses a country's readiness to begin negotiations.

Having examined its application for EU membership, the EU Council formally recognises the country as candidate, thus granting the country **candidate status**. The commission and a candidate country examine its laws and the those of the EU to determine the differences between them. The Council then recommends opening negotiations on legal harmonisation with the candidate country (European Commission 2015, 2016b).

When the candidate starts formal membership negotiations it becomes an **accession country**. The negotiations are held between ministers and ambassadors of the EU governments and the accession country. Negotiations are essentially a matter of agreeing on how and when the candidate will adopt and effectively implement EU rules and procedures. The rules as such are non-negotiable. Candidates consequently have an incentive to implement the necessary reforms rapidly and effectively. Some of these reforms require considerable and sometimes difficult transformations of a country's political and economic structures (European Commission 2015, 2016b).

When negotiations on all the chapters have been completed to the satisfaction of both sides, the results are incorporated into a draft **Accession Treaty**. The treaty is then signed and ratified by the candidate country and all of the member states and institutions of the Union. The accession treaty contains the detailed terms and conditions of membership, all transitional arrangements and deadlines, as well as details of financial arrangements and any safeguard clauses (European Commission 2015, 2016b).

Once the accession treaty has been signed, the **acceding state** is entitled to certain preliminary privileges. It acquires "active observer status" in most EU bodies and agencies, where it is entitled to speak, but not to vote; it can comment on draft EU proposals, communications, recommendations or initiatives. This means it is expected to become a full EU member on the date laid down in the treaty, providing the treaty has been ratified (European Commission 2015, 2016b).

Once a country enters the EU, it gets all its privileges: free movement of goods, services, capital and persons. **The EU accession** implies the fulfilment of a number of economic, political, and legal criteria (European Commission 2015, 2016b).

Membership in the EMU is an important step in the process of deepening integration but it does not necessarily require a radically different analytical approach to the question of investment behaviour in Europe.

One of the main objectives of economic and monetary union in Europe is to encourage cross-border investment in EU economies by removing the exchange-rate uncertainty that was believed to discourage such investment there. The architects of EMU expected that the single currency would be a powerful stimulus to investment between EU states and also hoped that, by consolidating the Single European Market and emerging as a global currency to rival the dollar, the euro would encourage investment from outside.

The euro has certainly facilitated consolidation of European industry and made cost comparisons easier across European countries.

All countries in the CEE had and have their own timing for the process of integration into the EU. The stages are summarised in Table 2.3.

The first commitment to accepting countries from CEE was made in 1993 by the European Council in Copenhagen. At this summit, three criteria for membership (widely known as the "Copenhagen Criteria") were proposed (European Parliament 1993). They were:

(1) a political criterion, requiring a demonstration of stability of institutions that guarantee democracy, rule of law, human rights and the protection of minorities.
(2) an economic criterion, under which a country must be a functioning market economy, able to cope with competitive pressures and market forces within the EU.
(3) a legal criterion, according to which the country must be able to take on the obligations of membership, that is harmonious its national law with the acquis, the entire body of Community law.

Of course, the European Union in addition had to have the capacity to absorb new members. The accession should take place as soon as an associated country is able to accept the obligations of membership (European Parliament 1993; Albi 2005).

The first country to apply for EU membership was Hungary in March 1994. Until January 1996, when the Czech Republic applied, 10 other CEECs also formally applied (See Table 2.3, column 4).

The list of all steps of the pre-accession strategy was presented in a White Paper at the Cannes European Council in June 1995. It described administrative and technical structures which were needed to ensure that legislation as effectively implemented and enforced, outlining how technical assistance from the EU could be focused to best effect. For countries in transition, the formal economic accession criteria focused first and foremost on the establishment of a functioning market economy. The guidance provided by the European Commission and other institutions helped these countries to undergo one of the most rapid modernisation processes in history (European Commission 2015, 2016b).

In July 1997 the Commission formally reacted to the applications by issuing *Agenda 2000: For a stronger and Wider Union*. This document suggested accepting countries in two waves (See Table 2.3, column 5). The first wave included the Czech Republic, Estonia, Hungary, Poland and Slovenia plus Cyprus (Albi 2005; Commission of the European Communities 1997).

The Luxembourg European Council opened formal negotiations for the first wave of countries on March 30, 1998 (Table 2.3, column 6). The second round of countries (Bulgaria, Latvia, Lithuania, Romania, and Slovakia) was invited to join the accession negotiations in December 1999 in the Helsinki European Council (Table 2.3, column 5); however, the negotiations were only opened in February 2000 (Table 2.3, column 6).

As these countries became candidate countries, they were regularly monitored by the Commission. Before long, the Council's decision was seen to be mistaken. One reason for this was that some of the "second wave countries" began to narrow the

Table 2.3 Integration stages towards membership of CEE in the EU and EMU

Country	AA (signed)	AA (Entry into force)	Potential candidate	Candidate country	Accession country	Acceding country	EU member state	Euro area member
1	2	3	4	5	6	7	8	9
Hungary	16.12.1991	01.02.1994	31.03.1994	12.12.1997[a]	31.03.1998	13.12.2002	01.05.2004	–
Poland	16.12.1991	01.02.1994	05.04.1994	12.12.1997[a]	31.03.1998	13.12.2002	01.05.2004	–
Czech Republic	04.10.1993	01.02.1995	17.01.1996	12.12.1997[a]	31.03.1998	13.12.2002	01.05.2004	–
Slovakia	04.10.1993	01.02.1995	27.06.1995	12.12.1997[b]	15.02.2000	13.12.2002	01.05.2004	01.01.2009
Bulgaria	08.03.1993	01.02.1995	14.12.1995	12.12.1997[b]	15.02.2000	17.12.2004	01.01.2007	–
Romania	01.02.1993	01.02.1995	22.06.1995	12.12.1997[b]	15.02.2000	17.12.2004	01.01.2007	–
Estonia	12.06.1995	01.02.1998	24.11.1995	12.12.1997[a]	31.03.1998	13.12.2002	01.05.2004	01.01.2011
Latvia	12.06.1995	01.02.1998	13.09.1995	12.12.1997[b]	15.02.2000	13.12.2002	01.05.2004	01.01.2014
Lithuania	12.06.1995	01.02.1998	08.12.1995	12.12.1997[b]	15.02.2000	13.12.2002	01.05.2004	01.01.2015
Slovenia	10.06.1996	01.02.1999	10.06.1996	12.12.1997[a]	31.03.1998	13.12.2002	01.05.2004	01.01.2007
Croatia	29.10.2001	01.02.2005	21.02.2003	18.06.2004	30.10.2005	30.01.2011	01.07.2013	–
Macedonia	09.04.2001	01.04.2004	22.03.2004	17.12.2005	–	–	–	–
Albania	12.06.2006	01.04.2009	28.04.2009	24.06.2014	–	–	–	–
Montenegro	15.10.2007	01.05.2010	15.12.2008	17.12.2010	29.06.2012	27.06.2013		
Bosnia and Herzegovina	01.06.2008	01.06.2015	15.02.2016	–	–	–	–	–
Serbia	29.04.2008	01.09.2013	22.12.2009	01.03.2012	21.01.2014	24.03.2015	–	–
Ukraine	27.06.2014[c]		–	–	–	–	–	–
Moldova	27.06.2014 [c]	01.07.2016	–	–	–	–	–	–
Georgia	27.06.2014 [c]	01.07.2016						

Source: Author's own work based on European Commission (2015, 2016a)
[a]The first wave countries according to Agenda 2000
[b]The second wave countries according to Agenda 2000
[c]Political provisions of the AAs signed on 21 March 2014, remaining provisions and DCFTA signed on 27 June 2014

gap with first wave countries. According to the EU Commission, evaluation the criterion of a "functioning market economy" was completed by 2000s. Thus, the rapid transformation in the CEE candidates helped to fulfil the Copenhagen criteria and harmonise their legislation (based on the 1995 Cannes "White Book"). In December 2002, the European Commission recommended admitting to the EU eight candidate countries from CEE in 2004 (Table 2.3, columns 7, 8). Bulgaria and Romania were expected to be ready to join the EU in 2007 (Albi 2005).

Croatia applied for EU membership in 2003, in 2004 Commission approved Croatia's application for EU membership, and it was in negotiations from 2005 until 2011. On December 9, 2011 leaders from the EU and Croatia signed the accession treaty. The country became the 28th EU member country on July 1, 2013.

Nowadays, there are already five CEECs that have entered monetary union: Slovenia (in 2007), Slovakia (in 2009), Estonia (in 2011), Latvia (in 2014) and Lithuania (in 2015).

The Western Balkans (Serbia and Montenegro, FYR Macedonia, Albania, Bosnia and Herzegovina) were identified as potential candidates for EU membership during the Thessaloniki European Council summit in 2003. All EU Member States confirmed that these countries have a "European perspective". It means that they might join the EU if they fulfil all the necessary conditions. Accession criteria remained those defined by the 1993 Copenhagen European Council, but additional conditions for membership were set out in the so-called "Stabilisation and Association process", mostly relating to regional cooperation and good neighbour relations (European Commission 2016a).

These countries are at different stages of their transformation and, thus, in the integration progress. Montenegro and Serbia acceded in 2013 and 2015 respectively. FYR Macedonia is still being screened by the Commission (European Commission 2016a).

In 2009, Albania submitted its formal application for EU membership. In October 2012, the Commission recommended that Albania should be granted EU candidate status. Since then it had completed a number of reforms in the judicial and public fields. By 2014 it has achieved the necessary degree of compliance with the membership criteria and that year it was granted candidate status (European Commission 2016a).

Bosnia and Herzegovina applied for EU membership in February 2016. Ukraine, Moldova and Georgia have not yet applied for a membership in the EU.

The other dates of EU accession are shown in Table 2.3.

2.4.4 The Channels of Influence of the EU Integration on FDI Inflows

The EU represents the oldest, largest, most advanced and most successful regional integration organisation in the world. Since its establishment in 1958, the EU has gone through six rounds of enlargements:

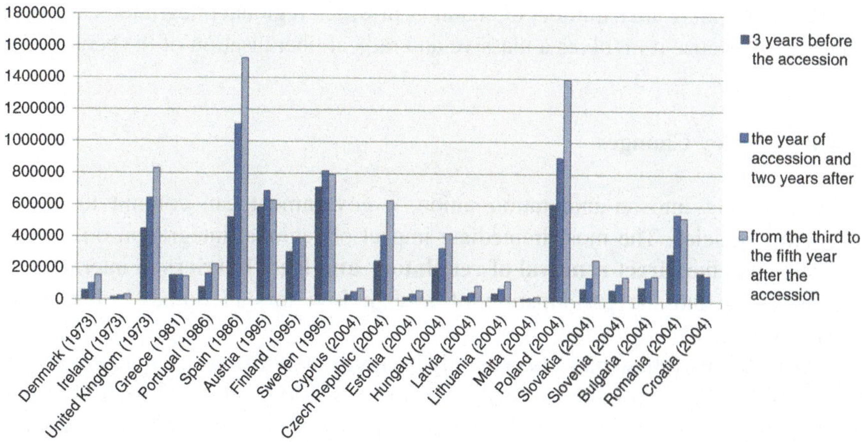

Fig. 2.11 FDI accumulated inflows before and after accession, in million US dollars. *Source*: Authors' elaboration based on the data from UNCTAD (2016b). *Note*: in brackets is the accession year

- 1973 (Denmark, Ireland and the United Kingdom);
- 1981 (Greece);
- 1986 (Portugal and Spain);
- 1995 (Austria, Finland and Sweden);
- 2004 the first wave (Cyprus, Czech Republic, Estonia, Hungary, Malta, Latvia, Lithuania, Poland, Slovakia and Slovenia); and 2007 the second wave (Bulgaria and Romania).
- 2013 Croatia

European integration over six decades has played an important role in FDI trends in Europe, judging from the FDI inflows into accession countries before and after the accession (Fig. 2.11).

The 2004 EU expansion to new members from Central and Eastern Europe (CEE) affected their FDI inflows more strongly and positively than was the case with earlier accessions (which all related to advanced market economies at the time of their entry to the EU).

EU integration helped to finish FDI liberalisation, raised protections and treatment standards for foreign investors, and assured investors about the irreversibility of reforms in the new accession countries, thus reducing transaction costs and the risk of investing in these countries. Moreover, EU funds have improved infrastructure or restructured inefficient state-owned enterprises, and, thus, have enhanced the long-term economic attractiveness of the CEE countries to FDI.

However, it is not clear when exactly the EU membership of CEE countries had an impact on the FDI inflows. One reason is that, since the early 1990s, these countries were linked to the EU through Association Agreements which, during the 1990s, gradually gave them free access to the EU market for manufactured goods—the greatest benefit in attracting export-oriented FDI.

Moreover, there are a number of channels in which regional integration can affect FDI flows because it involves a massive and radical liberalisation of the economies.

2.4.4.1 Policy Changes

When entering into an integration union, a government can commit to liberal economic policies. The most immediate impact of regional integration on foreign investment is the **direct removal of regulatory and legal barriers** to international capital flows and the participation of foreign investors in domestic firms and financial markets.

The removal of these barriers generally brings in more FDI as a country opens up new sectors, relaxes foreign ownership restrictions, and changes or abolishes local content requirements. However, the majority of integration agreements do not explicitly address FDI policy. The overall impact of the regional agreements on the policy framework for FDI therefore depends on whether an agreement contains provisions liberalising the movement of capital (including FDI capital).

In addition to explicit investment provisions, other agreements can influence FDI: trade in services, the setting and harmonising of standards, customs cooperation, and dispute settlement. A very important element of the policy changes is the commitment of the CEECs to adopt laws on economic and related issues that approximate EU laws. This includes competition rules and limits on state aid to industries. The protection of intellectual, industrial and commercial property is provided for at the same standard as applies within the Union. Economic, financial and cultural cooperation is also foreseen in integration Agreements. Although not directly related to investment, these features **improve the host economy's investment climate** and are thus likely to result in increased FDI inflows (Baldwin 1994).

Thus, membership in the European Union, either current or prospective, indicates a favourable investment climate, as it provides investors with a guarantee of the country's adherence to certain economic standards, as well as the adoption of regulations designed to harmonise its business and legal environment with the other member states. European Union membership also opens the possibility of a country adopting the euro, which further harmonises the country's macroeconomic policies with those of the rest of Europe. The gradual adoption of the acquis has vastly contributed to the improvement in business climate and made CEECs more attractive to foreign and domestic investors alike.

2.4.4.2 Economic Determinants

The reduction of trade barriers is the first step of any integration process. The key determinant of the sign and magnitude of this effect depends on the issue of whether FDI and trade are substitutes or complements. The effect of the reduction of trade barriers also depends on the country of FDI origin (Yeyati et al. 2003).

By lowering or eliminating tariffs between participants of the integration process, preferential liberalisation removes incentives for intraregional investment, and therefore negatively influences FDI inflows. On the other hand, such elimination of trade barriers creates favourable conditions for foreign companies to access regional markets for final and intermediate production, which in turn stimulates more FDI.

While the aggregate relationship between trade and FDI remains unclear, the connection between host **market size** and FDI is well established. The extended common market effect on FDI is not automatic, and its magnitude depends on the economic and geographic proximity of the partners, although preferential liberalisation can potentially bring some FDI benefits even for distant countries. Thus, membership in the EU allows countries that have small domestic markets to expand their market size. Firms located in the EU get access to the entire EU and are associated with EU countries (El-Kady and Zimny 2009).

Since the same definition of market size would apply to all member countries, other determinants come to play a much more important role in the location decisions of TNCs. For small countries, the size of their domestic market will no longer deter market-seeking foreign investors in tradable goods since they will now have access to the region's market, and not just the host country's market (El-Kady and Zimny 2009).

Regional integration also influences TNCs' **access to resources**. In many integration unions, TNCs can access the skills, technologies or other strategic assets available in member countries other than those in which their production operations are located. The European Union, for example, allows all foreign affiliates regardless of their location within the Union to participate in European Union-sponsored R&D projects—subject to certain restrictions on the transfer of technology to non-member countries (Brewer and Young 2000).

2.4.4.3 Business Factors

The primary effect of integration on business facilitation FDI determinants is to reduce intra-regional business transaction costs. Such costs arise directly from inadequacies of information, asymmetries in doing business in different countries, the heterogeneity of administrative procedures, and differences in business support measures. Recognising the importance of business facilitation obstacles, some integration unions seek to harmonise efforts to remove them or replace them with comprehensive region-wide programs for FDI facilitation.

In the case of the European Union, for example, the removal of internal tariff barriers was insufficient for creating a unified regional market because of other obstacles to intraregional transactions, especially in services.

Thus, if European integration can be seen to have stimulated investment flows in Europe, it can also affect the choice of location of economic activity more broadly.

2.5 Appendix

2.5.1 *Appendix A*

Table 2.4 FDI inflows in selected Central and Eastern European countries by source countries, 1998, in %

Home region and country	Host country and year														
	Bosnia and Herzegovina	Bulgaria	Croatia	Czech Republic	Estonia	Hungary	Latvia	Lithuania	Macedonia, FYR	Moldova, Republic	Poland	Romania	Slovakia	Slovenia	Ukraine
	1998	1998	1998	1998	1998	1998	1998	1998	1998	1998	1997	1998	1998	1998	1998
Central and Eastern Europe	23	4,8	2,7	3,4	2	1,1	13	3	0,7	32	1	1	10	9,4	6,7
Croatia	17	–	..	..	–	..	..	..	1,1	..	–	–	..	3,3	..
Czech Republic	..	0,7	0,2	–	..	0,1	..	..	–	..	..	..	..	5,4	..
Hungary	..	0,1	0,3	0,2	..	..	..	..	..	..	..	..	..	0,2	..
Russian Federation	..	2,8	0,3	0,1	2	..	9	..	..	29	–	–	..	0,1	6,7
Developed countries		76,1	93,6	94,6		94,7			41,2					89,8	52,8
European Union	30	58,3	60,6	82,7	77	64	53	57	19,5	23	77	60	71	81,2	28,1
Austria	4	7,2	19,3	11,5	2	11,7	1	..	7,4	1	4	5	20	37,5	2,8
Belgium	..	..	0,7	1,1	–	3,9	–	..	..	6	2	5	..	0,3	..
Denmark	3	0,1	0,7	0,9	5	0,4	16	4	–	..	4	–	..	1,4	..
Finland	..	–	..	0,1	27	0,6	4	19	..	..	1	..	..	..	..
France	3	1,3	1,6	4,7	–	6,1	–	..	0,2	..	11	7	7	12,8	..
Germany	17	8	27,9	29,6	3	28	8	7	1,3	6	22	10	20	12,3	8,3
Greece	..	7,8	..	–	..	–	..	..	3,2	4	–	2	..	..	..
Ireland	..	0,1	–	0,1	..	0,3	..	..	..	..	..	..	..	–	..
Italy	4	1,3	1,4	0,9	1	3,2	–	..	1,3	..	5	8	..	6,6	..
Luxembourg	..	..	–	0,4	–	..	..	..	1,6	..	..	..	..	0,3	..
Netherlands	..	5,8	3,9	27,1	2	15,5	3	..	4	..	22	15	8	3,8	9,5
Portugal	..	0,1	..	–	..	–	..	..	..	..	..	..	..	..	..
Spain	..	4,1	..	0,2	..	0,1	..	..	..	..	..	..	..	1,1	..
Sweden	..	0,2	2,6	1,4	32	0,7	7	22	..	..	2	2	..	0,3	..

United Kingdom	–	12,2	2,5	4,7	4	6,4	8	5	0,4	..	4	5	13	4,8	7,5
Other Western Europe		4,8	2,8	2,8		16,2			18,5					4	6,3
Liechtenstein	..	..	1,3	0,1	–	..	–	..	18,1	–	..	..	..	–	3,1
Norway	..	0,1	..	0,7	..	0,3	..	..	..	..	..	..	..	..	..
Switzerland		4,7	1,5	1,8	5	2,9	4	..	0,4	6	3	2	..	3,3	3,2
Other developed countries		13,1	30,3	9,1		14,5			3,3					4,6	18,3
Canada	..	–	0,7	0,3	..	0,2	..	..	..	..	..	..	..	–	..
Japan	..	0,7	..	0,5	–	1,9	..	..	..	..	–			0,1	..
United States	..	12,2	28,4	8,2	5	12,2	11	16	3	19	12	7	11	4,4	18,3
Developing countries		4,8	1,6	2		2,1			55,8					0,8	15
Africa	..	–	0,1	0,1	..	0,6	..	..	–	..	..	..	..	–	..
Latin America and the Caribbean	..	–	1,5	0,3	..	0,3	..	..	..	..	..	..	..	0,1	3
Developing Asia		4,8	–	1,6		1,2			55,8					0,7	12,1
Cyprus	..	..	–	1,2	..	..	–	..	55,4	1	–	2	..	0,3	5,4
Korea, Republic of	..	2,6	..	–	..	0,8	..	..	..	..	2	6	..	..	6,7
Kuwait	21	..	..	..	..	..	..	..	..	..	..	..	..	..	..
Turkey	12	1,4	..	–	–	–	..	..	0,4	..	–	5	..	0,1	..
The Pacific	..	..	..	..		..	..	..	..	..	..	..	..	..	..
Other and not specified	13	14,2	6	..	11	2,2	20	24	2,3	20	5	13	9	–	25,5
Memorandum item															
Commonwealth of Independent States	..	3,2	0,3	0,1	..	0,5	..	..	..	..	..	..	..	0,1	6,7
Total	100	100	100	100	100	100	100	100	100	100	100	100	100	100	100

Source: UNCTAD FDI/TNC database
Double periods denote N/A and Dashes denote "0"

Table 2.5 Privatization-related FDI inflows in selected Central and Eastern European countries, 1991–1999

Country	Indicator	1991	1992	1993	1994	1995	1996	1997	1998	1999	Total
Bulgaria	Total FDI[a]	..	..	40	105	90	109	492	505	476	1817
	Privatization-related	..	..	3	28	63	36	340	216	227	912
	Privatization-related as share of total (per cent)	..	..	8	26	70	33	69	43	48	50
Croatia	Total FDI[a]	..	..	88	105	83	437	320	591	1146	2769
	Privatization-related	..	..	53	92	79	4	169	449	951	1798
	Privatization-related as share of total (per cent)	..	..	61	88	95	1	53	76	83	65
Czech Republic	Total FDI[a]	..	..	654	869	2562	1428	1300	2540	4877	14,230
	Privatization-related[b]	..	..	568	862	2559	1317	1038	..	..	6344
	Privatization-related as share of total (per cent)	..	..	87	99	100	92	80	..	..	45
Hungary	Total FDI[a]	1459	1471	2339	1146	4453	1788	1811	1410	1675	17,552
	Privatization-related	325	488	651	99	3025	577	272	12	0	5449
	Privatization-related as share of total (per cent)	22	33	28	9	68	32	15	1	0	31
Macedonia, FYR	Total FDI[a]	..	..	..	20	1	5	9	103	10	148
	Privatization-related	..	..	..	..	..	..	5	26	3	34
	Privatization-related as share of total (per cent)	..	..	..	..	..	..	57	25	35	23
Republic of Moldova	Total FDI[a]	..	..	14	28	65	21	70	57	37	292
	Privatization-related	..	..	14	28	64	17	39	..	..	161
	Privatization-related as share of total (per cent)	..	..	100	100	97	82	55	..	..	55
Poland	Total FDI[a]	892	298	892	884	1807	2845	2663	4323	..	14,604
	Privatization-related[c]	127	213	176	104	480	423	464	300	..	2287
	Privatization-related as share of total (per cent)	14	72	20	12	27	15	17	7	..	16
Romania	Total FDI[a]	..	..	37	188	207	151	655	1346	656	3240
	Privatization-related	..	..	6	33	82	16	335	1131	..	1604
	Privatization-related as share of total (per cent)	..	..	17	17	40	11	51	84	..	49

Russian Federation	Total FDI[a]	..	..	1211	640	1451	1822	5014	1378	1240	12,756
	Privatization-related	..	..	..	..	..	..	2155	1	0	2156
	Privatization-related as share of total (per cent)	..	..	..	..	..	..	43	0	0	17

Source: Hunya (2000), UNCTAD FDI/TNC database
Note: The data presented in this table are not strictly comparable because the definition of "privatization-related inflows" varies from country to country
[a]FDI equity inflows paid in cash only
[b]Including reinvestments and additional investments
[c]Capital (indirect) privatization only
Double periods denote N/A and Dashes denote "0"

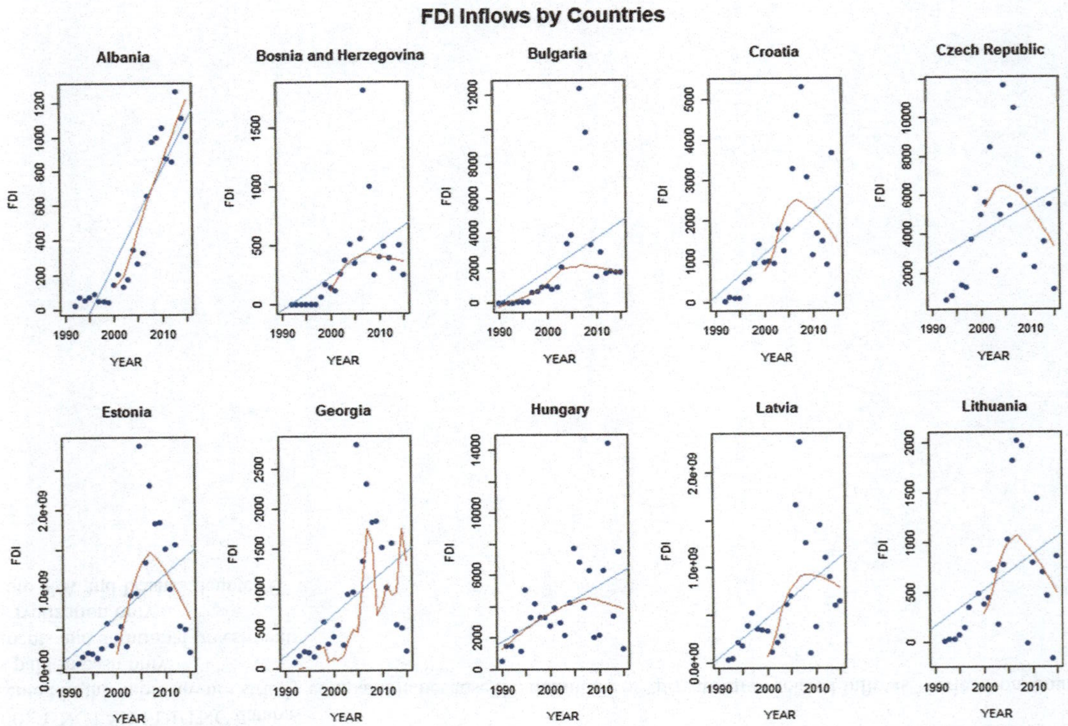

Fig. 2.12 Scatter plots of FDI inflows by countries. *Source*: Author's calculation based on UNCTAD (2016b). *Note*: Blue line is trend line, red line is LOWESS (locally weighted scatterplot smoothing)

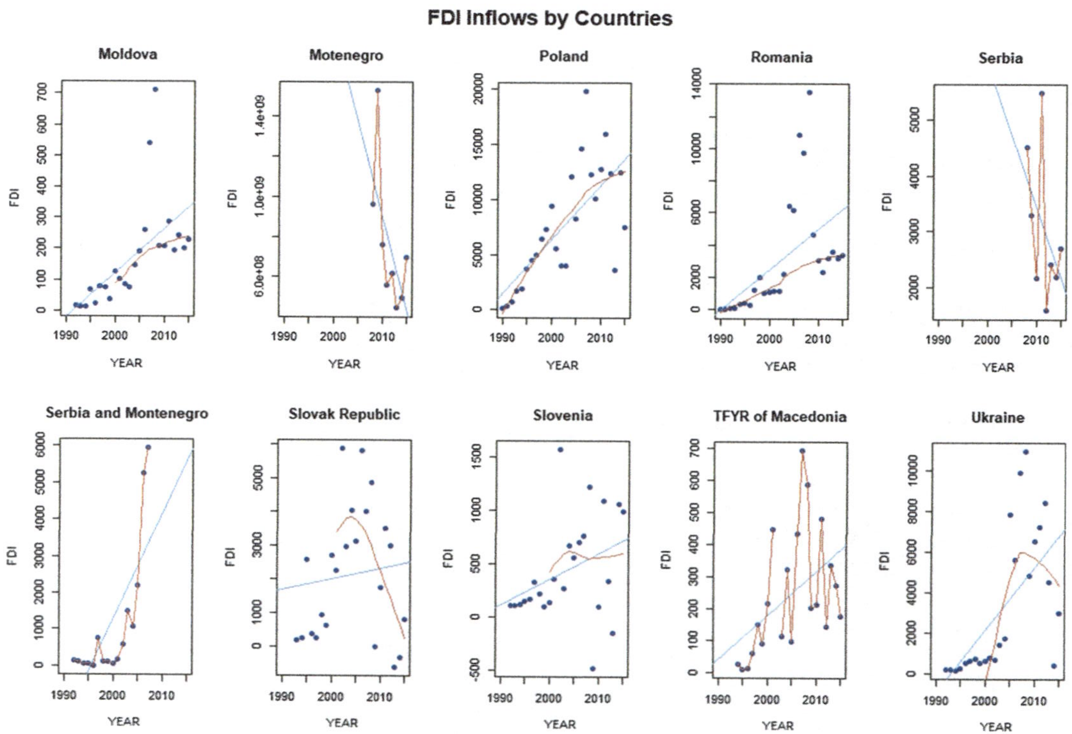

Fig. 2.13 Scatter plots of FDI inflows by countries (part 2). *Source*: Author's calculation based on UNCTAD. *Note*: Blue line is trend line, red line is LOWESS (locally weighted scatterplot smoothing)

2.5.2 *Appendix B*

Table 2.6 Empirical literature overview

	Proxy	Effect	Data source	Location	Studied period	Author
Market size	GDP	+		CEE	1992–2001	Clausing and Dorobantu (2005)
		+		CEE accession countries and Ukraine	1994–1998, 1994–2000	Bevan and Estrin (2000, 2004)
		+		8 accession CEECs	1997	Janicki and Wunnava (2004)
		+		CEE and SE	2000–2008	Kinoshita (2011)
		+		SE	1996–2002	V. Botric and L. Skuflic (2006)
		+		CEE and Ukraine	1994–2000	S. Estrin and K.E. Meyer (2011)
		0		25 transition economies	1991–1999	P. Garibaldi et al. (2002)
		+		25 transition economies	1994–1998	Tondel (2001)
		+	WDI	16 CEEC countries	1996–2009	C. Tintin (2011)
		+		10 EU accession countries	1987–2001	J.W.B. Bos and M. van de Laar (2004)
		+		CEE and SE	1991–1993	Brada et al. (2003)

		+		CEE and other regions	1992–1995	P. Brenton et al. (1998)
		+		143 countries	1980–2003	D. Medvedev (2006)
		+		25 transition economies	1994–1998	Tondel (2001)
	GDP per capita	+		CEE	1992–2001	Clausing and Dorobantu (2005)
		+		25 transition countries	1990–1998	Campos and Kinoshita (2002)
		+	The World Bank Group	CEE and SE	2001–2006	M. Mateev (2009)
		+		CEE and CIS	1991–2003	A. Johnson (2006)
		–		SE	1996–2002	V. Botric and L. Skuflic (2006)
		+		CEE accession countries	1990–1995	Resmini (2000)
		+		SE	1995–2000	E. Hengel (2011)
		+	WIIW	CE	1990–1993	D. P. Woodward (2000)
		+		25 transition economies	1994–1998	Tondel (2001)
		+		CEE and SE	1991–1993	Brada et al. (2003)
		0		CEE accession countries + Ukraine and Turkey	1990–2009	Güngör, Hakan; Oğuş, Ayla (2010)
	Discounted GDP of a country by its average distance from the "core" European regions (Frankfurt).	+		CEE and MED	1990–1997	Altononte and Guagliano (2003)

(continued)

Table 2.6 (continued)

	Proxy	Effect	Data source	Location	Studied period	Author
	Market potential (the host's internal transportation costs proxied by the distance in minutes and the transportation cost between the host and the home country)	+		CEE	1993–1999	K. Carstensen and F. Toubal (2004)
	GDP (ln)/internal distance	+	World Bank WDI, CEPII	CEE	1995–2000	A. Seric (2011)
	GDP adjusted to PPP (ln)	+		25 transition economies	1991–1999	P. Garibaldi et al. (2002)
		+		15 transition economies	2000–2002	Dimitri G. Demekas et al. (2005), Ribakova et al. (2005)
	Population	+	The World Bank Group	CEE and SE	2001–2006	M. Mateev (2009)
		+		CEE and CIS	1991–2003	A. Johnson (2006)
		–		SE	1996–2002	V. Botric and L. Skuflic (2006)
		+		CEE accession countries	1990–1995	Resmini (2000)
		+	WIIW	CE	1990–1993	D. P. Woodward (2000)
		0		25 transition economies	1991–1999	P. Garibaldi et al. (2002)
		+		CEE	1998–2008	C. T. Albulescu et al. (2010)
		0		10 EU accession countries	1987–2001	J.W.B. Bos and M. van de Laar (2004)

		+		CEE and SE	1991–1993	Dimitri G. Demekas et al. (2005), Ribakova et al. (2005)
		–		CEE and other regions	1992–1995	P. Brenton et al. (1998)
Market growth	GDP growth	+		25 transition economies	1991–1999	P. Garibaldi et al. (2002)
		0		25 transition economies	1994–1998	Tondel (2001)
		+		143 countries	1980–2003	D. Medvedev (2006)
	GDP per capita growth rate	0		CEE accession countries + Ukraine and Turkey	1990–2009	Güngör, Hakan; Oğuş, Ayla (2010)
Labor costs	Unit labour cost	–		CEE	1992–2001	Clausing and Dorobantu (2005)
		–		CEE accession countries and Ukraine	1994–1998, 1994–2000	Bevan and Estrin (2000, 2004)
		–		CEE and Ukraine	1994–2000	S. Estrin and K.E. Meyer (2011)
		–		15 transition economies	2000–2002	Dimitri G. Demekas et al. (2005), Ribakova et al. (2005)
	Labor cost relative to other potential costs	–		CE	1990–1994	Lansbury et al. (1996)
	Relative labor cost between host and source countries	+	European Economy (European Commission 2002), WIIW (2001), ILO (2016)	CEE	1993–1999	K. Carstensen and F. Toubal (2004)
	Labor cost (average annual wages in 1995–1999 in manufacturing sector)	–		8 accession CEECs	1997	Janicki and Wunnava (2004)

(continued)

Table 2.6 (continued)

	Proxy	Effect	Data source	Location	Studied period	Author
	Labor productivity (ln)	+	Eurostat database	CEE	1998–2008	C. T. Albulescu et al. (2010)
	Labor force (ln)	–		10 EU accession countries	1987–2001	J.W.B. Bos and M. van de Laar (2004)
	Changes in costs of labor (%)	–		CEE and SE	2001–2006	M. Mateev (2009)
	Wages	0	WIIW	CE	1990–1993	D. P. Woodward (2000)
		+		25 transition economies	1994–1998	Tondel (2001)
		0	Average gross wage in euro, index (US = 100)	CEE and SE	2000–2008	Kinoshita (2011)
		0		SE	1996–2002	V. Botric and L. Skuflic (2006)
		0		CEE accession countries + Ukraine and Turkey	1990–2009	Güngör, Hakan; Oğuş, Ayla (2010)
		0	UNECE 'Economic Survey of Europe'	25 transition countries	1990–1998	Campos and Kinoshita (2002)
	Average Monthly manufacturing wages	–	ILO (2016)	CEE and CIS	1991–2003	A. Johnson (2006)
		0		25 transition economies	1991–1999	P. Garibaldi et al. (2002)
	Wage differentials between the host and source countries	0		CEE accession countries	1990–1995	Resmini (2000)
	Compensation of employment/total hours worked	+		CEE	1995–2000	A. Seric (2011)
	Gross value added/total hours worked	+		CEE	1995–2000	A. Seric (2011)
	Income per capita	+		CEE and SE	2000–2008	Kinoshita (2011)

	Per capita income to per capita income in the US	–		143 countries	1980–2003	D. Medvedev (2006)
Labor quality	General secondary school enrollment rate	+		25 transition countries	1990–1998	Campos and Kinoshita (2002)
		+		25 transition economies	1994–1998	Tondel (2001)
		+		CEE and SE	1991–1993	
	The general tertiary education enrollment rate	–		CEE and MED	1990–1997	Altononte and Guagliano (2003)
		+		CEE and SE	2000–2008	Kinoshita (2011)
		0	UNESCO	CEE and SE	2001–2006	M. Mateev (2009)
	The relation of skilled to total labor	+	UNICEF (2001), World Development Indicators	CEE	1993–1999	K. Carstensen and F. Toubal (2004)
Capital cost	The interest rate differential between host and source countries	0		CEE accession countries and Ukraine	1994–1998, 1994–2000	Bevan and Estrin (2000, 2004)
		0		CEE and Ukraine	1994–2000	S. Estrin and K.E. Meyer (2011)
	Real domestic treasury bill rate (if not available = 0)	0		25 transition economies	1991–1999	P. Garibaldi et al. (2002)
	Real domestic deposit rate		World economic outlook, IMF	25 transition economies	1991–1999	P. Garibaldi et al. (2002)
	Lending-deposit rate	+		CEE and SE	1991–1993	Brada et al. (2003)
	Lending rate	–	EBRD	CEE	1998–2008	C. T. Albulescu et al. (2010)
Natural resources	Endowments of natural resources (dummy 'poor' (=0), 'moderate' (=1), and 'rich' (=2))	0		25 transition countries	1990–1998	Campos and Kinoshita (2002)
		+		25 transition economies	1991–1999	P. Garibaldi et al. (2002)

(continued)

Table 2.6 (continued)

	Proxy	Effect	Data source	Location	Studied period	Author
	Dummy variable. Proxy for oil and gas abundance, equal to 1 for Azerbaijan, Kazakhstan, Russia and Turkmenistan, zero otherwise	0	Based on Shiells (2003)	CEE and CIS	1991–2003	A. Johnson (2006)
	Production of crude oil in thousand barrels per day	0	EIA	CEE and CIS	1991–2003	A. Johnson (2006)
	Energy consumption	0		CE	1990–1994	Lansbury et al. (1996)
	Total production of primary energy	0		CEE	1995–2000	A. Seric (2011)
	Relative factor endowments	+	Gross fixed capital formation is taken from EBRD (2001). Employment is taken from the World Development Indicators	CEE	1993–1999	K. Carstensen and F. Toubal (2004)
Openness	Export+Import to GDP	+		CEE and SE	2000–2008	Kinoshita (2011)
		0	Export + Import to GDP	CEE and SE	2001–2006	A. Johnson (2006)
		+		SE	1996–2002	V. Botric and L. Skuflic (2006)
		+		CEE accession countries	1990–1995	Resmini (2000)
		+		CEE	1995–2000	A. Seric (2011)
		+		SE	1995–2000	E. Hengel (2011)
		+	WDI	16 CEEC countries	1996–2009	C. Tintin (2011)
		+		CEE	1998–2008	C. T. Albulescu et al. (2010)

		+		CEE and SE	1991–1993	Brada et al. (2003)
		+		143 countries	1980–2003	D. Medvedev (2006)
	Share of trade between two countries to total trade	0		CE	1990–1994	Lansbury et al. (1996)
	Total imports (% GDP)	+		CEE accession countries and Ukraine	1994–1998, 1994–2000	Bevan and Estrin (2000, 2004)
		+		8 accession CEECs	1997	Janicki and Wunnava (2004)
	Tariff revenues (percentage of imports to the trade cost of country)	–	EBRD (2001)	CEE	1993–1999	K. Carstensen and F. Toubal (2004)
	Tariff revenue/imports	–		15 transition economies	2000–2002	Dimitri G. Demekas et al. (2005), Ribakova et al. (2005)
	Import per capita	+		CEE accession countries + Ukraine and Turkey	1990–2009	Güngör, Hakan; Oğuş, Ayla (2010)
	Goods export (ln)	–	IFS statistics	10 EU accession countries	1987–2001	J.W.B. Bos and M. van de Laar (2004)
	Goods import (ln)	+	IFS statistics	10 EU accession countries	1987–2001	J.W.B. Bos and M. van de Laar (2004)
	Services export (ln)	0	IFS statistics	10 EU accession countries	1987–2001	J.W.B. Bos and M. van de Laar (2004)
	Services import (ln)	0	IFS statistics	10 EU accession countries	1987–2001	J.W.B. Bos and M. van de Laar (2004)

(continued)

Table 2.6 (continued)

	Proxy	Effect	Data source	Location	Studied period	Author
	Income credit (ln)	–	IFS statistics	10 EU accession countries	1987–2001	J.W.B. Bos and M. van de Laar (2004)
	Income debit (ln)	+	IFS statistics	10 EU accession countries	1987–2001	J.W.B. Bos and M. van de Laar (2004)
	Capita account credit (ln)	–	IFS statistics	10 EU accession countries	1987–2001	J.W.B. Bos and M. van de Laar (2004)
	Capital account debit (ln)	+	IFS statistics	10 EU accession countries	1987–2001	J.W.B. Bos and M. van de Laar (2004)
	Openness (host countries' import to GDP ratios on population and population squared)	+		CEE	1992–2001	Clausing and Dorobantu (2005)
EU accession	EU announcements (dummy)	+		CEE accession countries and Ukraine	1994–1998, 1994–2000	Bevan and Estrin (2000, 2004)
	EU announcements (dummy)	+		CEE	1992–2001	Clausing and Dorobantu (2005)
	EU membership (dummy)	+		CEE	1992–2001	Clausing and Dorobantu (2005)
	EU membership (dummy)	+		16 CEEC countries	1996–2009	C. Tintin (2011)
	EU Membership Interaction Term (EU membership dummy*GDP)	–		16 CEEC countries	1996–2009	C. Tintin (2011)

	EU accession phases of host countries (dummy, 0 = EU does not approve the country as a candidate; 1 = candidate country of EU; 2 = accession negations begin; 3 = the membership of EU)	+		CEE accession countries + Ukraine and Turkey	1990–2009	Güngör, Hakan; Oğuş, Ayla (2010)
PTA and FTA membership	Dummy variable for duration of membership in CEFTA/BAFTA	+		CEE	1995–2000	A. Seric (2011)
	Dummy variable for duration of membership in CEFTA or CEFTA 2006	0		SE	1995–2000	E. Hengel (2011)
	Preferential relations between countries (dummy)	0		CEE and other regions	1992–1995	P. Brenton et al. (1998)
	Sum of GDP of PTA partners	0		143 countries	1980–2003	D. Medvedev (2006)
	PTA concluded (dummy)	0		143 countries	1980–2003	D. Medvedev (2006)
	Number of PTA	0		143 countries	1980–2003	D. Medvedev (2006)
Financial incentives	Corporate income tax rates	–		CEE	1992–2001	Clausing and Dorobantu (2005)
		–	PriceWaterhouse Coopers	CEE	1993–1999	K. Carstensen and F. Toubal (2004)
		–		CEE	1995–2000	A. Seric (2011)
		–		15 transition economies	2000–2002	Dimitri G. Demekas et al. (2005), Ribakova et al. (2005)
	Tax holidays (whether the country has a 5-year or longer tax holiday: 1 yes; 0 no)	0		15 transition economies	2000–2002	Dimitri G. Demekas et al. (2005), Ribakova et al. (2005)
		+	PriceWaterhouse	CE	1990–1993	D. P. Woodward (2000)

(continued)

Table 2.6 (continued)

	Proxy	Effect	Data source	Location	Studied period	Author
	Number of years a tax loss can be carried forward to offset income in future years	+	PriceWaterhouse	CE	1990–1993	D. P. Woodward (2000)
	Aggregate financial stability index	+		CEE	1998–2008	C. T. Albulescu et al. (2010)
	Restrictions on capital inflows	0	Binici et al. (2009)	CEE and SE	2000–2008	Kinoshita (2011)
Infrastructure	The number of main telephone lines	+		25 transition countries	1990–1998	Campos and Kinoshita (2002)
	The number of telephone lines per 100 inhabitants	0		SE	1996–2002	V. Botric and L. Skuflic (2006)
	The number of internet connections	0		SE	1996–2002	V. Botric and L. Skuflic (2006)
	Index of infrastructural reform	+	EBRD	CEE and SE	2000–2008	Kinoshita (2011)
		+	EBRD	CEE	1995–2000	A. Seric (2011)
		+	EBRD	SE	1995–2000	E. Hengel (2011)
		0	EBRD	CEE and SE	2001–2006	M. Mateev (2009)
		+	EBRD	15 transition economies	2000–2002	Dimitri G. Demekas et al. (2005), Ribakova et al. (2005)
		+	EBRD	CEE and SE	1991–1993	Brada et al. (2003)
	Highways (ln)	+	CIA factbook	10 EU accession countries	1987–2001	J.W.B. Bos and M. van de Laar (2004)
Privatisation	Privatisation method (by direct sale, by voucher, insider)	+	Holland and Pain (1998)	CEE accession countries and Ukraine	1994–2000	Bevan and Estrin (2000)

		0	Holland and Pain (1998)	CEE and SE	2001–2006	M. Mateev (2009)
		+		CEE and CIS	1991–2003	A. Johnson (2006)
		+	Holland and Pain (1998), EBRD, Böhm and Simoneti (1993), Böhn (1994–1996)	CEE	1993–1999	K. Carstensen and F. Toubal (2004)
		– for direct sale, insider	EBRD transition report	25 transition economies	1991–1999	P. Garibaldi et al. (2002)
	Privatization revenue	0	EBRD	CEE and SE	2000–2008	Kinoshita (2011)
	Private sector (% GDP)	+		SE	1996–2002	V. Botric and L. Skuflic (2006)
		+	EBRD	CEE	1993–1999	K. Carstensen and F. Toubal (2004)
		0		CEE and SE	1991–1993	Brada et al. (2003)
		+		CE	1990–1994	Lansbury et al. (1996)
	Change in share of private sector	+		CEE and SE	1991–1993	Brada et al. (2003)
	Large-scale privatisation	+		SE	1996–2002	V. Botric and L. Skuflic (2006)
	Index of privatization reform	+	EBRD	SE	1995–2000	E. Hengel (2011)
		0	EBRD	CEE	1995–2000	A. Seric (2011)
Transition and liberalisation	Early transition (dummy: is based on Blanchard (1998): 'if the countries started transition in 1991' = 1, otherwise = 0)	0	Blanchard (1998)	CEE and SE	2000–2008	Kinoshita (2011)
	Transition performance	+	Constructed based on indicators in EBRD	CEE and CIS	1991–2003	A. Johnson (2006)

(continued)

Table 2.6 (continued)

	Proxy	Effect	Data source	Location	Studied period	Author
		0, only for CEE and BS		25 transition economies	1994–1998	C. Tintin (2011)
	Index of competition reform	0	EBRD	CEE	1995–2000	A. Seric (2011)
		+	EBRD	SE	1995–2000	E. Hengel (2011)
	Index of enterprise restructuring	0	EBRD	CEE	1995–2000	A. Seric (2011)
		+	EBRD	SE	1995–2000	E. Hengel (2011)
	Index of the overall quality of institutions	+	Fraser Institute	CEE	1995–2000	A. Seric (2011)
	Liberalisation index	+	De Melo et al. (1996) based on EBDR indicates	25 transition economies	1991–1999	P. Garibaldi et al. (2002)
		+	De Melo et al. (1996)	25 transition countries	1990–1998	Campos and Kinoshita (2002)
Corruption	"Bribe tax"	–	Transition Report and Transition (EBRD)	CEE accession countries and Ukraine	1994–2000	Bevan and Estrin (2000)
		0		15 transition economies	2000–2002	Dimitri G. Demekas et al. (2005), Ribakova et al. (2005)
	Corruption Index	+	Transparency International	CEE and SE	2001–2006	M. Mateev (2009)
		0	Transparency International	CEE and CIS	1991–2003	A. Johnson (2006)
Stability	Credit rating of country	+	Institutional Investor	8 accession CEECs	1997	Janicki and Wunnava (2004)

		0	Institutional Investor	CEE accession countries and Ukraine	1994–1998, 1994–2000	Bevan and Estrin (2000, 2004)
		+	Moody's Sovereign	CEE and SE	2001–2006	M. Mateev (2009)
	Country risk rating	+	Euromoney	CE	1990–1993	D. P. Woodward (2000)
		–	Euromoney	25 transition economies	1991–1999	P. Garibaldi et al. (2002)
		0	Euromoney	10 EU accession countries	1987–2001	J.W.B. Bos and M. van de Laar (2004)
	The political risk index	–	Euromoney	CEE	1993–1999	K. Carstensen and F. Toubal (2004)
		+	Euromoney	10 EU accession countries	1987–2001	J.W.B. Bos and M. van de Laar (2004)
	Economic risk	0		10 EU accession countries	1987–2001	J.W.B. Bos and M. van de Laar (2004)
	Economic freedom index	–	Johnson (2006)	CEE and other regions	1992–1995	P. Brenton et al. (1998)
	Economic freedoms	+	Heritage Foundation	16 CEEC countries	1996–2009	C. Tintin (2011)
	Business environment index	+	BERI S.A.	CEE and MED	1990–1997	Altonontе and Guagliano (2003)
		0	BERI S.A.	CEE accession countries	1990–1995	Resmini (2000)
	Overall government-business interface	0	World Development Report 1997 Survey	25 transition economies	1991–1999	P. Garibaldi et al. (2002)

(continued)

Table 2.6 (continued)

	Proxy	Effect	Data source	Location	Studied period	Author
	Risk (net debt/exports ratio; import/reserves ratio; government deficit/GDP ratio; inflation)	0		CE	1990–1994	Lansbury et al. (1996)
	Risk (the variance in growth rates, inflation or exchange rate stability, institutional stability reflected in policies towards FDI, tax regimes, the transparency and effectiveness of the commercial legal code, and the extent of corruption and political stability, represented by measures of political freedom)	0		CEE and Ukraine	1994–2000	S. Estrin and K.E. Meyer (2011)
	Political stability and security of property	0	World Development Report 1997 Survey	25 transition economies	1991–1999	P. Garibaldi et al. (2002)
Institutional quality	Rule of laws	+	Campos (2000)	25 transition countries	1990–1998	Campos and Kinoshita (2002)
		0	ICRG	CEE and SE	2000–2008	Kinoshita (2011)
	Predictability of laws and policies	0	World Development Report 1997 Survey	25 transition economies	1991–1999	P. Garibaldi et al. (2002)
	Efficiency of government in providing services	0	World Development Report 1997 Survey	25 transition economies	1991–1999	P. Garibaldi et al. (2002)
	Index of the completeness of the local legal framework	+	The World Bank	CEE and MED	1990–1997	Altononte and Guagliano (2003)
	Political rights	+	Freedom House	16 CEEC countries	1996–2009	C. Tintin (2011)
	Civil liberties	+	Freedom House	16 CEEC countries	1996–2009	C. Tintin (2011)
	State fragility index	0	Polity IV Database	16 CEEC countries	1996–2009	C. Tintin (2011)

Bureaucracy	Quality of bureaucracy	+	Campos (2000)	25 transition countries	1990–1998	Campos and Kinoshita (2002)
		0	ICRG	CEE and SE	2000–2008	Kinoshita (2011)
		–	World Development Report 1997 Survey	25 transition economies	1991–1999	P. Garibaldi et al. (2002)
Economic stability	Inflation rate	0		25 transition countries	1990–1998	Campos and Kinoshita (2002)
		0		CEE and SE	2000–2008	Kinoshita (2011)
		–	Transition Report Update (EBRD 2000)	CEE accession countries and Ukraine	1994–1998	Bevan and Estrin (2000)
		0		SE	1996–2002	V. Botric and L. Skuflic (2006)
		0		SE	1995–2000	E. Hengel (2011)
		0		25 transition economies	1991–1999	P. Garibaldi et al. (2002)
		0		CEE accession countries + Ukraine and Turkey	1990–2009	Güngör, Hakan; Oğuş, Ayla (2010)
		–		143 countries	1980–2003	D. Medvedev (2006)
	Cumulative inflation 1990–1993	–		CEE and SE	1991–1993	Brada et al. (2003)
	Unemployment	0		SE	1996–2002	V. Botric and L. Skuflic (2006)
	Change in unemployment rate	–		CEE and SE	1991–1993	Brada et al. (2003)
	Macroeconomic stability (inflation +unemployment rates, ln)	–		CEE	1992–2001	Clausing and Dorobantu (2005)

(continued)

Table 2.6 (continued)

Proxy	Effect	Data source	Location	Studied period	Author
Government balance (% GDP)	+	Transition Report Update (EBRD 2000)	CEE accession countries and Ukraine	1994–1998	Bevan and Estrin (2000)
	+		25 transition economies	1991–1999	P. Garibaldi et al. (2002)
	+		CEE and SE	1991–1993	Brada et al. (2003)
	0		CEE and SE	2000–2008	Kinoshita (2011)
External debt	0		SE	1996–2002	V. Botric and L. Skuflic (2006)
	–	Transition Report Update (EBRD 2000)	CEE accession countries and Ukraine	1994–1998	Bevan and Estrin (2000)
Real effective exchange rate	+	EUROSTAT	CEE	1995–2000	A. Seric (2011)
The annual percentage change in the real effective exchange rate	–		143 countries	1980–2003	D. Medvedev (2006)
Exchange rate	–		10 EU accession countries	1987–2001	J.W.B. Bos and M. van de Laar (2004)
	–		10 EU accession countries	1987–2001	J.W.B. Bos and M. van de Laar (2004)
Multiple exchange rates	0	Annual report on exchange Arrangements and Restrictions	25 transition economies	1991–1999	P. Garibaldi et al. (2002)

	Preannounced exchange rate regime (dummy)	+ for fixed	Annual report on exchange Arrangements and Restrictions	25 transition economies	1991–1999	P. Garibaldi et al. (2002)
Structure of economy	The manufacturing sector (% GDP)	+	Transition Report Update (EBRD 2000)	CEE accession countries and Ukraine	1994–2000	Bevan and Estrin (2000)
		–		CEE accession countries	1990–1995	Resmini (2000)
	Industrial share (% GDP, ln)	0		10 EU accession countries	1987–2001	J.W.B. Bos and M. van de Laar (2004)
	Services share (% GDP, ln)	0		10 EU accession countries	1987–2001	J.W.B. Bos and M. van de Laar (2004)
	Agriculture (% GDP, ln)	–		10 EU accession countries	1987–2001	J.W.B. Bos and M. van de Laar (2004)

Source: Author's work

References

Albi A (2005) EU enlargement and the constitutions of Central and Eastern Europe. Cambridge University Press, Cambridge. ISBN: 9780521607360. http://www.loc.gov/catdir/enhancements/fy0632/2005046525-d.html

Albulescu CT, Briciu L, Coroiu SI (2010) Determinants of foreign direct investment in CEECs: the role of financial stability. Analele Stiintifice ale Universitatii "Alexandru Ioan Cuza" din Iasi—Stiinte Economice 2010:85–96 https://ideas.repec.org/a/aic/journl/y2010vsep85-96.html

Altenburg T (2000) Linkages and spill-overs between transnational corporations and small and medium-sized enterprises in developing countries: opportunities and policies. German Development Institute, Berlin. ISBN: 3-88985-217-3. http://www.die-gdi.de/CMS-Homepage/openwebcms3.nsf/%28ynDK_contentByKey%29/ENTR-7BZCCT/

Altomonte C (1998) FDI in the CEEC's and the theory of real options: an empirical assessment. https://ideas.repec.org/p/lic/licosd/7698.html

Altomonte C, Guagliano C (2001) Competing locations? Market potential and FDI in Central and Eastern Europe vs the Mediterranean. https://ideas.repec.org/p/lic/licosd/10801.html

Altomonte C, Guagliano C (2003) Comparative study of FDI in Central and Eastern Europe and the Mediterranean. Econ Syst 27(2):223–246

Ash TN, Hare PG (1994) Privatisation in the Russian federation: changing enterprise behaviour in the transition period. Camb J Econ 18(6):619–634 https://ideas.repec.org/a/oup/cambje/v18y1994i6p619-34.html

Assenov I (2003) Market reforms and foreign investment: what drives capital flows to transition economies? Ōsaka-Daigaku-keizaigaku 53(1):99–118

Baldwin RE (1994) Towards an integrated Europe. Centre for Economic Policy Research, London. ISBN: 1898128138

Bellak C, Leibrecht M (2007) How to make FDI in Central and Eastern European countries sustainable. In: Liebscher K, Christl J, Mooslechner P, Ritzberger-Grünwald D (eds) Foreign direct investment in Europe. Edward Elgar, Cheltenham. ISBN: 9781847208798

Benacek V, Gronicki M, Holland D, Sass M (2000) The determinants and impact of foreign direct investment in Central and Eastern Europe: a comparison of survey and econometric evidence. Transl Corp 9(3):163–212 http://pure.iiasa.ac.at/5953/

Bengoa M, Sanchez-Robles B (2003) Foreign direct investment, economic freedom and growth: new evidence from Latin America. Eur J Polit Econ 19(3):529–545

Bevan AA, Estrin S (2000) The determinants of foreign direct investment in transition economies, 2638

Bevan AA, Estrin S (2004) The determinants of foreign direct investment into European transition economies. J Comp Econ 32(4):775–787

Blanchard O (1998) The economics of post-communist transition. Clarendon Press (Clarendon lectures in economics), Oxford

Binici M, Schindler M, Hutchison MM (2009) Controlling capital? Legal restrictions and the asset composition of international financial flows. International Monetary Fund, Washington, DC (IMF working papers, Working paper no. 09/208). Online verfügbar unter. http://elibrary.imf.org/view/IMF001/10473-9781451873559/10473-9781451873559/10473-9781451873559.xml

Böhn A (ed) (1994–1996) Privatization in central and Eastern Europe. Annual conference series. CEEPN, Ljubjana, pp 5–7

Böhm A, Simoneti M (eds) (1993) Privatization in central and Eastern Europe. Annual conference series. CEEPN, Ljubjana, p 4

Bos J, van de Laar M (2004) Explaining foreign direct investment in Central and Eastern Europe: an extended gravity approach, 8

Botrić V, Škuflić L (2006) Main determinants of foreign direct investment in the southeast European countries. Transit Stud Rev 13(2):359–377

Brada JC (1996) Privatization is transition. Or is it? J Econ Perspect 1996(2):67–86

Brada JC, Kutan AM, Yigit TM (2003) The effects of transition and political instability on foreign direct investment: Central Europe and the Balkans. https://ideas.repec.org/p/zbw/zeiwps/b282003.html

Brada JC, Kutan AM, Yigit TM (2006) The effects of transition and political instability on foreign direct investment inflows. Econ Transit 14(4):649–680

Brenton P (1999) Removing obstacles to deeper economic integration in the broad European trade area: Report of the CEPS working party on trade and investment in an enlarging Europe. CEPS, Brussels. ISBN: 9290792574

Brenton P, DiMauro F, Lücke M (1998) Economic integration and FDI: an empirical analysis of foreign investment in the EU and in Central and Eastern Europe. http://EconPapers.repec.org/RePEc:kie:kieliw:890

Brewer TL, Young S (2000) The multilateral investment system and multinational enterprises. Oxford University Press, Oxford. ISBN: 9780198293156

Campos FN (2000) Context is everything. Measuring institutional change in transition economies. The World Bank, Washington, DC. Online verfügbar unter http://elibrary.worldbank.org/content/workingpaper/10.1596/1813-9450-2269

Campos NF, Kinoshita Y (2002) Foreign direct investment as technology transferred. Some panel evidence from the transition economies. Manch Sch 70(3):398–419

Carstensen K, Toubal F (2004) Foreign direct investment in Central and Eastern European countries: a dynamic panel analysis. J Comp Econ 32(1):3–22

Chaudhuri S, Mukhopadhyay U (2014) Foreign direct investment in developing countries: a theoretical evaluation. Springer, New Delhi. ISBN: 978-81-322-1897-5

Clark D (1997) Enlargement and integration of the European Union: issues and strategies. Routledge, London. ISBN: 0203195876. http://gbv.eblib.com/patron/FullRecord.aspx?p=168593

Clausing K, Dorobantu C (2005) Re-entering Europe: does European Union candidacy boost foreign direct investment? Econ Transit 13(1):77–103 http://EconPapers.repec.org/RePEc:bla:etrans:v:13:y:2005:i:1:p:77-103

COMM/PRESS/01 (2015) European Commission – Press release – The DCFTA Facilities for SMEs. http://europa.eu/rapid/press-release_MEMO-15-5013_en.htm. Accessed 05 Nov 2016

Commission of the European Communities (1997) Agenda 2000. Commission of the European Communities, Luxembourg, (97) 2000 final

Commission of the European Communities (2003) Report from the Commission. The stabilisation and association process for South East Europe Second Annual Report. Commission of the European Communities

de Melo M, Denizer C, Gelb AH (1996) From plan to market: patterns of transition. World Bank, Policy Research Department, Transition Economics Division, Washington, DC

Declaration № 142-H 1991 of the Soviet of the Republics of the Supreme Soviet of the Soviet Union. https://en.wikisource.org/wiki/Declaration_no._142-N_of_the_Soviet_of_the_Republics_of_the_Supreme_Soviet_of_the_USSR

Demekas DG, Horváth B, Ribakova E, Wu Y (2005) Foreign direct investment in Southeastern Europe; How (and how much) can policies help? https://ideas.repec.org/p/imf/imfwpa/05-110.html

Dunning JH (1973) The determinants of international production. Oxf Econ Pap 25(3):289–336 http://EconPapers.repec.org/RePEc:oup:oxecpp:v:25:y:1973:i:3:p:289-336

Dunning JH (1993) Multinational enterprises and the global economy. Addison-Wesley, Wokingham. ISBN: 0201175304

Dunning JH, McQueen M (1981) The eclectic theory of international production: a case study of the international hotel industry. Manag Decis Econ 2(4):197–210

EBRD (2000) Transition report 2000. Employment, skills and transition. European Bank for Reconstruction and Development, London

EBRD (2001) Energy in transition. Europ. Bank for Reconstruction and Development, London (Transition report, 8.2001)

Egger P, Pfaffermayr M (2004) Foreign direct investment and European integration in the 1990s. World Econ 27(1):99–110 https://ideas.repec.org/a/bla/worlde/v27y2004i1p99-110.html
El-Kady H, Zimny Z (2009) The role of international investment agreements in attracting foreign direct investment to developing countries. United Nations, New York. United Nations Conference on Trade and Development. ISBN: 9789211127812. http://search.ebscohost.com/login.aspx?direct=true&scope=site&db=nlebk&db=nlabk&AN=348985
Estrin S (1994) Privatisation in the transitional economies of Central and Eastern Europe: issues and progress. Bus Strateg Rev 5(4):81–96
Estrin S, Meyer KE (2011) Foreign direct investment in transition economies. Strengthening the gains from integration. In: Globalization and economic diversification: policy challenges for economies in transition. Bloomsbury Academic, London, pp 155–177. ISBN: 978-1-8496-6532-2
Estrin S, Uvalic M (2013) Foreign direct investment into transition economies: are the Balkans different? London School of Economics (LSE) 'Europe in Question' series
European Commission (ed) (2002) STATISTICAL ANNEX of European economy
European Commission (2015) Enlargement: extending European values and standards to more countries. Publications Office, Luxembourg. ISBN: 978-92-79-49209-9
European Commission (2016a) European neighbourhood policy and enlargement negotiations. http://ec.europa.eu/neighbourhood-enlargement/
European Commission (2016b) Steps towards joining. http://ec.europa.eu/neighbourhood-enlargement/policy/steps-towards-joining_en
European Parliament (1993) European Council in Copenhagen. http://www.europarl.europa.eu/summits/copenhagen/default_en.htm. Accessed 17 April 2002
European Parliament (1999) Briefing no 38: The role of the European parliament in the enlargement process. http://www.europarl.europa.eu/enlargement/briefings/38a2_en.htm
Faeth I (2009) Determinants of foreign direct investment—A tale of nine theoretical models. J Econ Surv 23(1):165–196
Fiscal Affairs Department (2005) Issues with taxation in the enlarged EU. International Monetary Fund, Washington, DC
Garibaldi P, Mora N, Sahay R, Zettelmeyer J (2002) What moves capital to transition economies? IMF, Washington, DC (IMF working paper, 02/64)
Grabbe H (1999) A partnership for accession? The implications of EU conditionality for the Central and East European applicants. Robert Schuman Centre, European University Institute, San Domenico
Grcic B, Babic Z (2003) The determinants of FDI: evaluation of transition countries attractiveness for foreign investors
Gungor H, Binatli AO (2010) The effect of European accession prospects on foreign direct investment flows. https://ideas.repec.org/p/izm/wpaper/1006.html
Hengel E (2011) Determinants of FDI location in South East Europe (SEE). OECD J Gen Pap 2010 (2):91–104
Holland D, Pain N (1998) The determinants and impact of foreign direct investment in the transition
Hunya G (2000) Recent FDI trends, policies and challenges in South-East European countries. Wiener Institut für Internationale Wirtschaftsvergleiche, Vienna
ILO (2016) ILO database of labour statistics: mean nominal monthly earnings of employees. http://ilo.org/global/statistics-and-databases/lang--en/index.htm
International Monetary Fund (2005) Balance of payments manual. International Monetary Fund, Washington, DC. ISBN: 9781557753397. http://elibrary.imf.org/view/IMF071/00546-9781557753397/00546-9781557753397/00546-9781557753397.xml
International Monetary Fund and Organisation for Economic Co-operation and Development (2010) Foreign direct investment statistics: how countries measure FDI 2001. International Monetary Fund, Washington, DC. ISBN: 1-58906-220-5. http://search.ebscohost.com/login.aspx?direct=true&scope=site&db=nlebk&db=nlabk&AN=449527

Janicki HP, Wunnava PV (2004) Determinants of foreign direct investment: empirical evidence from EU accession candidates. Appl Econ 36(5):505–509

Johnson A (2006) The effects of FDI inflows on host country economic growth. Working paper series in economics and institutions of innovation. Royal Institute of Technology, CESIS – Centre of Excellence for Science and Innovation Studies, p 58. Online verfügbar unter https://EconPapers.repec.org/RePEc:hhs:cesisp:0058

Kalotay K, Hunya G (2000) Privatization and FDI in Central and Eastern Europe. Transl Corp 9 (1):39–66

Kinoshita Y (2011) Sectoral composition of foreign direct investment and external vulnerability in Eastern Europe. International Monetary Fund, Washington, DC (IMF working papers, working paper No. 11/123). Online verfügbar unter http://elibrary.imf.org/view/IMF001/11856-9781455263400/11856-9781455263400/11856-9781455263400.xml

Kinoshita Y, Campos N (2003) Why does FDI go where it goes? New Evidence from the transition economies. IMF Working Papers. International Monetary Fund (03/228). http://EconPapers.repec.org/RePEc:imf:imfwpa:03/228

Lankes H-P, Venables AJ (1996) Foreign direct investment in economic transition: the changing pattern of investments. Econ Transit 4(2):331–347

Lansbury M, Pain N, Šmídková K (1996) Foreign direct investment in Central Europe since 1990: an econometric study. Natl Inst Econ Rev 156(1)

Marinova ST, Marinov MA (2003) Foreign direct investment in Central and Eastern Europe. Ashgate Publishing Group, Aldershot. ISBN: 9780754630265

Mateev M (2009) Determinants of foreign direct investment in Central and Southeastern Europe: new empirical tests. Oxf J Spl Issue 8(1):133–149 http://mateevfinance.com/re_pdfs/1440238611_pdf_Determinants%20of%20Foreign%20Direct%20Investment%20in%20Central%20and%20Southeastern%20Europe_2009.pdf

Medvedev D (2006) Preferential trade agreements and their role in world trade. World Bank Development Prospects Group, Washington, DC (Policy research working paper, 4038)

Merlevede B, Schoors K (2004) Reform, FDI and economic growth: tale of the tortoise and the hare. William Davidson Institute, Ann Arbor, MI http://www.bus.umich.edu/KresgeLibrary/Collections/Workingpapers/wdi/wp730.pdf

Meyer K (1998) Direct investment in economies in transition. University, Dissertation – London. Elgar, Cheltenham. ISBN: 978 1 85898 736 1

OECD (2009) OECD benchmark definition of foreign direct investment 2008. Organisation for Economic Co-operation and Development, Paris. ISBN: 9789264045743. http://gbv.eblib.com/patron/FullRecord.aspx?p=474058

Resmini L (2000) The Determinants of foreign direct investment in the CEECs: new evidence from sectoral patterns. Econ Transit 8(3):665–689

Ribakova E, Horváth B, Demekas DG, Wu Y (2005) Foreign direct investment in Southeastern Europe. How (And how much) can policies help? International Monetary Fund, Washington, DC (IMF working papers, Working paper no. 05/110). Online verfügbar unter http://elibrary.imf.org/view/IMF001/02589-9781451861297/02589-9781451861297/02589-9781451861297.xml

Rodin S (2001) Requirements of EU membership and legal reform in Croatia. Politička misao XXXVIII(5):87–105

Sapienza E (2009) FDI and growth in Central and Southern Eastern Europe. https://ideas.repec.org/p/ufg/qdsems/12-2009.html

Seric A (2011) Determinants of FDI location in Central and Eastern Europe (CEE). OECD J Gen Pap 2010(2):77–90

Shenkar O, Luo Y (2004) International business. Recording for the Blind & Dyslexic, Princeton, NJ

Shiells CR (2003) FDI and the investment climate in the CIS countries. http://www.imf.org/external/pubs/cat/longres.aspx?sk=16950

Stern N (1997) The transition in Eastern Europe and the former Soviet Union: some strategic lessons from the experience of 25 countries over six years

Tintin C (2011) Do institutions matter for FDI? Evidence from Central and Eastern European countries. In: Proceedings of ETSG 2011

Tondel L (2001) Foreign direct investment during transition: determinants and patterns in Central and Eastern Europe and the former Soviet Union. Chr. Michelsen Institute, Development Studies and Human Rights, Bergen. ISBN: 9788290584936

UNICEF (2001) A decade of transition. The MONEE project; CEE, CIS, Baltics. UNICEF Innocenti Research Centre, Florence (Regional monitoring report, 8)

UNCTAD (1994) World investment report: transitional corporations, employment and the workplace. ISBN: 9211044359

UNCTAD (1999) Foreign direct investment and the challenge of development. United Nations, New York. ISBN: 92-1-112440-9

UNCTAD (2003) World investment report: FDI policies for development: national and international perspectives. United Nations, New York. ISBN: 92-1-112580-4

UNCTAD (2004) World investment report: the shift towards services. United Nations, New York. ISBN: 92-1-112644-4

UNCTAD (2009a) UNCTAD training manual on statistics for FDI and the operations of TNCs. United Nations, New York. ISBN: 978-92-1-112766-9. http://search.ebscohost.com/login.aspx?direct=true&scope=site&db=nlebk&db=nlabk&AN=348983

UNCTAD (2009b) World investment report: transnational corporations, agricultural production and development. United Nations, New York. ISBN: 978-92-1-112775-1

UNCTAD (2014a) Bilateral FDI statistics. http://unctad.org/en/Pages/DIAE/FDI%20Statistics/FDI-Statistics-Bilateral.aspx. Accessed 03 Nov 2016

UNCTAD (2014b) World investment report: investing in the SDGs: an action plan. United Nations, New York. ISBN: 978-92-1-112873-4

UNCTAD (2015) World investment report: reforming international investment governance. United Nations, New York. ISBN: 978-92-1-112891-8

UNCTAD (2016a) Investor nationality: policy challenges. United Nations, New York. ISBN: 978-92-1-112902-1

UNCTAD (2016b) UNCTADstat: Foreign direct investment: inward and outward flows and stock, annual, 1970–2015 Table summary. http://unctadstat.unctad.org/wds/TableViewer/tableView.aspx?ReportId=96740

UNCTAD (2016c) UNCTADstat: Gross domestic product: total and per capita, current and constant (2005) prices, annual, 1970–2015. http://unctadstat.unctad.org/wds/TableViewer/tableView.aspx?ReportId=96

UNCTAD (2016d) UNCTADstat: Total and urban population, annual, 1950–2050. http://unctadstat.unctad.org/wds/TableViewer/tableView.aspx?ReportId=97

Wacker KM (2013) On the measurement of foreign direct investment and its relationship to activities of multinational corporations. https://ideas.repec.org/p/ecb/ecbwps/20131614.html

WIIW (ed) (2001) WIIW handbook of statistics. Countries in transition. Vienna Institute for International Economic Studies, Vienna

Witkowska J (2007) Foreign direct investment in the changing business environment of the European Union's new member states. Glob Econ J 7(4):1–30. https://doi.org/10.2202/1524-5861.1233

Witkowska J (2008) The role of foreign direct investor policies in creating a knowledge—Based economy in the new member states of the European Union. Compar Econ Res: Central and Eastern Europe 11(3):53–72

Woodward DP (2000) Taxation and the location of foreign direct investment in Central Europe. In: The new world order: internationalism, regionalism and the multinational corporations. Pergamon, Amsterdam, pp 192–208

Yeyati EL, Stein E, Daude C (2003) Regional integration and the location of FDI. Inter-American Development Bank Research Department, Washington, DC http://www.iadb.org/res/publications/pubfiles/pubWP-492.pdf

Chapter 3
Theoretical Model

As we have seen in Sect. 2.3, there is broad empirical evidence showing that regional integration considerably influences the choice of firms to invest in the CEE countries. To date, the theoretical literature addressing these issues is rather limited. The structure of empirical models usually follows the theoretical findings of Dunning (1993)—the framework of ownership, location and internalisation advantages (OLI). However, the traditional theory of FDI does not fully capture the effects linked with regional integration.

In this chapter, we present a theoretical model that helps us organise our thinking about the FDI determinants in CEE after closer integration in the EU. We construct a model where firms are making strategic location decisions in choosing how to serve their target markets: in other words, making strategic choices between export and FDI. These choices are sensitive to the economic environment in which they are made.

If we are correct in arguing that market accessibility affects the exporting vs. FDI choice, then our analysis is as relevant to developments in NAFTA and ASEAN as it is to the EU.

We begin this chapter with the examination of the related literature. In the second section, we study a model offered by Neary (2002) with fully symmetrical countries. Following the general model set-up, three scenarios are considered: high trade costs, preferential trade costs in the integrating region, and, in the final scenario, the zero trade costs between member countries.

In the third part of the chapter, we supplement the literature findings by adding the heterogeneous countries in the basic set-up. Countries differ in market sizes, external tariffs, labour and installation costs. Thus, we analyse how previous findings can be implemented in the world of heterogeneous countries. And finally, we derive FDI equation in part four.

H. Makhavikova, *Determinants of FDI in Central and Eastern Europe*,
Contributions to Economics, https://doi.org/10.1007/978-3-319-91878-5_3

3.1 Literature Overview

3.1.1 *Classification of the Regional Integration Theories*

The principal aim of this section is to examine the main features of the theoretical models intended to explain FDI in the integrating countries, and critically assess their predictions and policy implications.

There are two families of international trade model most appropriate for dealing with the location effects of trade agreements (see Table 3.1).

The first group of models is new economic geography (NEG) theory. This depicts the geographical pattern of the distribution of production in the presence of economies of scale. The other is the **theory of multinational firms and FDI**. This explains the (location) choices of multinational firms. In both models, trade costs are a crucial variable affecting firms' choice of location for production and therefore, a discriminatory reduction of tariffs in these models directly affects their decision making.

Table 3.1 Classification of the models according to the type of analysis and models used

	New economic geography models	Multinational firms and FDI models	
		General equilibrium	Partial equilibrium
Symmetrical countries	Krugman and Venables (1995) Baldwin et al. (1995) Baldwin and Ottaviano (1998) Puga and Venables (1997)	Ragoussis and Miroudot (2009)[a]	Motta (1992) Smith (1987) Motta and Norman (1996) Bertrand and Madariaga (2003) Ito (2013) Donnenfeld (2003)
Asymmetrical countries	Helpman (1984) Helpman and Krugman (1985) Horstmann and Markusen (1992) Rowthorn (1992) Brainard (1993) Markusen and Venables (1998)[b] Ono and Davis (2005) Baldwin and Venables (1995) Altomonte (2007) Head and Mayer (2004) Fujita et al. (1999)	Yeaple (2003)[b]	Neary (2002) Bjorvatn and Cappelen (2004) Haller (2010) Ekholm et al. (2007) Montout and Zitouna (2005) Yeaple (2003)[b] Neary (2009)

Source: Author's work
[a]Different distance costs
[b]Both general and partial equilibrium for different set ups

There are two features that distinguish NEG models from those including FDI. As it was already mentioned, NEG models focus on the agglomeration factors which induce firms to concentrate geographically, while models with FDI do not consider agglomeration. Secondly, NEG theories have been developed in a general equilibrium framework. The general equilibrium studies examine the external factors that are likely to determine the location and magnitude of direct investment by multinationals (Chaudhuri and Mukhopadhyay 2014).

Thus, general equilibrium models are essentially based on the trade-off between, on the one hand, locating production close to a local market, thereby saving variable trade and distance costs and, on the other hand, concentrating production in one location to profit from plant-level scale economies, which involves additional fixed costs (Markusen 1984; Brainard 1993; Markusen and Venables 1998; Helpman 1984; Helpman and Krugman 1985).

Models including FDI are usually exploit partial equilibrium model. The basic idea of partial equilibrium models is that it examines the internal firm-specific factors that motivate a firm to become a TNC a foreign firm wants to enter a foreign market with a homogenous good. And it makes strategic choice between exports and FDI facing trade or installation costs correspondingly (Smith 1987; Horstmann and Markusen 1992; Motta 1992; etc.).

Both theoretical branches study either fully equal or heterogeneous countries. Asymmetries between countries include different market sizes, labour or installation costs. However, it is rare that all or at least several of the country differences are discussed in the same papers at once.

An additional difference among the papers—which is not included in Table 3.1—is the kind of regional agreement (see Table 3.2). In most papers regional integration basically means a reduction (or an elimination) of internal trade barriers—a Free Trade Area (FTA). Other papers consider the "hub-and-spoke" agreements, that is, bilateral free trade agreements of one country, the hub, with several other countries, the spokes. These type of arrangements gives one region (the hub) better access to other regions (the spokes) than these have to each other (see, Baldwin and Venables 1995; Puga and Venables 1997; Altomonte 2007). In a hub-and-spoke arrangement thus gives, hub firms get access to relatively larger markets.

3.1.2 New Economic Geography Models

3.1.2.1 The Earliest "New Trade" Models

Helpman (1984) and Helpman and Krugman (1985) initiated the NEG models with the idea that different factor prices across countries might be a reason for a firm to set up production in a low-cost country. They found that if countries are different enough in their relative factor endowments, trade does not equalise factor prices. Therein, firms have an incentive to divide activities among countries, placing the

Table 3.2 Classification of models according to the type of regional agreements

Regional agreements	Hub-spoke and core-periphery agreements	Multilateral agreements
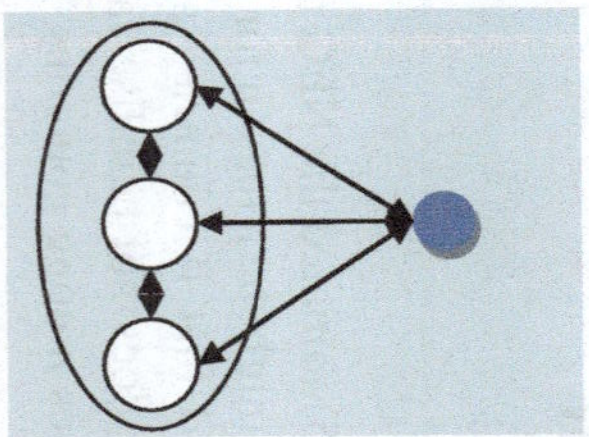	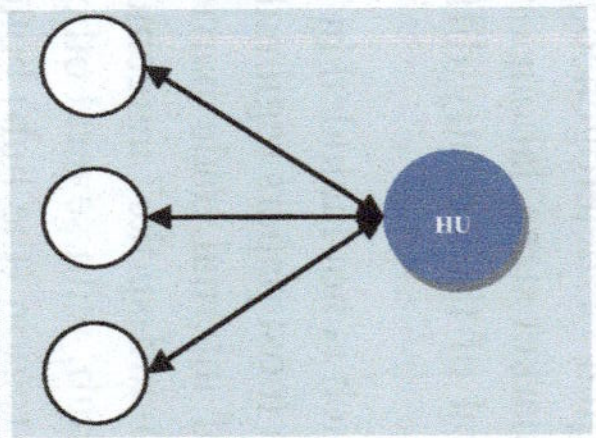	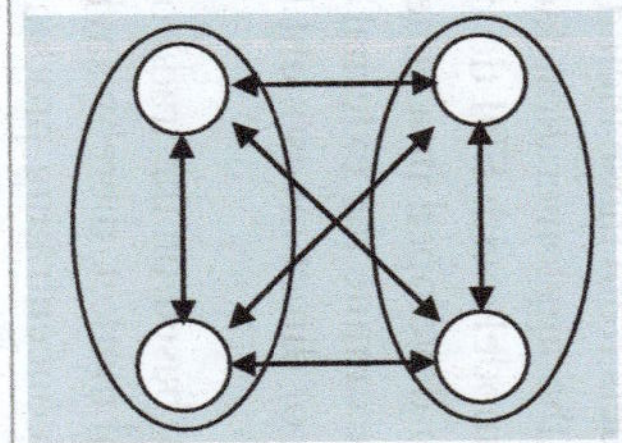
Motta (1992) Helpman (1984) Helpman and Krugman (1985) Baldwin et al. (1995) Head and Mayer (2004) Smith (1987) Motta and Norman (1996) Neary (2002) Bjorvatn and Cappelen (2004) Bertrand and Madariaga (2003) Haller (2010) Ekholm et al. (2007) Montout and Zitouna (2005) Yeaple (2003) Ragoussis and Miroudot (2009) Neary (2009) Baldwin and Venables (2004)	Krugman and Venables (1995) Horstmann and Markusen (1992) Rowthorn (1992) Brainard (1993) Markusen and Venables (1998) Ono and Davis (2005) Baldwin and Venables (1995) Baldwin and Ottaviano (1998) Puga and Venables (1997) Altomonte (2007)	Donnenfeld (2003) Ito (2013)

Source: Author's work

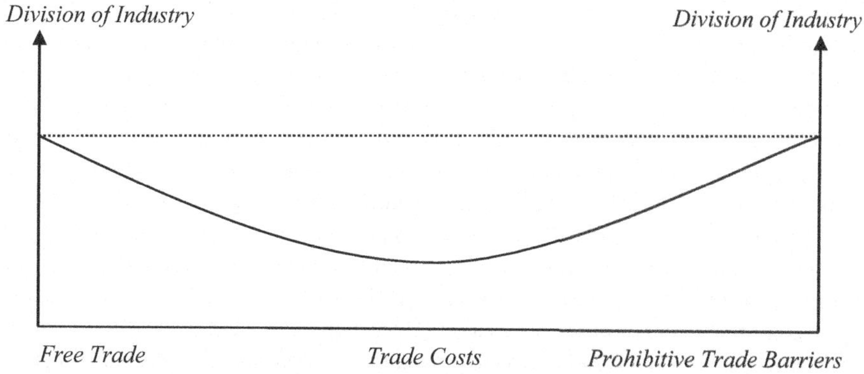

Fig. 3.1 The U-shape relation of concentration and openness. *Source*: Reprinted from Krugman and Venables (1990)

most capital-intensive part (e.g. headquarter services) in the capital-abundant country and production in the labour-abundant economy.

Krugman and Venables (1990, 1995) showed that the link between trade barriers and industry location is not simple and monotonic. They considered two identical countries under two extreme cases: prohibitive trade costs and no trade costs. With no trade costs, firms would tend to spread out in search for low cost immobile factors, such as land. A core-periphery spontaneously forms. A rise in trade barriers would lead to increasing concentration. The opposite happens at the other extreme. If trade costs are initially prohibitive, the location will be decentralised since firms would be forced to produce locally. They showed that at high transportation costs countries have equal sector structure. If trade barriers fall to just below the prohibitive level, some firms would relocate in search of bigger markets (Krugman and Venables 1995). The point is illustrated in Fig. 3.1.

Generally, the earliest "new trade" models of multinational corporations—e.g. Helpman (1984), Helpman and Krugman (1985), Krugman and Venables (1995)—did not focus on explaining FDI, but the effects of globalisation on real national incomes.

3.1.2.2 "Footloose Capital" Models

This subgroup of NEG models analytically (not numerically) explains the production location within asymmetrical countries that differ only by market size. Market size thus plays an important role in production location decisions.

Horstmann and Markusen (1992) set out the basic three-countries case—core-periphery model so as to investigate the effects of preferential agreements. The basic paradigm was pursued by Brainard (1993), Markusen and Venables (1998), and others.

According to Horstmann and Markusen (1992) firms can supply the foreign market via exports or via FDI. Given plant-level scale economies, exporting would always be the lowest cost option. However, when trade costs are high enough and the countries similar enough in size, it is cheaper to supply both markets from local plants instead of via trade. In this case, plants will be concentrated within some of the countries of the integration union—the core, while the rest will lose companies. Thus, preferential liberalisation is clearly welfare-improving for the "core", while the "periphery" is worse off. As liberalisation persists and internal trade barriers fall further, location becomes more sensitive to differences in production costs. The periphery of the integration area may once again become attractive because of low wages and free access to the core market (Horstmann and Markusen 1992).

Rowthorn (1992) extends upon Horstmann and Markusen (1992) in order to describe general patterns of trade without the use of numerical simulations. He found that intra-industry trade and FDI occur as the production costs and market size of two developed countries are similar. For any given level of trade costs, FDI occurs in equilibrium when barriers to investment are small. If there are large barriers to trade and therefore high trade costs, tariff-jumping FDI can be observed (Rowthorn 1992).

Brainard (1993) showed also that high transport costs stimulate FDI if fixed plant costs are relatively low, and if the increasing returns at the corporate level to the plant level are high. The model also establishes conditions for a mixed equilibrium in which exports and FDI coexist (Brainard 1993).

Markusen and Venables (1998) used a similar model, but added elements of increasing returns to scale, imperfect competition, and product differentiation. They found that the incentive to invest appears when transport and tariff costs and income are high. They also proved that if countries are more similar in incomes, relative factor endowments, and technologies, FDI will supplant intra-industry trade as economies converge (Markusen and Venables 1998).

A similar idea was developed in the paper of Ono and Davis (2005). In it, they described the patterns of trade and investments in a two-country model, and showed that international activities arise as the production costs and market size of the countries converge.

3.1.2.3 Regional Inequalities

Early works of Krugman (1991), Krugman and Venables (1995), Baldwin and Venables (1995) and Puga and Venables (1997) investigated the ways regional integration alters the distribution of economic activity within the integrated area, and thus increases regional inequality.

Baldwin and Venables (1995) addressed the question of how the formation of an integration area changes the static allocation of resources in participating economies. They found that the formation of an integration union tends to shift production of liberalised goods into the liberalising region. They referred to this as "production shifting". The most important conclusion is that—despite theoretical ambiguities—RIAs seem to have generated welfare gains for the participants with small, but possibly negative spill-over onto the rest of the world (Baldwin and Venables 1995).

Baldwin et al. (1995) studied the investment creation and investment diversion effects of the EU's Single Market Program. They employed a model with three identical countries, where two of them build a perfect economic union. The results show that foreign firms prefer to invest in the liberalising region. Since tradeable sectors are capital intensive relative to non-traded sectors, production shifting raises the rental rate in the integrating regions, and lowers it elsewhere. As a result, investment creation and diversion appear (Baldwin et al. 1995).

Baldwin and Ottaviano (1998) posit a quite different model in which two-way FDI arises due to imperfect competition, and exports and FDI go hand in hand.

If firms within each sector are similar, and countries have similar trade and investment barriers (sector-by-sector), the simple version of these models predicts that international commerce in each sector should be dominated either by intra-industry trade, or by FDI. As a consequence, tariff-jumping FDI models are not well-suited to explaining the close correlation between the observed patterns of trade and investment (Baldwin and Ottaviano 1998).

Puga and Venables (1997) showed how industrial location may be changed in response to concluding an integration agreement. They found similar results to Krugman and Venables (1995). During the initial stages of integration, high internal trade barriers provide an incentive to supply national markets locally. That raises the profitability of firms located in the liberalising nations and shifts industry towards them. All member states of the free trade area benefit identically from integration, while industry size and welfare fall outside the liberalising regions.

To encompass a source country of FDI within the analysis, Puga and Venables (1997) extended a core-periphery model to a multi-country case.

They showed that the effects of integration differ for countries after the fall of trade costs. This is because mutual reduction of trade barriers between integrating countries leads to hub-and-spoke relations (Figs. 3.2 and 3.3). During the early stages of integration, production is concentrated in the hub of the region because there is better access to other spokes. This effect is called hub-effect (Krugman 1993). Due to the agglomeration effect, industrial production accelerates further in the hub. However, the production of intermediaries can be shifted to the spokes as production costs and wages are lower than in the hub. This model however, predicts that just one of the spokes may see an increase in firms, while there will be a reduction in the others. As a consequence, deep hub-and-spoke integration may lead to a divergence between the spokes (Puga and Venables 1997).

Among other findings, they conclude that in a "hub and spoke" arrangement of trade liberalisation, like that between the European Union and each of the CEECs, firms will tend to concentrate in the 'hub', since firms located in "spoke" countries are penalised by a lower demand from both consumers and firms in other spokes compared to that enjoyed by hub firms (Puga and Venables 1997). This result however, contrasted sharply with the almost exponential increase of European FDI in the CEECs over the last decade (see Sect. 2.2).

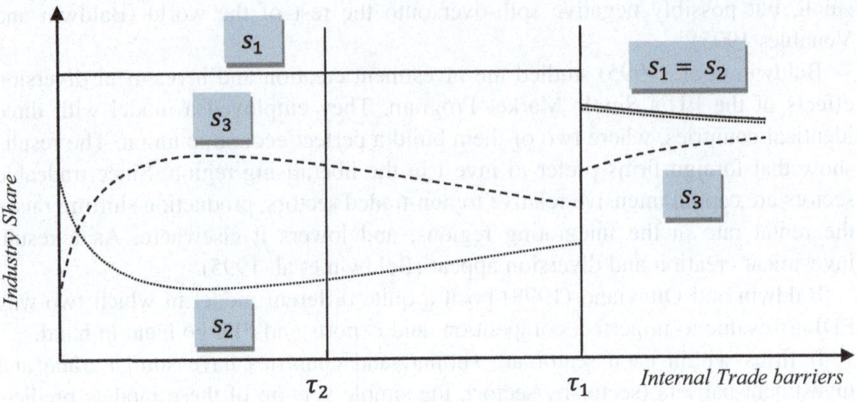

Fig. 3.2 The formation of a free trade area: share of industry in each country. *Source*: Reprinted from Puga and Venables (1997). *Note*: Trade barriers are higher than τ_1, there is no agglomeration of industry; a free trade area is formed between countries 1 and 2, and 3 is unchanged, this allows firms inside the free trade area to expand production and make positive profits, while profits located outside it contract production and make negative profits. Free entry and exit restores profits back to zero, as country 3 firm relocate into 1 and 2 (Puga and Venables 1997)

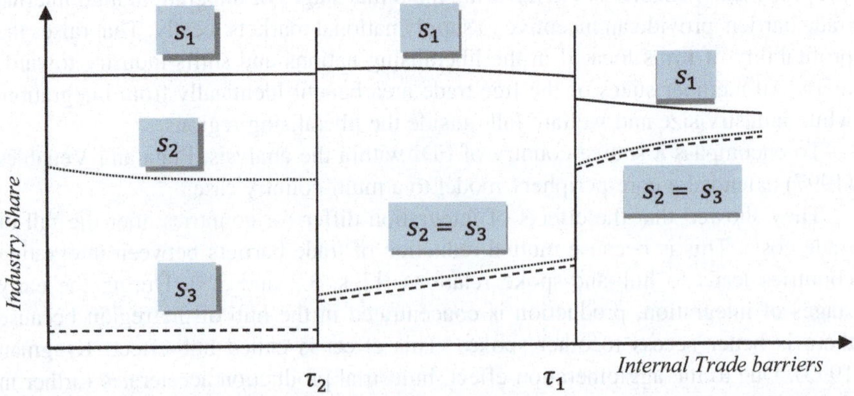

Fig. 3.3 A hub-spoke arrangement: share of industry in each country. *Source*: Reprinted from Puga and Venables (1997). *Note*: Initially, firms located in country 1 (the hub) can sell to consumers in 2 and 3 (the spokes) at lower trade costs than firm exporting from one spoke to the other. It shifts industry out of spokes (Puga and Venables 1997)

Head and Mayer (2004) developed a theoretical model of location choice under imperfect competition, and estimated the model empirically. According to their results, market size played an important role, however, it cannot fully explain the tendency of firms in the same industry to agglomerate. In doing so, they proved the importance of the agglomeration effect (Head and Mayer 2004).

Altomonte (2007) analysed a theoretical model of international location in the context of regional economic integration, where countries conclude multilateral

FTAs. The latest generations of RIAs in fact, tend to be of a multilateral nature, since they combine the traditional "hub and spoke" bilateral pattern of integration with arrangements in which the "spokes" enjoy free trade among themselves (e.g. FTAs and AAs in Europe).

Market conditions are supposed to differ between the "hub" and the "spokes". In the hub, market rules ensure free entry and exit of firms, leading to a zero-profit condition. In the spokes, national rules on FDI partially restrict the entry of foreign firms and hinder the full equalisation of production costs across locations within each RIA. In addition, it is supposed that there are no processes of economic integration among the alternative RIAs, i.e. regionalism rather than multilateralism prevails on the international scene (Altomonte 2007).

The analysis suggests that the dynamics of FDI inflow tend to be associated with positive changes in the degree of economic integration for a given configuration of regional integration agreements, in which both "hub" and "spoke" countries mutually liberalize trade (what has been called a "multilateral" RIA). In such a setup, progressively prevailing worldwide, a parallel evolution of FDI and trade flow is not a puzzle, but rather it is to be expected (Altomonte 2007).

3.1.3 Models with FDI

A limited number of papers have explicitly introduced FDI and multinational firms in theoretical models of regional integration.

3.1.3.1 Basic Models

Early works provide a model for international investments in an oligopolistic setting (Smith 1987; Motta 1992; Motta and Norman 1996). One of the advantages of this approach is that it shows the strategic role of FDI.

Smith (1987) showed why foreign firms decide to install a subsidiary in a host market rather than export its product, and how this choice may be influenced by government policy. The model offers an extremely simple characterisation of the technological advantages a multinational firm may possess over a host-country rival. In order to make production possible, a firm-specific fixed cost must be incurred in addition to the plant-specific fixed cost associated with the establishment of a plant in any particular location. However, tariffs neither play a role in location decision nor in change of market structure.

Motta (1992) analysed a situation where a foreign multinational chooses between direct investment and exports. Despite some slight modifications, this model can be seen as an extension of the Smith (1987) paper.

He showed that the existence of a tariff may cause a shift away from foreign investment or else induce tariff-jumping investment. The intuitive idea is that an increase in the size of the host market and export costs and a decrease in plant-specific costs and information costs would determine a shift from exports to investments (Motta 1992).

Motta and Norman (1996) analysed the effects of economic integration on oligopolistic multinationals in a three-country setup; two integrating (host) countries, and a country source of FDI which is external to the integration union. Their results have one important implication. This is that the effects of a decrease in the internal tariff in this model are very different from those of an enlargement of the market. While a decrease in the internal tariff induces export-platform FDI, an increase in market size leads to dispersed FDI. Thus, when member country market sizes are "small," improved market integration favours concentrated FDI plus intra-regional exports over extra-regional exports. Whereas increased market size is likely to lead to dispersed FDI, economic integration is more likely to lead to concentrated FDI, with the investing firm supplying the majority of the countries in the regional block by intra-regional exports (Motta and Norman 1996).

Neary (2002) developed a very similar model with analogous conclusions. Unlike in Motta and Norman (1996), the effects of a trade agreement are not determined by means of numerical simulations, but analytically. This implies more "reliable" results at the price of a more simplified setting.

He stressed three influences of regional integration on multinational firms. The first is the "tariff jumping" motive for FDI. This appears when trade barriers are high and multinationals invest in all countries to avoid protective trade barriers and supply countries from local plants. Moreover, he showed that the reduction of internal tariffs reduces the tariff-jumping incentive to establish more than one plant in the union market (Neary 2002).

Second, once internal trade barriers are reduced or eliminated, multinationals enjoy the export-platform motive, which allows exports to the other members of the integration union at reduced internal tariffs. It may induce a firm which has never exported to invest (Neary 2002).

Finally, reduced internal tariffs increase competition from domestic firms. This works against both FDI and exports and may lead to a "Fortress Europe" outcome in which multinationals leave the union market even though external tariffs remain unchanged (Neary 2002).

A paper by Montout and Zitouna (2005) expanded upon the model of Neary (2002) by considering countries with different production costs due to different wages. They showed that location choices depend on trade and fixed costs in addition to wage differences. The greater the difference in wages between the countries involved in an integration union, the more likely the outsider will invest in the low-wage country.

However, they found that over time market access in the low-wage country can be reduced under certain conditions. It usually implies an increase in the fixed costs of locating there. Indeed, if the trade liberalisation process negatively affects the insiders, they evict their competitors (eviction effect) (Montout and Zitouna 2005).

3.1.3.2 M&A and Greenfield Investments

Bertrand and Madariaga (2003) underlined the relevance of separating entry modes when studying FDI, Greenfield, and M&A investments. First, they presented a simple theoretical three-countries insider–outsider model framework, highlighting differences between the two modes of entry.

They found that only market size has a positive impact on the location of FDI, both for Greenfield and M&A. M&A are more concerned by tariff barriers. Moreover, M&A respond less strongly to institutional integration than Greenfield investment (Bertrand and Madariaga 2003).

Bjorvatn and Cappelen (2004) also demonstrated that increased competition following a process of economic integration may increase the profitability of cross-border acquisitions. However, economic integration doesn't necessarily increase the profitability of international mergers. The profitability of a cross-border acquisition depends on trade costs and Greenfield investment costs, and demonstrates that economic integration may indeed trigger international mergers, as well as when and why this takes place.

3.1.3.3 Horizontal and Vertical Investments

Ekholm et al. (2003) explored the reasons for the appearance of horizontal and vertical export-platforms in a region with asymmetric countries. They showed that trade liberalisation between large and small countries stimulates both outsiders and insiders to locate production in a country with low production costs (a small one). This is because there is free access to the partner's larger market.

Ekholm et al. (2007) expanded upon their previous findings by considering a fuller integration than just zero tariffs, such as the EU and NAFTA where insider firms enjoy many other advantages in trading goods and services. These include establishing subsidiaries, stationing personnel abroad, and so forth. They found that insider firms pursue home country export platform strategy, serving itself and the other high-income country from a low-cost country (Ekholm et al. 2007).

Yeaple (2003) used the same set-up as Ekholm et al. (2003) for the three investment opportunities of a foreign country; horizontal (investments in a developed country to supply a bigger market), vertical (investment in a developing country to produce more effectively), and investment in both, called complex integration strategy. Thus, production in a developing country will occur only when labour there is sufficiently cheap. Yeaple (2003) showed that complex integration strategies dominate other foreign investment strategies when the level of transport costs fall within an intermediate range. His analysis showed that whether two foreign locations are substitutes or complements depends critically on the initial level of transport costs (Yeaple 2003).

Neary (2009) also confirmed that most multinational corporations pursue what Yeaple (2003), following UNCTAD (1998) calls "complex integration strategies", which are those that do not fit neatly into either the horizontal or vertical categories. In his paper, he states an expectation that trade and FDI will be substitutes in the sense that a fall in trade costs should discourage FDI. However, this prediction conflicts with the experience of the 1990s, when trade and FDI appear to have been complementary. Throughout this period, trade costs fell dramatically due to trade liberalisation, market integration, and technological change, yet FDI grew much faster than trade. One broad conclusion of his work is that the distinction between horizontal and vertical FDI is useful for pedagogic purposes but otherwise not particularly helpful (Neary 2009).

Ragoussis and Miroudot (2009) described and illustrated new firm strategies of vertical specialisation and explored the policy implications of new patterns of trade and FDI. As becomes clear from the analysis, not all modes of FDI are associated with trade. Furthermore, when they are, significant differences in the nature and direction of the trade they enhance are observed. The results suggest a complementary relationship between vertical trade, FDI and sales of foreign affiliates, as all three variables are negatively affected by the distance between countries and positively by the size of markets (Ragoussis and Miroudot 2009).

3.1.3.4 Regional Blocks

Unlike the papers considered so far, Donnenfeld (2003) investigated location choices when two regional blocks are formed. He assumed that countries in both regions are fully symmetric.

Donnenfeld (2003) limited the amount of supply choices. Within his model, firms from one block can make FDI only in the other block, while within their own block they only export to partner countries, and firms can invest in the other block by locating just one plant from which they export to the other members. This means that the model considers only export-platform FDI, and not dispersed FDI within the blocks.

Moreover, he did not investigate the effect of integration on members of the same region. Despite these restrictive assumptions, the model has the advantage of taking into account two-way flows of FDI between the two blocks.

He found that in a such model, integration leads to the decline of the volume of world trade, but there is an increase in world output due to direct investment (Donnenfeld 2003).

Ito (2013) extends the model developed by Giorgio et al. (2006) to two-regions with two-countries and includes the possibility of export-platform FDI. The most important finding of this paper is that it describes all possible modes of supply, including exports, horizontal and vertical FDI, and horizontal and vertical export-platform FDI. It was proved that a decrease in inter-regional or intra-regional trade costs induces firms to choose the export-platform FDI.

More specifically, it is shown that regional trade agreements such as ASEAN or NAFTA, drive horizontal export-platform type FDI, while bilateral FTA such as

Japan's Economic Partnership Agreement in the context of the data this paper uses, induces the vertical export-platform type FDI in some cases (Ito 2013).

In summary, on the theory side, new geographic theory and the theory of FDI have created tools enabling rigorous analysis of the causes and consequences of multinational activity. However, as the literature review shows, existing theoretical models, for the most part, have not been tested empirically. This is why in our book, we construct a model that will theoretically explain the main determinants of FDI and then test it empirically.

3.2 Set Up of the Model

Integration with the EU has versatile effect on inward FDI. To explain the channels of influence we present a theoretical framework in this chapter. We start with the examination of the Neary's (2002) model what is the crucial for developing our own theoretical framework.

3.2.1 Specification of the Model

We start with the specification of our basic model.

Regions We consider an economic system in which all countries are identical, large open economies, with identical consumers. These are ŋ countries, a country $I \in \eta$ participates in international activities, and n countries ($n <$ ŋ) build an integration union ($I \notin n$).

The nature of integration depends on whether it takes the form of a preferential trade agreement in which internal trade barriers are lower than the external barriers, or a free trade area where all internal tariffs are eliminated. However, there are still obstacles to trade and to investment.

Firms There is a firm i in a country I that interested in selling its goods in all n countries. We do not allow new firms to enter our economic system. We also assume that i is the only supplier in the industry, thus, there is no competition between firms.

Regimes Since there are many possible configurations of how to supply foreign markets, we will make a number of restrictive assumptions to reduce the possibilities to a manageable number. The term *regime* will denote supply choices of a firm i in n countries: first, it can decide not to supply foreign markets, ($\varnothing$); second, i can export (X_n) to all countries; third, it can set up plants in all countries in the region (F_n); or it sets up subsidiaries in m countries and exports from these countries to the rest n-m countries (F_mX_{n-m}).The firm i never engages in both FDI and trade in the same country. Firms can easily switch regimes if needed.

Transfer Costs If a firm engages in exports, it is subject to a specific tariff *t*. *t* should be understood as a measure of the international trade barrier, which is zero if a firm locates a subsidiary in a country. We assume that trade barriers are not good specific.

Set-up cost Establishment by firm *i* of a subsidiary in any of *n* foreign countries requires a set-up cost *f*. This set-up cost may include the cost of purchasing or establishing a company as well as information costs, legal costs, and other costs of doing business.

Profits We assume that a firm *i* aims to maximize its aggregate profits in a country $j\,(j \in n)$, $\pi_{ij}(\cdot)$, through its location configuration. We assume that a firm's *i* operating profits only come from foreign markets, not from its home market, *I*. Moreover, $\pi_{ij}(\cdot)$ can be viewed as expected profits normalized to time 0.

$$\pi_j = \sum_{T=0}^{N} \frac{\pi_{jT}}{(1+r)^T} \tag{3.1}$$

r is the discount rate, T is time period.

Therefore, profits are comparable along time and host countries.

The aggregate potential profit Π_i of a generic regional agreement is given by the sum of all profits π_j obtainable in different locations *j* belonging to the regional agreement. Hence, we can write the operating profits of firm *i* as $\Pi_i = \sum_{j=1}^{n} \pi_j(\cdot)$, where all other determinants of profits, which are independent of how the market is served, are subsumed into the π function.

3.2.2 *Equal Barriers*

We consider the basic version of the model developed by Neary in 2002, in which all union countries are identical. The model explores different profit opportunities available in different location to a firm based in I.

We start from the case when the external trade barriers are equal between all countries (Fig. 3.20, Appendix C).

Neary (2002) determined only two regimes in this set-up: pure export and pure FDI strategies.

If firm *i* decides to export from its home country, it in turn pays transaction costs. The net operating profits, which a firm earns from supplying a single country facing a tariff t, are denoted by $\pi(t)$. Naturally, $\pi(t)$ is decreasing in *t* (Neary 2002). Its total profits to *n* countries in the export regime, denoted by Π_{Xn}, are therefore:

$$\Pi_{Xn} = n\pi(t) \tag{3.2}$$

For a sufficiently high tariff, defined implicitly by $\tilde{t}$ ($\pi(\tilde{t}) = 0$), it is not profitable to export to any country (Neary 2002).

Local production avoids trade barriers that might be incurred in supplying the market by imports. Thereupon, a multinational *i* may choose to set up plants in all foreign countries.

$$\Pi_{Fn} = n(\pi(0) - f) \tag{3.3}$$

In this case, a foreign firm has to pay set-up costs, denoted by *f*. Because all union countries are identical, and because there is no production cost advantage of locating in particular countries, firm *i* never installs less than *n* plants (Neary 2002).

Neary (2002) also compared profits from exporting and investing in a host country.

$$\Pi_{F1} - \Pi_{Xn} = \gamma(t, f) \tag{3.4}$$

where

$$\gamma(t, f) = \pi(0) - f - \pi(t) \tag{3.5}$$

He determined the function γ(t, f) measures the net gain from tariff-jumping into an individual union market: supplying it from a local plant with fixed cost *f*, rather than incurring the additional unit cost *t* of supplying it from home (Neary 2002).

Thus, the location choice of FDI is determined by relative profitability. When a company invests it gets benefits from avoiding trade costs. All things equal, the multinational will engage in FDI if and only if γ(t, f) is positive (Neary 2002).

Figure 3.4 illustrates the possible regimes in $\{f, t\}$ space, developed by Neary (2002). Profits from exporting, Π_{Xn}, are independent of *f*, and decreasing in *t*. Exporting is profitable only for tariffs below the threshold level $\tilde{t}$ (region Xn). By

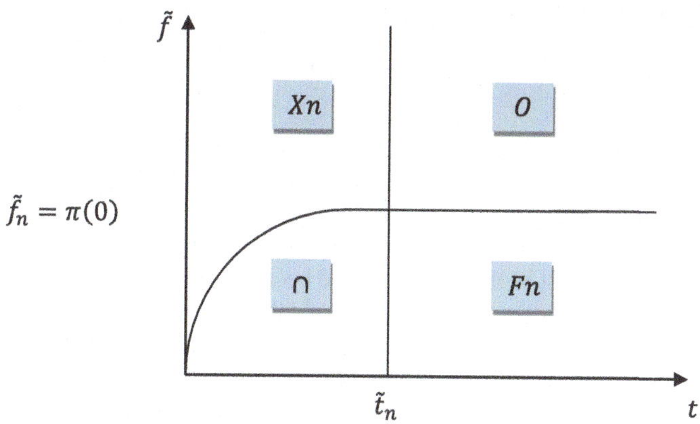

Fig. 3.4 Possible regimes when there are no trade agreements. *Source*: Reprinted from Neary (2002). *Note*: X_n are exports to n countries, F_n is FDI in all n countries, ∩ is mixed regimes where a firm i decides between exports and investment, O is the national strategy of a firm i

contrast, profits from FDI, Π_{Fn}, are independent of t, and decreasing in f. FDI is profitable only if the set-up costs are below a threshold level, $\tilde{f}$ (Neary 2002). From Eq. (3.3), $\tilde{f}$ equals to π (0).

If both trade costs and set-up costs are above their threshold values then a firm cannot make positive profits and decides not to serve foreign markets at all. It is region "O". Finally, if both costs are below their threshold values, a foreign firm is indifferent about the regime, ∩. The boundary separating the X and Fn regions, from Eq. (3.4), is defined by $\gamma(t, f)=0$, and must be increasing and concave as shown (Neary 2002).

3.2.3 Reduction in Internal Tariffs

Neary (2002) further considered the effects of preferential trade agreements on FDI. He assumed that internal trade barriers between partner countries are reduced from t to τ. The common external tariff remains at t, τ is set below $\tilde{t}$; if it is above prohibitive level $\tilde{t}$, nothing is affected (Neary 2002). An overview of the economic system is given in Fig. 3.21, Appendix C.

Regional integration improves market accessibility by lowering internal tariffs. Firm i can supply consumers in n markets by exporting or establishing subsidiaries in all countries, as in the previous section. Clearly, the profits from exporting and investing are not affected and are still given by Eqs. (3.1) and (3.4) respectively.

However, as the internal trade costs fall, the goods can now be exported from a single plant in the region:

$$\Pi_{F1Xn-1} = \pi(0) - f + (n-1)\pi(\tau) \tag{3.6}$$

Neary (2002) derived the difference between pure export regime and exporting from a plant in the region, which is given as:

$$\Pi_{F1Xn-1} - \Pi_X = \gamma(t, f) + \chi(t, \tau) \tag{3.7}$$

where

$$\chi(t, \tau) = (n-1)(\pi(\tau) - \pi(t)) \tag{3.8}$$

Neary (2002) found that the profits from locating a plant in one of the union countries are greater that in the previous case because full gains from FDI relative to exporting come from two sources. There is a gain from jumping into an individual market, $\gamma(t,f)$, a "tariff-jumping" gain. There is also $\chi(t,\tau)$ that denotes the gain from serving the partner countries in the integration region facing intra-union trade cost τ rather than higher common external trade cost t. This gain is called the "export-platform" gain. Unlike the "tariff-jumping" gain which can be positive or negative, the "export-platform" gain is always non-negative, since $\pi(\tilde{t})$ is equal to zero, $\pi(t)$ is decreasing in t, and τ smaller than $\tilde{t}$ by definition. Thus, as a preferential trade

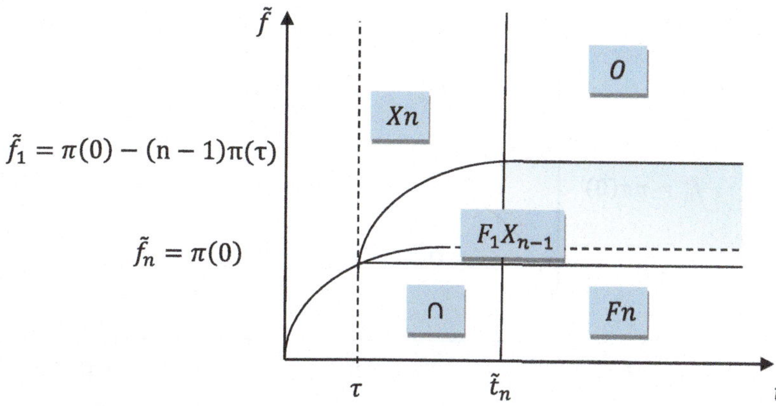

Fig. 3.5 Regimes with a reduced internal tariff. *Source*: Reprinted from Neary (2002). *Note*: X_n are exports to n countries, F_n is FDI in all n countries, F_1X_{n-1} is an installation of an export-platform, ∩ is mixed regimes where a firm i decides between exports and investment, O is the national strategy of a firm i

agreement is signed, FDI becomes more attractive relative to exporting even if $\gamma(t,f)$ is zero or negative. Hence, the lower is τ, the more attractive becomes "export-platform" to both other options (Neary 2002).

Thus, it is never profitable to have more than one and less than *n* plants in this set-up. Since all union countries are identical and all intra-union tariffs are the same, there is nothing to be gained from multiple export-platforms (Neary 2002).

Some further implications of this model can be derived from *{t,f}* space (Fig. 3.5).

In the region labelled "Fn" in Fig. 3.5, high trade costs and low set-up costs justify building a plant in all union countries. However, this region is smaller in size in comparison to Fig. 3.4 by the emergence of a new region labeled "F_1X_{n-1}". This regime implies the installation of a single plant and serving the other countries in the region. The export-platform motive also favors FDI over exporting and over not serving the market at all. The shaded area has FDI although X was never profitable there (Neary 2002).

Export-platform FDI is profitable for any set-up cost less than $\pi(0)+\pi(\tau)$ which is higher rather than $\pi(0)$.

A final implication of the Neary's model is that the same firm engages in both exports and FDI, albeit not across the same frontier: the firm engages in FDI in the host country and also in exports from there to the partner country. Hence exports and FDI become complements rather than substitutes in the aggregate data (Neary 2002).

3.2.4 No Barriers

In the last set-up Neary (2002) supposed that n countries form a free-trade area, so all trade costs between countries disappear. This situation is similar to the Treaty of

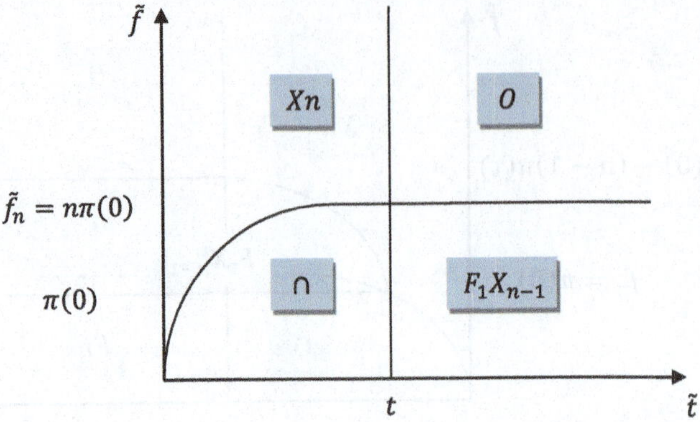

Fig. 3.6 Regimes with no internal tariffs. *Source*: Reprinted from Neary (2002). *Note*: X_n are exports to n countries, F_1X_{n-1} is an installation of an export-platform, ∩ is mixed regimes where a firm i decides between exports and investment, O is the national strategy of a firm i

Rome agreement, signed in 1957, that brought the elimination of internal tariffs and the harmonisation of external tariffs (see Fig. 3.22, Appendix C).

In a Customs Union, a firm *i* does not need to install its subsidiaries in all member countries because one subsidiary can supply the whole region without facing any trade barriers. Foreign direct investment is now even more attractive relative to exporting or not serving the union market (Neary 2002).

$$\Pi_{F1Xn-1} = n\pi(0) - f \tag{3.9}$$

A firm *i* puts its single plant in any country in the region and exports free to other (n−1) countries. Of course, it is still possible to serve n markets with exports if set-up costs are too high. The profits are given by Eq. (3.1).

So, in Fig. 3.6, the region F_1X_{n-1} expands to its maximum extent relative to the *X* and *O* regions. The foundation of a free-trade zone encourages a firm *i* to switch from exporting to foreign direct investment. However, the total amount of FDI in the region is lower in comparison to the previous two cases (Neary 2002).

Overall, Neary (2002) confirmed analytically, for some market equilibriums, the results of the simulations by Motta and Norman (1996). This implies more "reliable" results, at the price of a more simplified setting.

3.3 Heterogeneity Across Countries

In this section, we extend upon the model of Neary (2002) by adding four types of heterogeneity to the basic set-up (see Sect. 3.2): (1) different external tariffs, (2) different market size, (3) different production costs—namely labour costs, and (4) different costs of locating there, in terms of underlying differences in investment project costs, ease of doing business, government policies, and institutions, etc. The point of adopting this model is to identify which country's characteristics attract more FDI all other things being equal.

This analysis will help us to understand how location preferences change under influence of regional integration agreements. The findings of this section will be useful in deriving our FDI model. This section, however, does not provide a full model of FDI location. It gives us theoretical evidence that the importance of traditional FDI location determinants can change during the economic integration.

Significant location advantages for all forms of international activities, such as political stability, low exchange rate risk, or low inflation rates etc., are taken as read here but excluded from the considerations.

3.3.1 Different External Tariffs

We begin by analysing location decisions in countries with differing external trade barriers. All other country characteristics are unchanged. The schematic diagram (Fig. 3.23, Appendix C) provides an overview of the economy's structure.

This analysis is important because, first, it represents the real state of nature, and second, considers heterogeneity in a manner which former studies do not. Some authors however, have included the distance between countries as giving rise to additional trade costs. This assumption is difficult to implement to the CEE region because the countries are situated so closely to each other, have common borders and, thus, are equally distant from the third countries.

We range countries according to external trade barriers. $t_1 < \ldots < t_m < \ldots t_n$. Intra-regional trade barriers are identical and not preferential. For simplicity we suppose that they are equal to $t^* \geq t_n$, so that firm i does not possess any advantage in supplying countries from an export-platform.

In such a set-up, there are two different market entry strategies. First, firm i can serve country j by exports. In this case, its total profits in the region are:

$$\Pi_{\mathrm{Xn}} = \sum_{j=1}^{m} \pi_j(t_j), where\ m = 1, \ldots, n \tag{3.10}$$

It exports to all n countries only when all tariffs are lower than threshold tariff $\tilde{t}_n$, $(\pi(\tilde{t}_n) = 0)$. Once some of the tariffs exceed $\tilde{t}_n$, trade with those countries becomes non-profitable.

Setting $\pi_j(t_j)$ to zero, we solve the threshold value of trade barriers at which it is profitable to trade with country j.

$$\pi_j(\tilde{t}_j) = 0 \Rightarrow \tilde{t}_j(m), m = 0, \ldots, n$$

Thus, if the trade barriers are low enough and trade with all countries is possible, firm i enjoys additional profits from trading with a greater number of countries, $\upsilon(t)$:

$$\Pi_{\mathrm{Xn}} - \Pi_{\mathrm{Xm}} = \sum_{j=m+1}^{n} \pi_j(t_j) = v(t) \tag{3.11}$$

v(t) is decreasing in t and increasing in the number of countries (*n-m*) that can be additionally supplied.

As an opportunity, a firm *i* can invest in countries that have protective tariffs. It pays installation costs, but increases its profits by the amount of saved trade costs and number of countries served:

$$\Pi_{\mathrm{Fn-m\ Xm}} = \sum_{j=1}^{m} \pi_j(t_j) + \sum_{j=m+1}^{n} (\pi_j(0) - f), where\ m = 1, \ldots, n \tag{3.12}$$

The difference between exports and investments in countries with restrictive trade barriers is written as:

$$\Pi_{\mathrm{Fn-m\ Xm}} - \Pi_{\mathrm{Xn}} = \sum_{j=m+1}^{n} (\pi_j(0) - f - \pi_j(t_j)) = \sum_{j=m+1}^{n} \gamma_j(t_j,f) \tag{3.13}$$

Here the sum of γ_j shows profits gained from tariff-jumping. This extension can be negative, which means that it is unreasonable to supply *n-m* countries with FDI or at all.

Equation (3.13) shows that with an increase in external trade tariffs the tariff-jumping gain becomes bigger. This confirms the hypothesis that protective trade barriers stimulate FDI in a country. This finding has an important practical implication. If the government aim is to attract more FDI into a country, it can impose higher trade barriers on imports.

In our analysis we also apply *{t,f}* space offered by Neary (2002) to our set-up of countries with different external trade barriers (Fig. 3.7). X_n region represents a situation when t_n does not exceed $\tilde{t}_n$ and a firm *i* can export to all n countries. X_m is for the case when $t_m < \tilde{t}_m$, the trade with only m countries is possible. The region X_n is bigger than region X_m by measure of *v*(*t*).

When in some countries trade barriers are protective but installation costs, $\tilde{f}_n$, are still low enough, a multinational can decide between investing in all n countries or only in those with high trade costs depending on γ_j. In this case, investment and import regimes are both compliments in a country *j* and supplements in the region. It allows a firm *i* to supply a greater number of countries.

As in the previous section, we also gradually remove the internal trade barriers. We assume that internal trade barriers fall within the region to level τ, where $\tau \leq \tilde{t}_n$ (Fig. 3.24, Appendix C).

Aside from the aforementioned regimes, an export-platform can be installed in the region. Since all countries in the region are equal in their macroeconomic characteristics (installation and production costs and intraregional tariffs are the same among countries), a country of FDI location is chosen randomly. The profit function is given by Eq. (3.6).

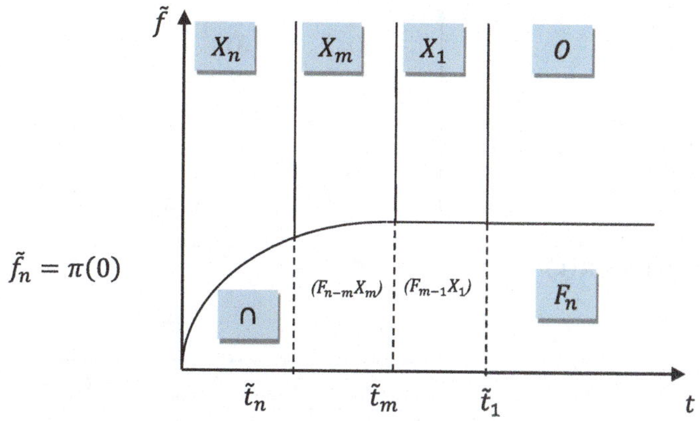

Fig. 3.7 Possible regimes with different external tariffs and no preferential trade agreements. *Source*: Author's work. *Note:* X_n, X_m, and X_1 are exports to n, m and 1 country correspondingly, F_n is FDI in all n countries, ∩, ($F_{n-m}X_m$), and ($F_{m-1}X_1$) are mixed regimes where a firm i decides between exports and investment, O is the national strategy of a firm i

In this case, the size of the export-platform gain varies between countries. The bigger the external tariffs are, the greater the additional gains which can be obtained by serving a country from a local plant.

$$\Pi_{F1Xn-1} - \Pi_{Xn} = \pi(0) - f - \pi(t_m) + \sum_{j=1}^{m-1} (\pi(\tau) - \pi(t_j)) + \sum_{j=m+1}^{n} (\pi(\tau) - \pi(t_j))$$
$$= \gamma_m(t_m; f) + \sum_{j=1}^{m-1} \chi(t_j; \tau) + \sum_{j=m+1}^{n} \chi(t_j; \tau), \textit{where } m = 1, \ldots, n \quad (3.14)$$

Thus, the reduction in intra-regional trade barriers reduces the tariff-jumping motive, and the incentive to install plants in all countries in the region. However, it increases the probability of the appearance of an export-platform in the region.

As can be seen in Fig. 3.8, when at least one plant has been installed, either further plants will be installed in the other countries, or it will be used as an export-platform to supply the other countries. The reduction in intra-regional trade barriers allows firm *i* to supply a greater number of countries at a lower cost.

Following Neary (2002), we also consider the case where all trade barriers within the region disappear. However, we assume that common external barriers are not introduced. This situation is similar to the Accession Agreements explained in Sect. 2.3. In our model, we also assume that transition of goods throughout the region is not possible, or customs clearance is required.

In this set-up, the foundation of more than one subsidiary is not reasonable (Eq. 3.9). Graphically the regimes are shown in Fig. 3.9.

We conclude that the reduction of internal trade barriers makes an installation of a single export-platform more attractive, though the location of FDI cannot be

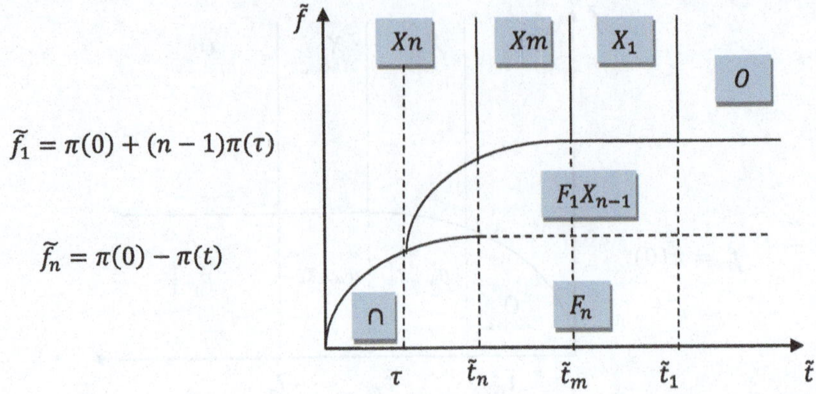

Fig. 3.8 Possible regimes with different external tariffs and with preferential trade agreements. *Source*: Author's work. *Note*: X_n, X_m, and X_1 are exports to n, m and 1 countries correspondingly, F_n is FDI in all n countries, ∩ is a mixed regime where a firm i decides between exports and investment, F_1X_{n-1} is an installation of an export-platform, O is the national strategy of a firm i

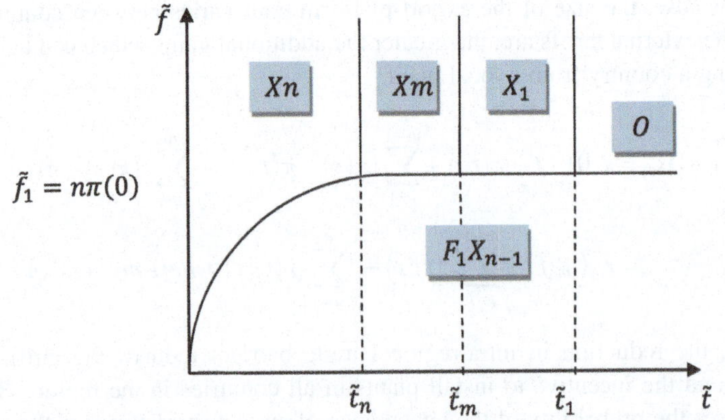

Fig. 3.9 Possible regimes with different external tariffs with no internal trade barriers. *Source*: Author's work. *Note*: X_n, X_m, and X_1 are exports to n, m and 1 countries correspondingly, F_1X_{n-1} is an installation of an export-platform, O is the national strategy of a firm i

influenced by authorities. On the contrary, in the presence of intra-regional trade costs, countries with high protective external trade barriers will attract more FDI.

Markusen (2002) also found that FDI positively related to the existence of trade barriers. However, these findings contradict the recent spectacular growth of FDI has actually taken place in parallel with the surge of integration agreements, in which barriers to trade between member countries are progressively reduced (see Sect. 2.2). Thus, we can suppose that high external trade barriers are not the single factors that attracts multinationals; and there are some factors that stimulate FDI inflows in countries especially when trade barriers between countries are reduced.

3.3.2 Market Size

The impact of differing market size alongside distance costs were investigated by Haller (2010). Thus, the specification here is based on the model by Neary (2002) and Haller (2010).

We assume that these countries are asymmetric in market size, but symmetric with respect to the other parameters. The countries are ordered according to market size; $1 \geq s1 \geq \ldots \geq sn > 0$ (see Fig. 3.26, Appendix C).

Firm *i*'s profits from exporting to a country *j* are given now by $\pi_j(s_j, t)$. They are increasing the size of the market, s_j, and as before, seeing a decrease in trade barrier cost, *t*. In general, the threshold level of external trade tariff, $\tilde{t}$, is defined by s_j: $\pi_j(\tilde{t}_j, s_j) = 0$. The smaller the market size of country *j*, the smaller the prohibitive level of trade barrier, $\tilde{t}_j$ (Haller 2010). Therefore, countries with a smaller market size are less attractive to multinationals because trade expenses are not compensated for by local demand.

As in the previous section, we assume that the intra-regional barrier t^* is higher than $\tilde{t}_n$ (there are no export-platform opportunities in this case).

Thus, profits from exporting are given by:

$$\Pi_{\mathrm{Xm}} = \sum_{\mathrm{j=1}}^{\mathrm{m}} \pi_{\mathrm{j}}(s_j, t), where\ m = 1, \ldots, n \qquad (3.15)$$

A firm *i* exports to a country only when it is profitable to do so. A multinational can set up a plant in a country with protective trade barriers. Quite naturally, if it sets up a plant, it faces the costs of setting-up, *f*, but no other supply costs $(\pi_j(s_j, 0) = \pi_j(s_j))$.

$$\Pi_{\mathrm{Fn-m-1Xm}} = \sum_{\mathrm{j=1}}^{\mathrm{m}} \pi_{\mathrm{j}}(s_j; t) + \sum_{\mathrm{j=m+1}}^{\mathrm{n}} (\pi_{\mathrm{j}}(s_j) - f), where\ m = 1, \ldots, n \qquad (3.16)$$

Following Haller (2010), we compare pure exports in n countries (Eq. 3.15) and FDI in the smallest countries,

$$\Pi_{\mathrm{FmXn-m}} - \Pi_{\mathrm{Xn}} = \sum_{j=m+1}^{n} (\pi_{\mathrm{j}}(s_j) - f - \pi_{\mathrm{j}}(s_j, t)) = \sum_{j=m+1}^{n} \gamma(s_j, t, f) \qquad (3.17)$$

where the term $\gamma(s_j, t, f)$ is the net gain from avoiding the trade barrier cost. As we found from the previous cases, $\gamma(s_j, t, f)$ is increasing with the trade barrier, *t*, and decreasing in set-up cost, *f*.

From the profit function, we can see that $\gamma(s_j, t, f)$ is also increasing in s_j. In addition, as noted by Haller (2010), $\gamma(s_j, t, f)$ depends on the market size of the country of investment and not on the market size of the countries where a firm *i* exports. However, the small market size of these countries also makes investment there relatively less attractive because market size, *s*, indirectly influences the threshold level of installation costs (Haller 2010).

So long as $\gamma(s_j, t, f)$ is positive, it makes sense to invest so as to avoid the trade barrier and increase the number of countries supplied. The profits from investing are:

$$\Pi_{\mathrm{Fn}} = \sum_{\mathrm{j}=1}^{\mathrm{m}} \left(\pi_{\mathrm{j}}(s_j) - f\right), where\ m = 1, \ldots, n \tag{3.18}$$

implying that fixed cost cannot exceed $\tilde{f} = \pi_{\mathrm{j}}(s_j)$ in each country *j*.

Thus, the firm's decision to invest is driven only by trade barrier and by market size. The larger the host market size, the greater the likelihood that multinationals will be able to recoup the fixed costs of their foreign plants.

For the set-up with different market sizes, we also worked out a *{t,f}* space to represent all possible regimes. We come to the conclusion that, unlike homogenous countries, market size, *s*, defines the threshold tariff level and thus, the threshold level of installation costs. The bigger a country is, the greater the likelihood it will be served by foreign companies (Fig. 3.10).

In a world without preferential trade agreements, the market size of a country plays a crucial role in defining which countries to serve.

Now we investigate what happens when intraregional barriers are reduced (see Fig. 3.27, Appendix C).

Pure export and investment strategies are given by Eqs. (3.15) and (3.18) correspondingly. For installation costs, *f*, higher than the threshold level, $\tilde{f}$, there are no changes: a firm *i* exports in m countries until its profits are positive (for $\tilde{t}_m$, $m = 1, \ldots, n$).

On the whole, preferential trade relations increase the incentive to install an export-platform FDI. Since all countries have identical installation and trade costs, and it is not observable how exactly market size enters the profit function, we assume that a single plant can be installed in any country in the region ($m = 1, \ldots, n$). The profits from operating an export-platform in country m are given by:

$$\Pi_{\mathrm{F1Xn-1}} = \pi_{\mathrm{m}}(s_m) - f + \sum_{\mathrm{j}=1}^{\mathrm{m-1}} \pi_{\mathrm{j}}(s_j, \tau) + \sum_{\mathrm{j=1+m}}^{\mathrm{n}} \pi_{\mathrm{j}}(s_j, \tau), where\ m = 1, \ldots, n \tag{3.19}$$

The relative profitability from establishing an export-platform is:

$$\Pi_{\mathrm{F1Xn-1}} - \Pi_{\mathrm{Xn}} = \gamma(s_m, t, f) + \chi(\mathrm{s_j}, \mathrm{t}, \tau) \tag{3.20}$$

where

$$\chi(\mathrm{s_j}, \mathrm{t}, \tau) = \sum_{\mathrm{j}=1}^{\mathrm{m-1}} \left(\pi_{\mathrm{j}}(s_j, \tau) - \pi_{\mathrm{j}}(s_j, t)\right) + \sum_{\mathrm{j=1+m}}^{\mathrm{n}} \left(\pi_{\mathrm{j}}(s_j, \tau) - \pi_{\mathrm{j}}(s_j, t)\right), where\ m = 1, \ldots, n \tag{3.21}$$

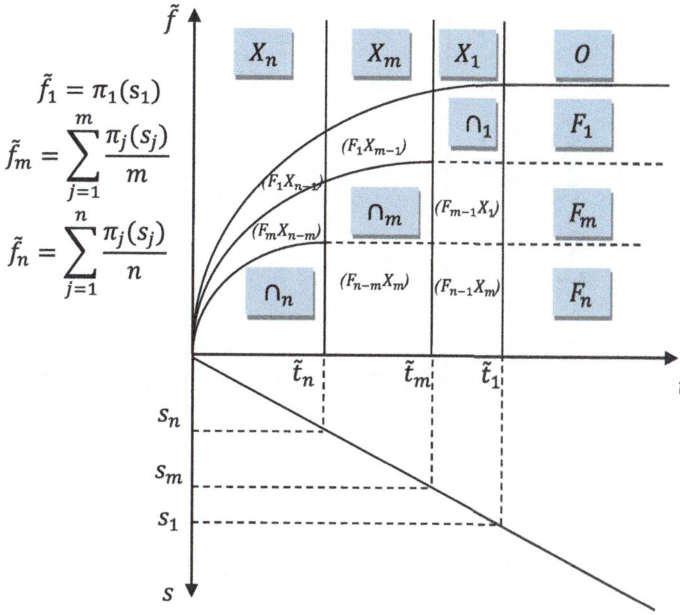

Fig. 3.10 Possible regimes with different market sizes and no trade agreements. *Source*: Author's work. *Note*: X_n, X_m, and X_1 are exports to n, m and 1 country correspondingly, F_n, F_m, and F_1 are FDI in all n, m or country 1, ∩, ($F_{n-m}X_m$), etc. are mixed regimes where a firm i decides between exports and investment, O is the national strategy of a firm i

The tariff-jumping gain $\gamma(s_m, t, f)$ has been explained previously. The second term $\chi(s_j, t, \tau)$ calculates the additional gains from exporting to $n-1$ countries at lower costs. Thus, this "export-platform" gain $\chi(s_j, t, \tau)$ is always positive. It is also increasing the market size of the region, not a single country. Put differently, this means that investing is less attractive the smaller the sum of market sizes of the countries that can be served in the integration union.

As we can see from Fig. 3.11, the reduction of intra-regional trade barriers lessens the importance of the host country's market size. However, the substantial market size of the region is attractive for foreign investors and attracts FDI in the member-countries.

In this set-up, the number of countries involved in international activity is never less than n if the installation of at least one subsidiary is possible. Since investors always intend to supply the maximum amount of countries, regime X_m, where $m = 1, \ldots, n-1$ arises only when FDI is not possible.

In the Customs Union (see Fig. 3.27), free trade between countries favours inward FDI and intra-regional exports over extra-regional exports, as other members do not require additional trade costs (Eq. 3.22).

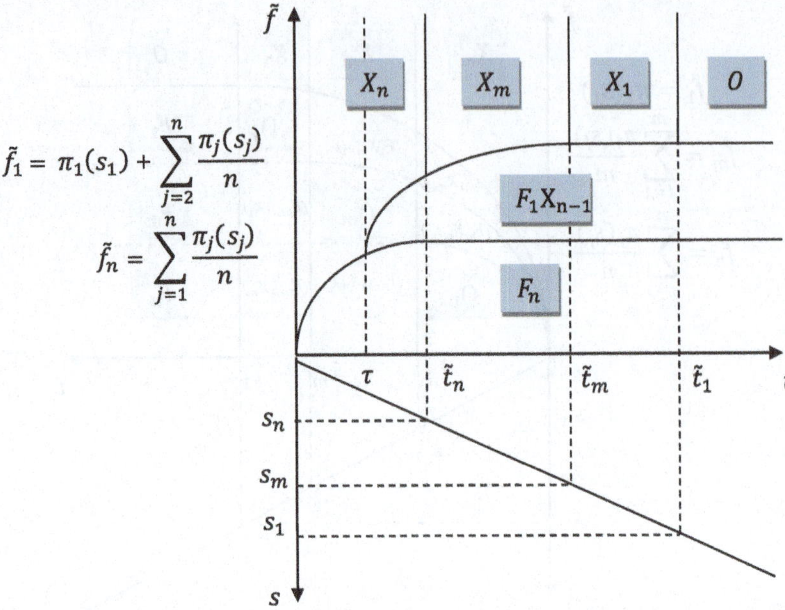

Fig. 3.11 Possible regimes with different market sizes and with preferential agreements. *Source*: Author's work. *Note*: X_n, X_m, and X_1 are exports to n, m and 1 countries correspondingly, F_n is FDI in all n countries, ∩ is a mixed regime where a firm i decides between exports and investment, F_1X_{n-1} is an installation of an export-platform, O is the national strategy of a firm i

$$\Pi_{F1Xn-1} = \sum_{j=1}^{n} \pi_j(s_j) - f \tag{3.22}$$

In this case, foreign firms are completely indifferent to the market size of the host country. This confirms the findings of Haller (2010), in that once a country opens its borders, market size loses its importance (Haller 2010).

Thus, the disappearance of trade barriers gives an opportunity for small countries to attract foreign investors, all other things being equal.

The findings in this section can be summarised as follows; in the case of protective trade barriers, multinationals choose to supply all countries with larger demand first. The statistics confirm these findings (see Sect. 2.2). FDI inflows were greater in large countries such as Poland, Hungary, and the Czech Republic etc., whilst smaller countries suffered from scant FDI inflow.

The gradual removal of trade barriers reduces the role of the host country's market size. Firms set up plants to supply not only the host country's market, but also the host nation's neighbouring markets. The market size of a country plays a less important role in the decision where to locate a subsidiary, however, the total market size of the region plays an important role, especially in defining the threshold level of installation costs (Fig. 3.12).

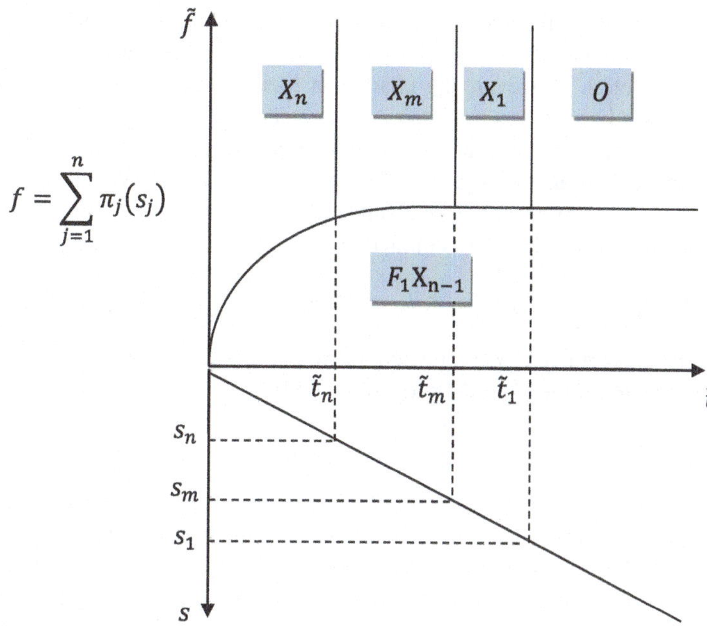

Fig. 3.12 Possible regimes with different market sizes and with no external trade barriers. *Source*: Author's work. *Note*: X_n, X_m, and X_1 are exports to n, m and 1 countries correspondingly, F_1X_{n-1} is an installation of an export-platform, O is the national strategy of a firm i

Ito (2013) confirms this finding, by calculating the ratio of exports to third countries to FDI from the US in 20 countries. He found that the smallest countries have the highest ratio of exports to third countries, large EU countries have a lower ratio, and finally, large non-EU countries have the lowest ratio. He explained it by the fact that non-EU countries do not have regional agreements and access to other markets. However, small countries that have access to large markets attract more FDI aimed at supplying both local and neighbouring markets (Ito 2013).

Chen (2009) also proved empirically that FDI is higher to the integrated countries. The effect from integration also rises in accordance with the number and size of associated countries (Chen 2009). Thus, regional agreements give small countries an advantage in attracting more FDI.

3.3.3 Labour Costs

In this section, we include the production costs difference outlined in Neary's model. Here, firm *i* chooses the location of production where cost plays the crucial role. The example given is differing labour costs in the Central European countries and Western Balkans.

The question of influence of production costs on regime choice have been analysed in a number of papers (Ekholm et al. 2003; Kim 2007; Montout and Zitouna 2005; etc.). However, the change in location choice during the gradual removal of trade barriers has not been investigated thus far.

In our set-up, the unit production costs vary according to country. The country with the cheapest production is 1, and the most expensive is n. We also assume that production in I is more expensive than in any foreign country (Fig. 3.29). The domestic costs of production are denoted as l:

$$0 < l_1 \leq \ldots \leq l_m \leq \ldots \leq l_n \ll l_i, where\ 1 < \ldots < m < \ldots < n$$

i's profits are written as $\pi_j(l_i; t)$ when a firm exports to a country j.

The aggregate profits from exports are given by:

$$\Pi_{\mathrm{Xn}} = n\pi(\mathrm{l_i}, \mathrm{t}) \tag{3.23}$$

Alternatively, a firm i can engage in FDI and locate a new plant in a host country j, $\pi_j(l_j) - f$. If a location is chosen as the destination of FDI, then from the investor's point of view, it must be more profitable to produce in that location than in the others. Thus, a firm i chooses the country with lowest production costs, l_1. In this case, it incurs a plant-specific installation cost, f, as in the previous sections, and earns operating profits from trade with the other countries from a plant situated in country 1:

$$\Pi_{\mathrm{F_1X_{n-1}}} = \pi(\mathrm{l_1}) - \mathrm{f} + (\mathrm{n}-1)\pi(\mathrm{l_1}, \mathrm{t}) \tag{3.24}$$

Following the analysis of Montout and Zitouna (2005), we define the relative profitability of FDI

$$\Pi_{\mathrm{F_1Xn-1}} - \Pi_{\mathrm{Xn}} = \gamma(\mathrm{t}; \mathrm{l_i}; \mathrm{l_1}) \tag{3.25}$$

where

$$\gamma(\mathrm{t}; \mathrm{l_i}; \mathrm{l_1}) = \pi(\mathrm{l_1}) - f - \pi(\mathrm{l_i}, \mathrm{t}) \tag{3.26}$$

If the production cost difference surpasses the installation cost, a multinational will install an off-shore there (see Eq. 3.25) to save on production costs. The "tariff-jumping" gain function γ is identical to that in the section with the homogenous countries, except now it depends on wages in a way that reflects its comparative advantage. The new element, $\gamma(\mathrm{t}; \mathrm{l_i}; \mathrm{l_1})$, is called the "off-shoring" gain. Not surprisingly, it depends negatively on the source country wage l_i and positively on the host-country wage, l_1, reflecting the importance of its comparative advantage. In addition, it is decreasing with the foreign trade tariff, t.

FDI thus becomes increasingly probable the higher the labour cost difference between the home and host country and the lower the set-up costs. Relatively similar labour costs do not lead to the possibility of exploiting differences in factor price, and do not stimulate inward FDI as they do not surpass installation costs (Motta and Norman 1996; Montout and Zitouna 2005).

To draw some additional conclusions, we developed *{t,f}* space for countries with different production costs following the idea of Neary (2002) to represent trade and installation thresholds in the same space.

When trade costs, *t*, are very high, a multinational installs subsidiaries until the comparative advantage from low production costs exceeds the installation costs, $\tilde{f}$.

$$\Pi_{\mathrm{Fn}} = \sum_{\mathrm{j}=1}^{\mathrm{m}} \left(\pi_{\mathrm{j}}(\mathrm{l}_{\mathrm{j}}) - \mathrm{f}\right), where\ m = 1, \ldots, n \tag{3.27}$$

This hypothesis is in line with the findings of Ekholm et al. (2003, 2007) and Kim (2007). They found that a foreign firm will choose FDI when the factor cost difference will allow them to recoup the installation costs (Fig. 3.13).

The firm's decision as to whether to construct only one affiliate abroad or a few thus depends on the unit labour cost difference, trade, and installation costs.

Now we assume that n countries conclude a preferential trade agreement (see Fig. 3.30). The export-platform becomes even more attractive for foreign investors since they can supply the rest of the countries at reduced costs τ:

$$\Pi_{\mathrm{F1X_{n-1}}} = \pi(\mathrm{l}_1) - \mathrm{f} + (\mathrm{n} - 1)\,\pi(\mathrm{l}_1, \tau) \tag{3.28}$$

Thus, the relative profitability from investing in a country *1* is:

$$\Pi_{\mathrm{F1Xn-1}} - \Pi_{\mathrm{X}} = \gamma(\mathrm{t}, \mathrm{l}_{\mathrm{i}}, \mathrm{l}_1) + \chi(\mathrm{t}, \tau, \mathrm{l}_{\mathrm{i}}, \mathrm{l}_1) \tag{3.29}$$

The total profitability from installation of an export-platform consists of two parts. The first one is a "tariff-jumping" gain, $\gamma(s_m; t_m; l_i; l_m)$, in a country *m*. The second one, $\chi(\mathrm{t}, \tau, \mathrm{l}_{\mathrm{i}}, \mathrm{l}_1)$, denotes the gain from serving the partner countries in the integration region facing intra-union trade cost, τ, rather than higher common

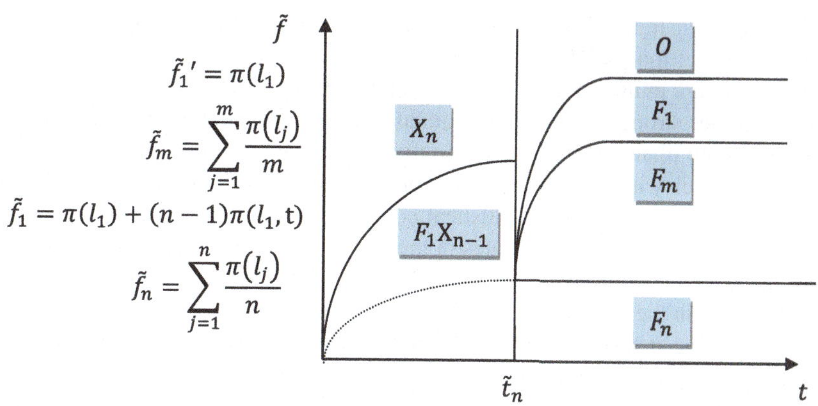

Fig. 3.13 Possible regimes with different production costs. *Source*: Author's work. *Note*: X_n *is* exports to n countries, F_n, F_m, F_1 are FDI in all n, m, and 1 countries, F_1X_{n-1} is an installation of an off-shore, O is the national strategy of a firm i

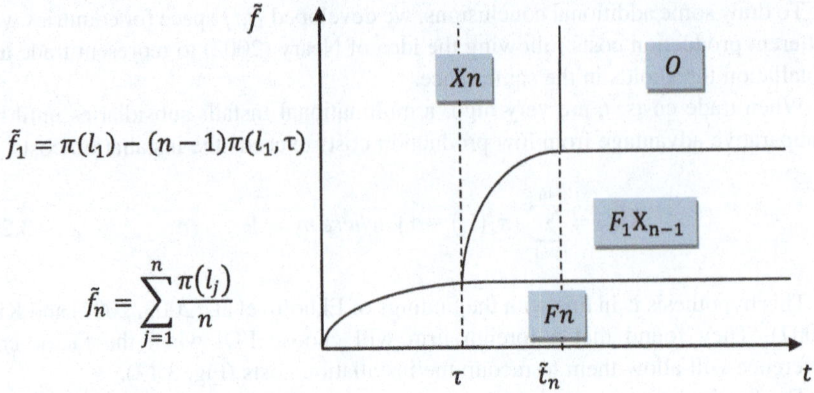

Fig. 3.14 Possible regimes with different production costs. *Source*: Author's work. *Note*: X_n *is* exports to n countries, F_n are FDI in all n countries, F_1X_{n-1} is an installation of an off-shore, O is the national strategy of a firm i

external trade cost, *t*. The lower the intraregional barrier, the more preferable an investment becomes. In addition to this, firm *i* invests in country m to save on production costs and to supply the others from the off-shore plant. Therefore, the greater the difference in wages between a host and a home country, the more likely FDI will arrive in a low-wage country.

Figure 3.14 points out that "off-shore" FDI has almost replaced pure export and investing strategies.

When n countries form a free trade area (see Fig. 3.31), the relative profitability of installing an export-platform increases by amount saved from trade at null tariffs. Therein, investing in a low-cost country becomes even more attractive:

$$\Pi_{F1X_{n-1}} = n\pi(l_1) - f \tag{3.30}$$

This case illustrates the strategic advantage for a low-wage country to join a free trade area to get more FDI.

Summing up, multinationals invest in countries with lower production costs. The effect becomes stronger in the line of gradual removal of intraregional trade barriers when a foreign plant gets free access to the regional market (Fig. 3.15).

In the model with differing production costs, we come to the most important results, in which a number of statistical confirmations are produced. For example, wages in the new EU member States in the early 2000s were about 60% lower than those in the EU-15 countries (UNCTAD 2005), which stimulated European TNCs to invest heavily in the automobile industry in Central and Eastern European countries. Moreover, since investing in the CEE countries allows overseas investors to jump over EU tariff barriers, investors (especially from Japan, the Republic of Korea and the United States) also became increasingly interested in the region. This resulted in the concentration of the automobile industry in four countries: the Czech Republic and Poland, followed by Hungary and Slovakia (e.g. Toyota and VW/Skoda in the

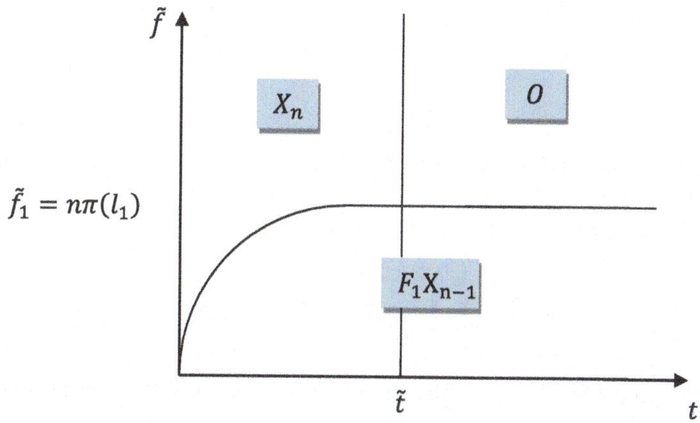

Fig. 3.15 Possible regimes with different production costs. *Source*: Author's work. *Note*: X_n is exports to n countries, F_1X_{n-1} is an installation of an off-shore, O is the national strategy of a firm i

Czech Republic; Suzuki and Audi in Hungary; Fiat, GM/Opel, Daewoo, VW in Poland; PSA/Peugeot and VW in Slovakia; and Renault in Slovenia, see UNCTAD (2003), p.61). According to the UNCTAD (2005) estimations, about one tenth of inward FDI stocks in Hungary, Poland and the Czech Republic were in the automobile industry (UNCTAD 2005).

3.3.4 Installation Costs

Here, we focus on differences in installation costs, and explore how they affect location decisions. The example given is of countries implementing policies that create incentives for FDI. In reality, many countries offer land at reduced prices and preferential tax rates to potential multinational firms who are interested in building plants. The costs of locating a plant can also differ between countries because of the harmonisation of technical and product standards or improved business relations across countries. Since these policies reduce the value of f, the FDI incentive policy may have some impact.

By convention, and without loss of generality, we assume that f is increasing among countries (so the countries are ordered by fixed cost).

$$f_1 \leq \ldots \leq f_m \leq \ldots \leq f_n, \text{ where } 1 < \ldots < m < \ldots < n$$

A firm i does not have any installation costs when it decides to produce in I.

The profits of a firm i from exports is given by Eq. (3.2). They are the same as in the economic system with homogenous countries. Once a firm i decides to supply n markets with FDI its profits become:

$$\Pi_{Fn} = m\pi(0) - \sum_{j=1}^{m} f_j, \textit{ where } m = 1, \ldots, n \tag{3.31}$$

Equation (3.31) shows that the net profits from investments drop with the increase of installation costs. Thus, the profits from investments can also be negative. In this case, a multinational refuses to invest in some counties. Therewith, the rest of the countries in the region can be served by trade if $t < \tilde{t}$:

$$\Pi_{FmXn-m-1} = m\pi(0) - \sum_{j=1}^{m} f_j + (n-m)\pi(t), \textit{ where } m = 1, \ldots, n \tag{3.32}$$

The gain in profits from establishing plants in m countries rather than supplying them with exports can be written as:

$$\Pi_{FmXn-m} - \Pi_{Xn} = m(\pi(0) - \pi(t)) - \sum_{j=1}^{m} f_j = \sum_{j=1}^{m} \gamma(t, f_j) \tag{3.33}$$

Here, (t, f_j), is the gain from tariff-jumping into an individual union country. However, unlike in earlier sections, tariff-jumping depends on the country under consideration. Thus, for some countries, γ is either positive (FDI are more profitable), or negative (a multinational prefers exports or does not supply foreign countries at all).

Setting γ equal to zero, we can determine the threshold value of installation costs. At this level of set-up costs, it will not be profitable to install further plants in the region:

$$\gamma(t, f_m) = 0 \Longrightarrow \tilde{f} = \tilde{f}(t, m), m = 0, \ldots, n \tag{3.34}$$

The threshold value of $\tilde{f}$ is increasing in t, since a higher external tariff increases the gains from tariff-jumping (Montout and Zitouna 2005).

We represent trade and installation costs threshold levels in Fig. 3.16. It shows that location in a country with higher installation cost reduces profits.

Sometimes it is not profitable to install subsidiaries in all countries, e.g. $\tilde{f}_n < f < \tilde{f}_m$, only m of n countries will be served (F_m). For t above the threshold level $\tilde{t}$, the profits from exports are negative and so the loci defined by (F) are independent of t, and become horizontal lines (Neary 2002).

If the internal tariffs are reduced to level τ (see Fig. 3.33), profits from establishing an export-platform are:

$$\Pi_{F1Xn-1} = \pi(0) - f_1 + (n-1)\pi(\tau) \tag{3.35}$$

As is the case with different production costs, a single plant will be installed in the country with the lowest installation costs.

Extending the logic of the relative profitability of an export-platform leads to:

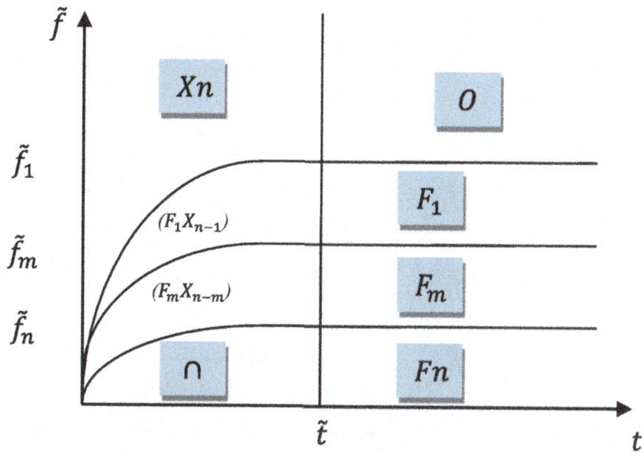

Fig. 3.16 Possible regimes with different installation costs. *Source*: Author's work. *Note*: X_n is exports to n countries, F_n, F_m, and F_1 are FDI in all n, m or country 1, ∩, $(F_{n-m}X_m)$, etc. are mixed regimes where a firm i decides between exports and investment, O is the national strategy of a firm i

$$\begin{aligned}\Pi_{F1Xn-1} - \Pi_{Xn} &= (\pi(0) - f_1 - \pi(\tau)) + (n-1)(\pi(\tau) - \pi(t)) \\ &= \gamma(t, f_1) + \chi(t, \tau)\end{aligned} \tag{3.36}$$

Setting this to zero, we can determine the threshold value of the installation cost parameter at which it is profitable to locate a single plant in the union:

$$\gamma(t, f_1) + \chi(t, \tau) = 0 \Rightarrow \tilde{f} = \tilde{f}(t, \tau) \tag{3.37}$$

The crucial feature is that $\tilde{f}$ is decreasing in τ. Hence a reduction in internal tariffs makes it more attractive to locate a single plant in the union than to export to it (Neary 2002). It is also increasing in t: high protective external trade barriers make the operation of the export-platform more profitable relative to export strategies (Fig. 3.17).

However, as τ falls, it becomes less profitable to locate more than one plant within the union. The total amount of FDI decreases (Neary 2002).

Once the trade barriers disappear (see Fig. 3.34), it becomes unreasonable to invest in more than one country with the cheapest installation costs, namely country *1* (see Eq. 3.30).

$$\Pi_{F1Xn-1} = n\pi(0) - f_1 \tag{3.38}$$

In our set-up with different installation costs, we come to very plausible conclusions; a country with a relatively more favourable business climate will attract more FDI. The reduction in internal trade barriers will stimulate the reallocation of production in countries with low business costs (Fig. 3.18).

For example, in 2000, the lowest corporate income tax rate among integrating countries was in Hungary, 18%, compared to 42% in Germany, 37,76% in France and 34,00% in Austria, what made it the third largest country in the region by FDI inflows.

In 2005, in eight CEE countries that just joined the EU the average tax corporate rate was 20,57%, and in France and Great Britain it was 34,93% and 30% respectively. The lowest rates were in Latvia (15%) and Hungary (16%) (OECD.Stat 2017; UNCTAD 2005). The opening of borders and free access to the EU market

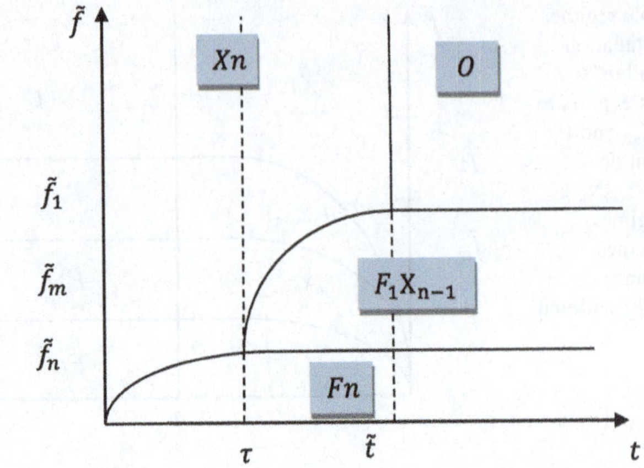

Fig. 3.17 Possible regimes with different installation costs. *Source:* Author's work. *Note*: X_n is exports to n countries, F_n is FDI in all n countries, ∩ is a mixed regime where a firm i decides between exports and investment, F_1X_{n-1} is an installation of an export-platform, O is the national strategy of a firm i

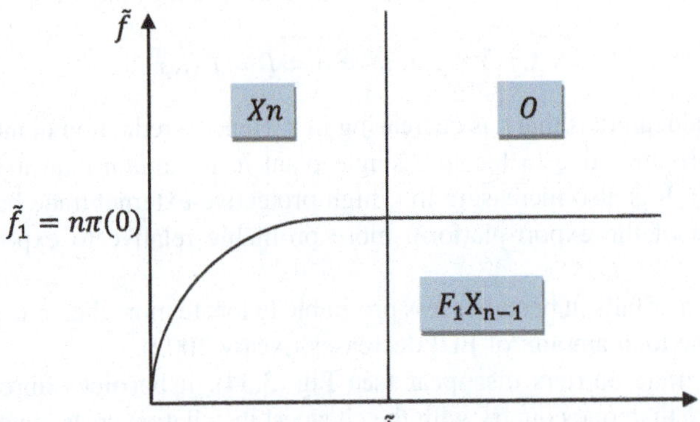

Fig. 3.18 Possible regimes with different installation costs with no intraregional trade barriers. *Source:* Author's work. *Note*: X_n is exports to n countries, F_1X_{n-1} is an installation of an export-platform, O is the national strategy of a firm i

stimulated FDI inflow from the third countries, and allocation of production within the region for the benefit of the new members of the EU (see Sect. 2.2).

According to Pomerleau and Potosky (2016), Montenegro, Macedonia, Bulgaria, Bosnia and Herzegovina, Moldova, Georgia and Albania were among 20 countries with the lowest marginal corporate tax rates in the World (from 9% in Montenegro to 15% in Albania), excluding countries without any corporate taxes (Pomerleau and Potosky 2016). Following the experience of the former enlargements, such low tax rates can attract investors in these countries once the countries get free access to the EU market.

Table 3.3 Determinants of FDI in the theoretical model

	No agreements	PTA	FTA
Homogenous countries	High external trade barriers (t)	High external trade barriers (t) Low intraregional trade barriers (τ)	High external trade barriers (t) Absence of intraregional trade barriers (τ)
Different external trade barriers	High external trade barriers (t)	High external trade barriers (t) Low intraregional trade barriers (τ)	High external trade barriers (t) Absence of intraregional trade barriers (τ)
Different market sizes	High external trade barriers (t) Large market size (s)	High external trade barriers (t) Low intraregional trade barriers (τ) Large market sizes of the whole region ($\sum s$)	High external trade barriers (t) Absence of intraregional trade barriers (τ) Large market sizes of the whole region ($\sum s$)
Different production costs	High external trade barriers (t) *or* Difference in production costs between the home and host countries (l_i and l_j) and Low trade barriers	High external trade barriers (t) Low intraregional trade barriers (τ) Difference in production costs between the home and host countries (l_i and l_j)	High external trade barriers (t) Absence of intraregional trade barriers (τ) Difference in production costs between the home and host countries (l_i and l_j)
Different installation costs	High external trade barriers (t) Low installation costs (f)	High external trade barriers (t) Low intraregional trade barriers (τ) Low installation costs (f)	High external trade barriers (t) Absence of intraregional trade barriers (τ) Low installation costs (f)

Source: Author's work

In Table 3.3, we summarise our main findings within this section by classifying the main determinants of FDI according to the types of heterogeneity and steps of integration.

Summing up, the incentive to invest or to export is explained by the concept of profit maximisation. If a location is chosen as the destination of FDI, then from the investor's point of view, it must be more profitable to produce in that location than in others, and FDI should be more profitable than other means. Thus, the location choice of FDI is determined by the relative profitability of a subsidiary and the motivations of investing firms (Dunning 1993). If the primary motive is to take advantage of the location as an export-platform, the costs related to the production of goods and their export cost to the rest of the region become an important factor.

3.4 FDI in the Model

Section 3.3 gave us a general overview of the separate cases of heterogeneity. In this section, we aim to combine them in one generalised theoretical model that will help us understand the investment motives. At the final stage of our theoretical analysis we derive a model of FDI locations. This explains why FDI may be sensitive not only to traditional FDI location determinants but also to integration specific factors.

3.4.1 *Generalised Theoretical Model*

We start our investigation from the standpoint of supply choices. There are four regimes for a firm *i* to choose from in order to supply a country m in the region: (1) it can export to m from its local plant, (2) it can invest, (3) it can invest with intent to supply the rest of the countries in the region, and (4) export in m from another country in the region. Foreign firms, in a world of heterogeneous firms, will use all possible means and their combinations to supply a bigger number of countries and increase their profits.

We can specify profit functions based on our findings in the previous sections.

$$\Pi_{Xim} = \pi_m(s_m; l_i; t_m), \textit{ where } m = 1, \ldots, n \tag{3.39}$$

Profits from exports (Π_{Xim}) are increasing in the size of the market, s_m, and decreasing in the trade barrier cost, t_m. l_i is home production costs.

A multinational can invest in a country to bypass import tariffs.

$$\Pi_{Fim} = \pi_m(s_m; l_m) - f_m, \textit{ where } m = 1, \ldots, n \tag{3.40}$$

Similarly, profits from investing depend on the market size, s_m, and local production and installation costs, l_m and f_m respectively. If the production costs difference surpasses installation costs, a multinational will install a plant there.

We define the relative profitability of FDI:

$$\Pi_{Fim} - \Pi_{Xim} = \pi_m(s_m; l_m) - f_m - \pi_m(s_m; l_i; t_m) = \gamma(s_m; t_m; l_i; l_m) \tag{3.41}$$

The "tariff-jumping" gain, $\gamma(s_m; t_m; l_i; l_m)$ depends negatively on the source country wage l_i and positively on the host-country wage, l_m. FDI, thus, become increasingly probable the higher the labour cost difference between the home and host country, the larger the market size and the lower the set-up costs. In addition, it decreases in the foreign trade tariff, t_m. Therefore, protective trade barriers stimulate FDI inflows.

A foreign firm can install an off-shore in *m* to supply other countries in the region. The profits are written as:

$$\Pi_{FimXn-1} = \pi_m(s_m; l_m) - f_m + \sum_{j=1}^{m-1} \left[\pi_j(s_j; l_m; t_m)\right] + \sum_{j=m+1}^{n} \left[\pi_j(s_j; l_m; t_m)\right],$$

$$\text{where } m = 1, \ldots, n \tag{3.42}$$

This regime allows the installation of a plant in a country with relatively high installation costs under the stipulation that it gets an additional gain from trading with the rest of the countries. This regime will not occur when the intra-regional trade barriers are the same as the extra-regional trade barriers, and there is no production comparative advantage.

The positive effect becomes evident once the preferential trade area is formed and import tariffs are reduced from t_m to τ, or eliminated completely.

To define the relative profitability of the export-platform, we compare profits from the installation of a single plant with exports to all n countries, which is the sum of profits in each country of the region.

Thus, the relative profitability from investing in a country m is:

$$\Pi_{Fi1Xn-1} - \Pi_{Xim} = \underbrace{\pi_m(s_m; l_m) - f_m + \sum_{j=1}^{m-1} \pi_j(s_j; l_m; \tau) + \sum_{j=m+1}^{n} \pi_j(s_j; l_m; \tau)}_{\textit{profits from export-platform in m}}$$

$$- \underbrace{\sum_{j=1}^{n} \pi_j(s_j; l_i; t_j)}_{\text{profits from exports to n countries}} = \gamma(s_m; t_m; l_i; l_m) + \chi(s_m; t_m, \tau, l_i; l_m) \tag{3.43}$$

where

$$\chi(s_m; t_m, \tau, l_i; l_m) = \sum_{j=1}^{m-1} \left(\pi_j(s_j; l_m; \tau) - \pi_j(s_j; l_m; t_m)\right)$$

$$+ \sum_{j=m+1}^{n} \left(\pi_j(s_j; l_m; \tau) - \pi_j(s_j; l_m; t_m)\right) \tag{3.44}$$

A firm i gets both "tariff-jumping" gain, $\gamma(s_m; t_m; l_i; l_m)$, in a country m and the gain from exporting in the partner countries at lower cost and producing more efficiently ($\chi(s, t, \tau, l_i, l_1)$). Moreover, it shows the benefit of servicing a larger market at more favourable conditions. Thus, when a preferential trade area is formed, foreign firms are motivated to move their production to the integrated bloc because the benefit of preferential market access is exclusive to inside firms.

An important implication of this model is that improved market access reduces the tariff-jumping FDI but increases off-shoring and export-platform FDI. Some countries can therefore experience a decline in inward FDI, while the other more attractive members of the union witness an increase. This is especially likely when countries in an integration union are highly heterogeneous. Countries with larger market sizes or with better access to neighbouring markets will attract more FDI inflow. Moreover, foreign investors are more likely to concentrate in countries with relatively low production and installation costs.

Once the trade barriers between countries disappear, an export-platform becomes even more preferable than other regimes. Moreover, the tariff-jumping motive (investments in countries with protective trade barriers) becomes unreasonable because now all countries in the region can be supplied from a single plant.

In a free trade area the local market size of a country plays no role in the decision where to locate, but the total size of the union, production and installation costs are important.

Finally, m imports from a plant situated in another country in the region:

$$\Pi_{FikXn-1} = \pi_k(s_k; l_k) - f_k + \sum_{j=1}^{k-1} \left(\pi_j(s_j; l_k; t_j)\right) + \sum_{j=k+1}^{n} \left(\pi_j(s_j; l_k; t_j)\right), \tag{3.45}$$

$$\text{where } k = 1, \ldots, n,\ m = 1, \ldots, n,\ m \neq k$$

The incentives to install a plant in a country k are the same as for country m.

All regimes occur when they are more profitable than other opportunities. Thus, a firm i will not export to a country m when it sees negative profits, $\Pi_{Xim} > 0$, or when it is less attractive than the other possible regimes, $\Pi_{Xim} \geq \Pi_{Fim}$, $\Pi_{Xim} \geq \Pi_{FimXn-1}$, $\Pi_{Xim} \geq \Pi_{FikXn-1}$. Non-strict inequalities mean that the exports here are more preferable, all other things being equal.

FDI occurs only when it is more profitable and more effective than the other opportunity regimes. Accordingly, a multinational installs an off-shore plant only when it is the best option of all.

The Eq. (3.46) describes the regime choice based on the given market sizes, production and installation costs as well as trade barriers. It includes pure exports, and investment regimes, as well as installation of a production plant in a country with relatively low labour costs to supply other countries. This equation also takes into account the regime of no international activities, if all strategies are non-profitable in a country m:

$$\begin{aligned}\Pi_{im} &= \iota\pi_m(s_m; l_i; t_m) + \kappa(\pi_m(s_m; l_m) - f_m) \\ &+ \lambda\left[\pi_m(s_m; l_m) - f_m + \sum_{j=1}^{m-1} \left(\pi_j(s_j; l_m; t_j)\right) + \sum_{j=m+1}^{n} \left(\pi_j(s_j; l_m; t_j)\right)\right] \\ &+ \mu\left[\pi_k(s_k; l_k) - f_k + \sum_{j=1}^{k-1} \left(\pi_j(s_j; l_k; t_j)\right) + \sum_{j=k+1}^{n} \left(\pi_j(s_j; l_k; t_j)\right)\right],\end{aligned} \tag{3.46}$$

$$\text{where } k = 1, \ldots, n,\ m = 1, \ldots, n,\ m \neq k$$

ι, κ, λ, and μ are introduced to exclude the possibility that the same country will be supplied by both exports and FDI.

We define:

$$\iota = \begin{cases} 1, \Pi_{Xim} > 0, \Pi_{Xim} \geq \Pi_{Fim}, \Pi_{Xim} \geq \Pi_{FimXn-1}, \Pi_{Xim} \geq \Pi_{FikXn-1} \\ 0, otherwise \end{cases}, \quad \text{where } m = 1, \ldots, n \tag{3.47}$$

By means of κ we limit the probability of a non-effective international trade strategy. Analogously, we define

$$\kappa = \begin{cases} 1, \Pi_{Fim} > 0, \Pi_{Fim} \geq \Pi_{Xim}, \Pi_{Fim} \geq \Pi_{FimXn-1}, \Pi_{Fim} \geq \Pi_{FikXn-1} \\ 0, otherwise \end{cases}, \quad \text{where } m = 1, \ldots, n \tag{3.48}$$

$$\lambda = \begin{cases} 1, \Pi_{FimXn-1} > 0, \Pi_{FimXn-1} \geq \Pi_{Xim}, \Pi_{FimXn-1} \geq \Pi_{Fim}, \Pi_{FimXn-1} \geq \Pi_{FikXn-1} \\ 0, otherwise \end{cases}, \quad \text{where } m = 1, \ldots, n \tag{3.49}$$

and

$$\mu = \begin{cases} 1, \Pi_{FikXn-1} > 0, \Pi_{FikXn-1} \geq \Pi_{Xim}, \Pi_{FikXn-1} \geq \Pi_{Fim}, \Pi_{FikXn-1} \geq \Pi_{FimXn-1} \\ 0, otherwise \end{cases}, \quad \text{where } k = 1, \ldots, n,\ m = 1, \ldots, n,\ m \neq k$$

In order to keep the analysis focused on the relationship between economic integration and FDI flow, we analyse the motivation for FDI in the integration region. Foreign investment is supposed to arise only when positive profit opportunities are available in these locations. In our model, FDI appears in two cases: to supply each country separately, and to establish an export-platform to supply all members of the integration union. In the second case, multinational corporations move their production to countries that have lower production costs and better access to larger markets.

In Eq. (3.46), by definition, f equals FDI because it includes the costs of buying or establishing a company.

Thus, FDI is observed in a country m, when profits are not negative:

$$f_m = \pi_m(s_m; l_m) + \lambda \underbrace{\left(\sum_{j=1}^{m-1} \pi_j(s_j; l_m; t_j) + \sum_{j=m+1}^{n} \pi_j(s_j; l_m; t_j) \right)}_{\text{the rest countries in the region}} \tag{3.50}$$

The first part of the equation captures the traditional factors of FDI—market size and production costs in a host country, whereas the second part displays the export-platform motive. Thus, the multinational's incentive to invest in the participating countries of the regional agreement is especially high in those countries that are integrated with larger markets and have lower production costs. The hypothesis has however, not been tested empirically in the former studies. The next chapter will address this issue.

From Eq. (3.50) the basic formulation of the log-linear model is:

$$f_{jT} = \beta_0 + \beta_1 s_{jT} + \beta_2 l_{jT} + \beta_3 \sum s_{n-1} + \beta_4 t_{jT} + \nu_{jT}, j = 1, \ldots N, T = 1, \ldots \text{y} \quad (3.51)$$

where s_{jt} is the host market size, l_{jT} is local production costs and $\sum s_{n-1}$ is the market size of the neighbouring markets, t_{jT} is the country's trade barriers. T is for the year. βs are the coefficients of the regression variables.

Despite the fact that our theoretical model analyses FDI only from third countries, our theoretical findings can also explain FDI within the region. Thus, a distinction should be made between members and non-members of the regional integration area.

If trade barriers are protective, there is no difference between insiders and outsiders—foreign firms invest to supply the host countries governed by the tariff-jumping motive. Once the trade barriers fall, insiders are encouraged to reallocate production to low-wage countries and re-export their output to their local markets. However, if there is no difference in production costs, we would expect a reduction in FDI from the members of the regional integration agreement, relative to exports. That is, exports should become more profitable as a means of servicing the foreign market within the integration union.

On the other hand, the opposite may become true for non-members (but only in the case of a customs union). The creation of a regional integration area leads previous exporters to directly invest in the union, in order to both avoid the tariff and access a larger market that is then free of tariffs. Outsiders are encouraged to locate to the low-wage country in order to benefit from improved access to the partner's market.

The next chapter is devoted to the validation of the conjectures derived in this section. For this purpose, we analyse the impact of economic integration on FDI while controlling for traditional FDI macroeconomic determinants (Eq. 3.51).

3.4.2 Export-Platform

In the previous section we highlighted that market access to a greater number of countries may stimulate FDI inflows (export-platform FDI). In this section, we want to analyse how the market access of the CEECs has changed during the time horizon and according to the agreements signed.

We should distinguish between three different integration agreements: FTAs within Europe (such as CEFTA, CEFTA 2006, and BAFTA), Association Agreements with the EU, and membership in the EU.

As was described in Sect. 2.4, the agreements governing the CEFTA and BAFTA assure duty-free trade only among CEFTAs or BAFTA nations correspondingly, and preferential or free trade with the EU (see Table 2.2).

Therefore, regarding the early stages of integration of CEE it is useful to think of integration in terms of multi-regional unions, where members of the small integration blocks had free trade access only to other members of these blocks.

In the early 1990s the CEECs signed a number of AAs with the EU. Association Agreements govern the bilateral relations between the EU and partner countries. In most of the countries AAs were in force simultaneously with FTAs. The exceptions are Ukraine and Georgia. As Baldwin (1994) noted, intra-CEE trade agreements are a perfect solution to avoid hub-spoke relations (see Fig. 3.19) because they provide an access to some associated with the EU countries.

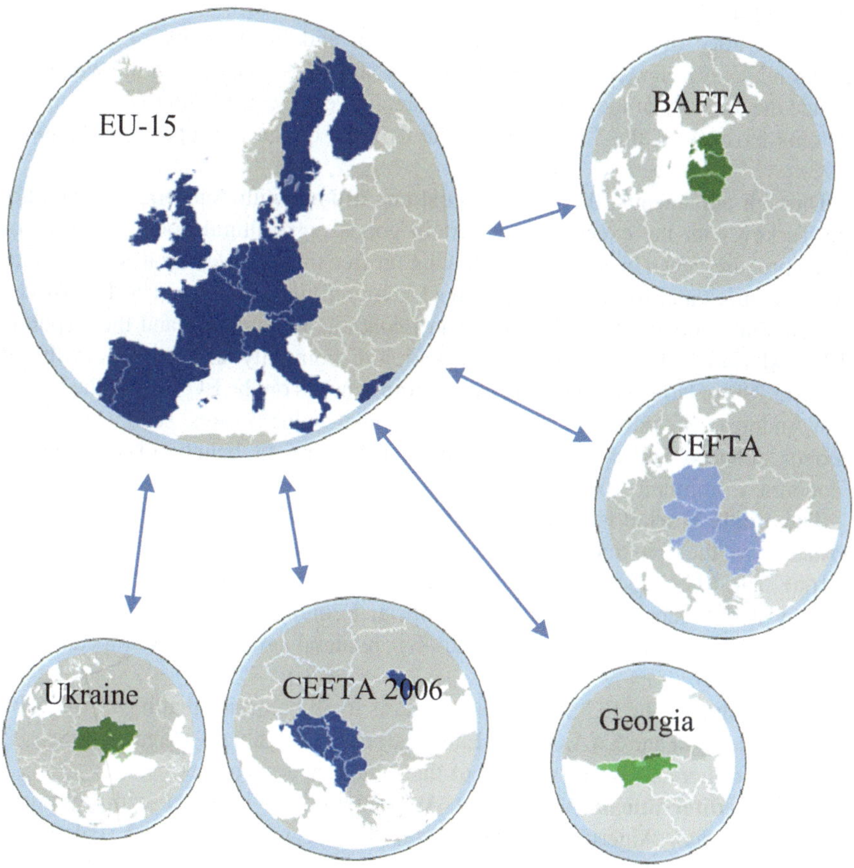

Fig. 3.19 FTAs and AAs in CEE. *Source*: Author's work

Consequently, the signing of the Accession Treaty provides access not only to all members of the EU but also to the European single market, the EU Customs Union, and a number of countries that have bilateral and multilateral free trade and association agreements with the EU.

The customs union imposes a common external tariff on all goods entering the area. The European Customs Union consists of all the member states of the European Union, except some territories, such as Denmark's Faroe Islands and Greenland, Germany's island of Heligoland and the territory of Büsingen, Spain's Ceuta and Melilla, French New Caledonia, Saint-Pierre and Miquelon, Wallis and Futuna Islands, French Polynesia and French Southern and Antarctic Territories, Italy's municipalities of Livigno and Campione d'Italia and the national waters of Lake Lugano which are between the bank and the political frontier of the area between Ponte Tresa and Porto Ceresio, the UK's Channel Islands and the Isle of Man, and some non-controlled territories of Cyprus (The Council of the European Communities 1992). These territories do not participate in the customs union, usually as a result of their geographic remoteness. However, most of these regions have bilateral FTAs with the EU (see Table 3.4).

The territory of the principality of Monaco, and the territory of the United Kingdom's Sovereign Base Areas of Akrotiri and Dhekelia, in Cyprus, which are outside the territory of the Member States, are, however, considered to be part of the customs territory of the Community (The Council of the European Communities 1992).

Through agreements, the EU is in **customs unions** with Andorra, San Marino, and Turkey with the exceptions of certain goods (agricultural goods, services or public procurement). In addition to allowing for free trade between states, it provides these countries and the EU with the most favoured nation status (The EC-Turkey Association Council 1995; The European Economic Community and the Republic of San Marino 1991; The European Economic Community and the Principality of Andorra 1990). However, there are full customs checks on the EU side on the border with Andorra, as Andorra has low VAT and other indirect taxes, such as those for alcohol, tobacco and petrol, from which visitors might benefit (The European Economic Community and the Principality of Andorra 1990).

The Single Market is a territory without any internal borders or other regulatory obstacles to the free movement of goods and services (European Commission 2016h). The EU single market includes three additional EFTA members (Iceland, Norway and Liechtenstein) via the European Economic Area agreement, and a remaining EFTA member—Switzerland—via bilateral agreements (European Commission 2016h).

Membership of the EU also provides access to all countries that have **AAs with the EU.** The AAa and SAAs within Europe were thoroughly investigated in Sect. 2. 3. However, there are also a number of inter-regional agreements.

Euro-Mediterranean Association Agreements are in force with European Union, Morocco, Algeria, Tunisia, Egypt, Jordan, Lebanon, Israel, Palestinian National Authority (in Syria and Libya the agreements were suspended) (European Commission 2016e).

Table 3.4 Agreements in force in 2016 implying free trade

State	Signed	In force since	Notes	Relations
Akrotiri and Dhekelia	2003	2004	Customs Union	
Albania	2006	2009	SAA	Candidate for EU accession
Algeria	2002	2005	EMAA	The EU-Algeria Association Agreement
Andorra	1990	1991	Customs Union	The "Agreement between the European Economic Community and the Principality of Andorra"
Bosnia and Herzegovina	2008	2015	SAA	Potential candidate for EU accession
Chile	2002	2003	AA	The EU-Chile Association Agreement
Egypt	2001	2004	EMAA	The EU-Egypt Association Agreement
Faroe Islands	1996	1997	Autonomous entity of Denmark	Fisheries Agreement (1977) and a Free Trade Agreement (1991, revised 1998)
Georgia	2014	2016	AA (DCFTA)	Association Agreement set up by the DCFTA
Channel Islands (Bailiwick of Jersey and Bailiwick of Guernsey)	1972	1973	Customs Union	
Iceland	1992	1994	EFTA	Negotiating for EU accession The agreement on the European Economic Area (EEA)
Isle of Man	1972	1973	Customs Union	Fisheries Agreement (1977) and a Free Trade Agreement (1991, revised 1998)
Israel	1995	2000	EMAA	The EU-Israel Association Agreement
Jordan	1997	2002	EMAA	The EU-Jordan Association Agreement
Kosovo	2015	2016	SAA	Potential candidate
Lebanon	2002	2006	EMAA	The EU-Lebanon Association Agreement
Liechtenstein	1992	1995	EFTA	The agreement on the European Economic Area (EEA)
Republic of Macedonia	2001	2004	SAA	Candidate for EU accession
Mexico	1997	2000	Economic Partnership FTA	Political Coordination and Cooperation Agreement The EU-Mexico Free Trade Agreement
Moldova	2014	2016	AA (DCFTA)	Association Agreement set up by the DCFTA

(continued)

Table 3.4 (continued)

State	Signed	In force since	Notes	Relations
Monaco		1958	Customs Union	Franco-Monegasque Treaty
Montenegro	2007	2010	SAA	Acceding country
Morocco	1996	2000	EMAA	The Association Agreement, EU-Morocco Fisheries Partnership Agreement
Norway	1992	1994	EFTA	The agreement on the European Economic Area (EEA)
EU's overseas countries and territories[a]	2001	2001	FTA	Association of the OCTs with the EU
Palestinian Authority	1997	1997	EMAA	Euro-Mediterranean AA
San Marino	1991	2002	Customs Union	Co-operation and CU Agreement 1991
Serbia	2008	2013	SAA	Acceding country
South Africa	1999	2004	TDCA	Interim Trade, Development and Co-operation Agreement Trade, Development and Cooperation Agreement (TDCA)
South Korea	2010	2015	FTA	The EU-South Korea Free Trade Agreement
Switzerland	1972 1999 2004	1973 2002	FTA	The Free Trade Agreement, Bilaterals I, Bilaterals II
Tunisia	1995	1998	EMAA	U-Tunisia Association Agreement by the Deep and Comprehensive Free Trade Area (DCFTA)
Turkey	1995	1995	Customs Union	the Ankara Association Agreement 1963 The EC-Turkey association Council Negotiating for EU accession

Source: European Commission (2016b)

[a]Overseas territories of the United Kingdom: Anguilla, Bermuda, British Antarctic Territory, British Indian Ocean Territory, British Virgin Islands, Cayman Islands, Falkland Islands, Montserrat, Pitcairn Islands, Saint Helena, Ascension and Tristan da Cunha, South Georgia and the South Sandwich Islands, Turks and Caicos Islands; the French overseas territories: French Scattered Islands, Saint-Pierre and Miquelon, Saint Barthélemy, French Polynesia, Wallis, Futuna, New Caledonia; Dutch overseas territories: Aruba, Curaçao, and Sint Maarten, Bonaire, Sint Eustatius, Saba; and Greenland (The Council of the European UN 2013)

This agreement created the Euro-Mediterranean Free Trade Area, which removes all barriers to trade and investment between within the EMFTA and with the EU. EMAAs also include a Free Trade Agreement (FTA) between the EU and third countries. It covers the EU, the EFTA, the EU customs unions, the EU candidate states, and the partners of the Barcelona Process (European Commission 2016e).

The **EU-Chile Association Agreement** covers all the areas of trade relations between Chile and the EU. The agreement eliminates barriers to trade, and creates a free trade area in goods, services and government procurement (European Commission 2016d).

EU members have access to the distant regions through **FTAs**: see the FTA with South Africa, for example. The reason for this agreement is that the European Union (EU), particularly through immigration from the Netherlands, the United Kingdom, Germany, France, and Greece has strong cultural and historical links to this country (European Commission 2016g).

The current **Economic Partnership, Political Coordination and Cooperation Agreement** (the Global Agreement) between the EU and Mexico includes trade provisions that were developed in a comprehensive Free Trade Agreement. Recently (in June 2016) the EU and Mexico began the first round of negotiations to modernise their trade agreement (European Commission 2016f).

Other agreements with a trade component between the EU and many countries worldwide are currently being negotiated or are awaiting ratification. They include the **Economic Partnership Agreements (EPAs)** between the EU and African, Caribbean and Pacific (ACP) countries. In June 2012 the EU signed an ambitious and comprehensive **Trade Agreement with Colombia and Peru**. In July 2014 negotiations were concluded for the accession of Ecuador to the Trade Agreement with Colombia and Peru (European Commission 2016c).

Partnership and Cooperation Agreements between the EU and Azerbaijan, Armenia, Kazakhstan, Kyrgyzstan, Tajikistan and Uzbekistan do not imply any preferential trade relations, however, they prohibit quantitative restrictions in bilateral trade (European Commission 2016a).

Thus, membership of the EU allows countries that have small domestic markets to expand their market size. Membership in the EU provides an access to a greater amount of markets on preferable conditions. Among those markets are Turkey, Norway, Switzerland and many other large markets all around the world (see Table 3.4).

For the purposes of this section, one main working hypothesis can be derived: the greater the degree of trade integration in a given regional integration agreement, the larger the increase in each integration's market potential and hence the higher the profits obtainable by relocation production through FDI.

3.5 Appendix C

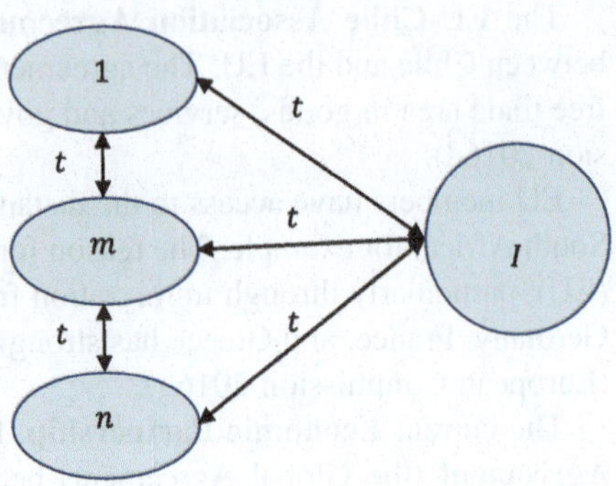

Fig. 3.20 Schematic map of the economic system with homogenous countries and no PTAs. *Source*: Author's work

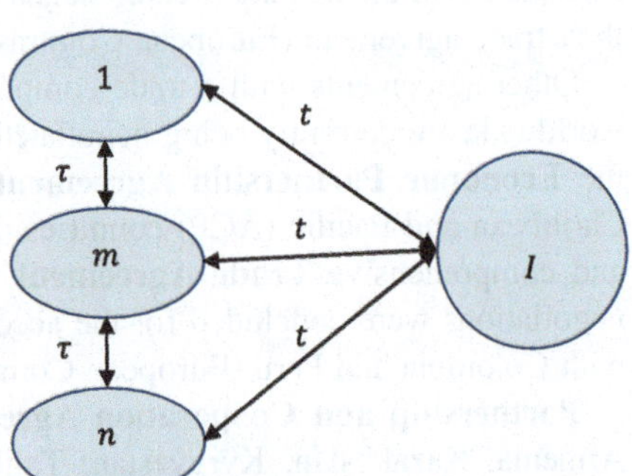

Fig. 3.21 Schematic map of the integration union with homogenous countries and with PTAs. *Source*: Author's work

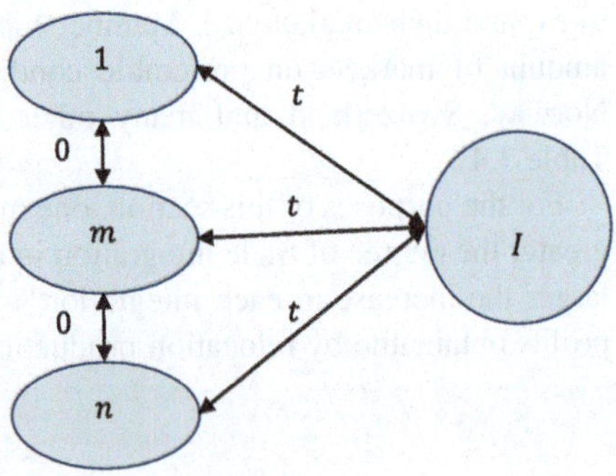

Fig. 3.22 Schematic map of the free trade zone with homogenous countries. *Source*: Author's work

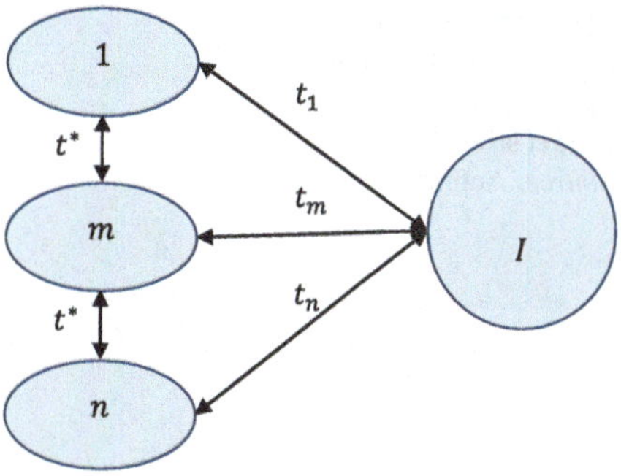

Fig. 3.23 Schematic map of the integration union with heterogeneous countries (different external trade barriers) and no PTAs. *Source*: Author's work

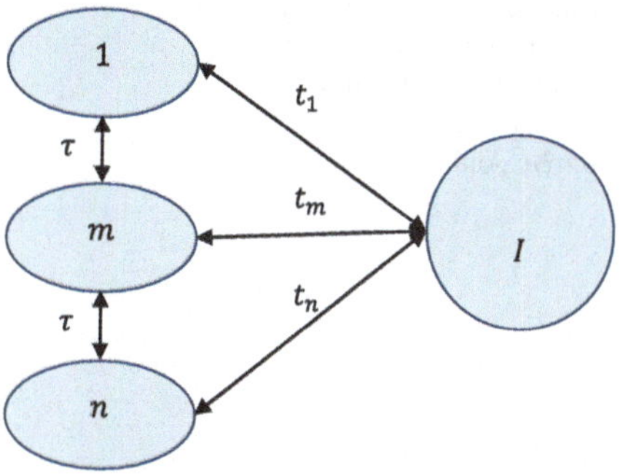

Fig. 3.24 Schematic map of the integration union of the countries with different external trade barriers and with PTAs. *Source*: Author's work

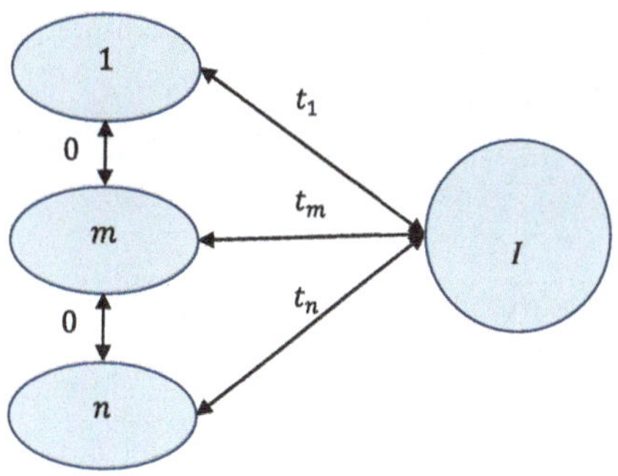

Fig. 3.25 Schematic map of the free trade zone of the countries with different external trade barriers. *Source*: Author's work

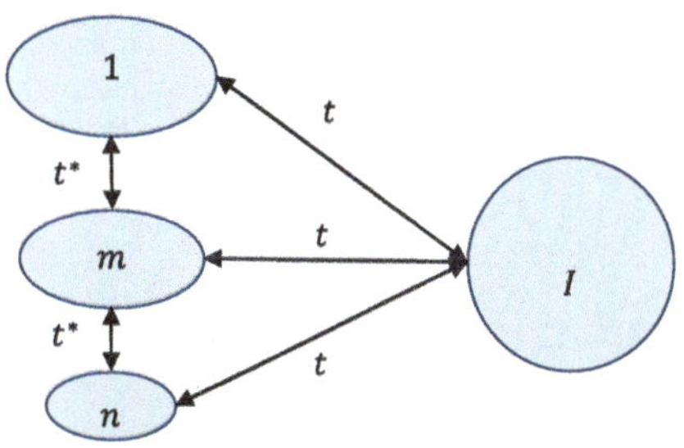

Fig. 3.26 Schematic map of the integration union of the countries with different market sizes and with no PTAs. *Source*: Author's work

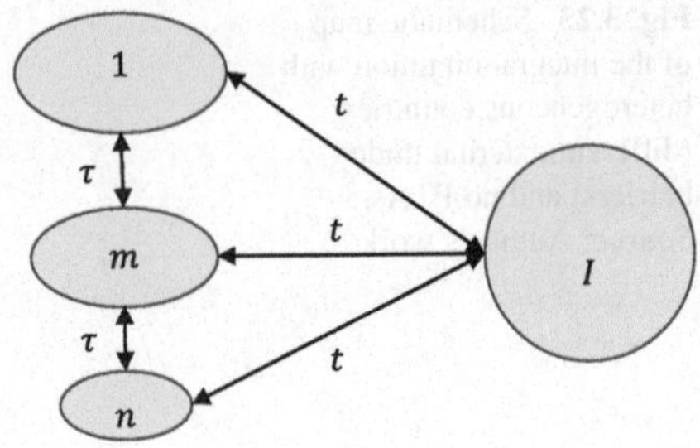

Fig. 3.27 Schematic map of the integration union of the countries with different market sizes and with PTAs. *Source*: Author's work

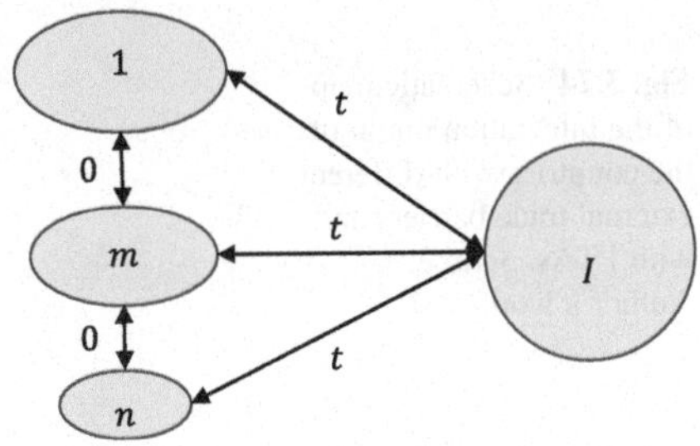

Fig. 3.28 Schematic map of the integration union of the countries with different market sizes and with no external trade barriers. *Source*: Author's work

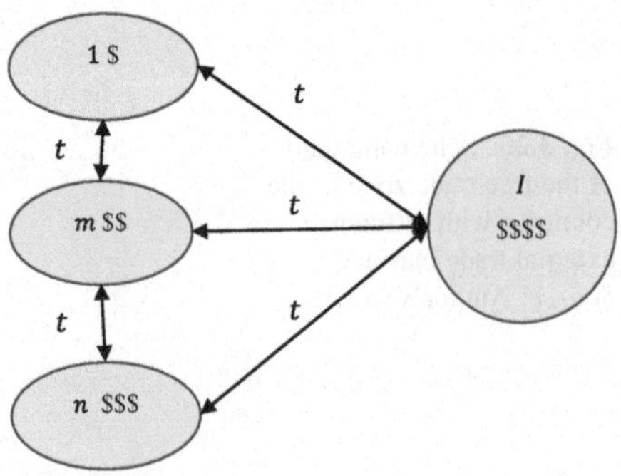

Fig. 3.29 Schematic map of the integration union of the countries with different production costs and with no PTAs. *Source*: Author's work

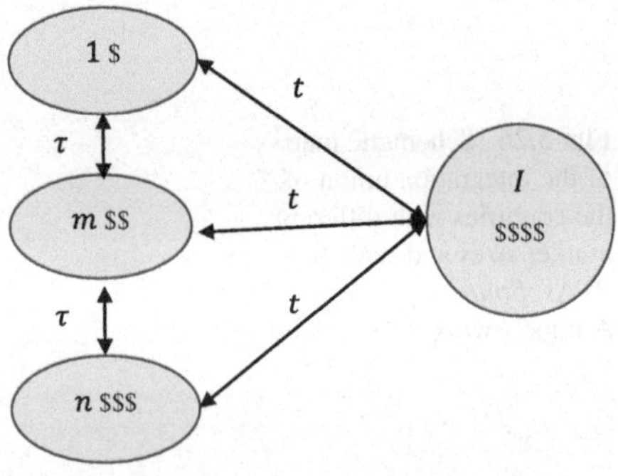

Fig. 3.30 Schematic map of the integration union of the countries with different production costs and with PTAs. *Source*: Author's work

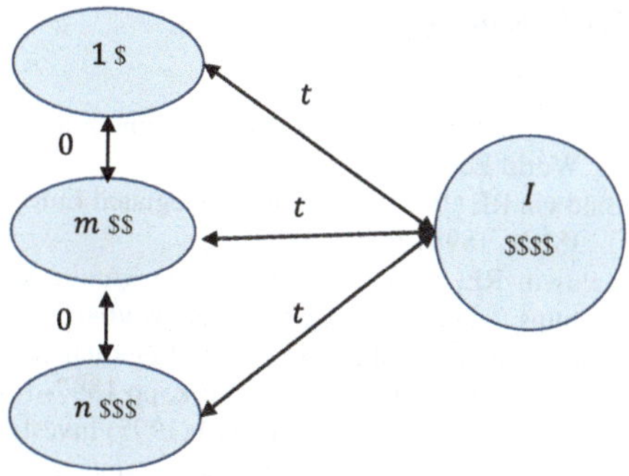

Fig. 3.31 Schematic map of the integration union of the countries with different production costs and without trade barriers. *Source*: Author's work

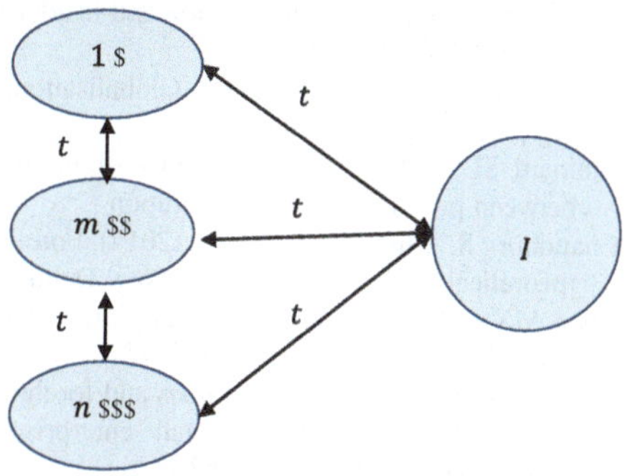

Fig. 3.32 Schematic map of the integration union of the countries with different installation costs and with no PTAs. *Source*: Author's work

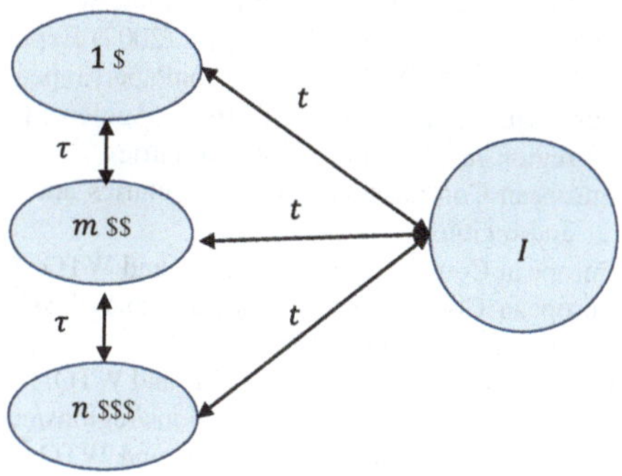

Fig. 3.33 Schematic map of the integration union of the countries with different installation costs and with no PTAs. *Source*: Author's work

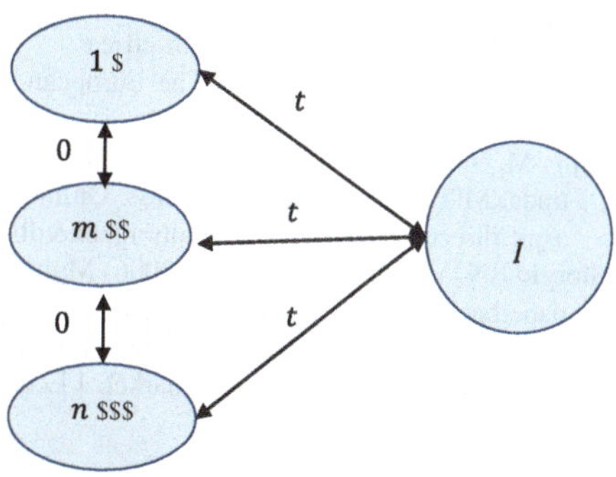

Fig. 3.34 Schematic map of the integration union of the countries with different installation costs and with PTAs. *Source*: Author's work

References

Altomonte C (2007) Regional economic integration and the location of multinational firms. Rev World Econ 143(2):277–305

Baldwin RE (1994) Towards an integrated Europe. Centre for Economic Policy Research, London. ISBN: 1898128138

Baldwin RE, Ottaviano GIP (1998) Multiproduct multinationals and reciprocal FDI dumping. https://ideas.repec.org/p/nbr/nberwo/6483.html

Baldwin RE, Venables AJ (1995) Regional economic integration. In: Handbook of international economics. Elsevier, New York, pp 1597–1644. ISBN: 9780444815477

Baldwin RE, Forslid R, Haaland J (1995) Investment creation and investment diversion: simulation analysis of the single market programme. https://ideas.repec.org/p/nbr/nberwo/5364.html

Bertrand O, Madariaga N (2003) U.S. Greenfield Investments and M&A location: impact of American continental integration and insider vs outsider position. http://EconPapers.repec.org/RePEc:ecj:ac2003:22

Bjorvatn K, Cappelen AW (2004) Globalisation, inequality and redistribution. https://ideas.repec.org/p/zbw/cegedp/33.html

Brainard SL (1993) A simple theory of multinational corporations and trade with a trade-off between proximity and concentration

Chaudhuri S, Mukhopadhyay U (2014) Foreign direct investment in developing countries: a theoretical evaluation. Springer, New Delhi. ISBN: 978-81-322-1897-5

Chen MX (2009) Regional economic integration and geographic concentration of multinational firms. Eur Econ Rev 53(3):355–375

Donnenfeld S (2003) Regional blocs and foreign direct investment. Rev Int Econ 11(5):770–788

Dunning JH (1993) Multinational enterprises and the global economy. Addison-Wesley, Wokingham. ISBN: 0201175304

Ekholm K, Forslid R, Markusen J (2003) Export-platform foreign direct investment. http://EconPapers.repec.org/RePEc:nbr:nberwo:9517

Ekholm K, Forslid R, Markusen J (2007) Export-platform foreign direct investment. J Eur Econ Assoc 5(4):776–795 http://EconPapers.repec.org/RePEc:tpr:jeurec:v:5:y:2007:i:4:p:776-795

European Commission (2016a) Agreements. http://ec.europa.eu/trade/policy/countries-and-regions/agreements/#_other-countries

European Commission (2016b) Countries and regions. http://ec.europa.eu/trade/policy/countries-and-regions/

European Commission (2016c) EU and WTO: Africa, Caribbean, Pacific (ACP)

European Commission (2016d) EU and WTO: Chile. http://ec.europa.eu/trade/policy/countries-and-regions/countries/chile/

European Commission (2016e) EU and WTO: Euro-Mediterranean partnership. http://ec.europa.eu/trade/policy/countries-and-regions/regions/euro-mediterranean-partnership/

European Commission (2016f) EU and WTO: Mexico. http://ec.europa.eu/trade/policy/countries-and-regions/countries/mexico/

European Commission (2016g) EU and WTO: South Africa. http://ec.europa.eu/trade/policy/countries-and-regions/countries/south-africa/

European Commission (2016h) The European single market. https://ec.europa.eu/growth/single-market_en

Fujita M, Venables A, Krugman PR (1999) The spatial economy. Cities, regions and international trade. MIT Press, Cambridge, Mass. Online verfügbar unter http://search.ebscohost.com/login.aspx?direct=true&scope=site&db=nlebk&db=nlabk&AN=9243

Giorgio BN, Venables A, Barry F (2006) Multinational firms in the world economy. 2. printing, 1. paperback printing. Princeton University Press, Princeton, NJ

Haller SA (2010) More intra-region direct investment through economic integration? Modelling the experience of the EU's single market. J Econ Integr 25(3):427–456

Head K, Mayer T (2004) Market potential and the location of Japanese investment in the European Union. Rev Econ Stat 86(4):959–972

Helpman E (1984) A simple theory of international trade with multinational corporations. J Polit Econ 92(3):451–471

Helpman E, Krugman PR (1985) Market structure and foreign trade: increasing returns, imperfect competition, and the international economy. MIT Press, Cambridge, MA. ISBN: 9780262580878

Horstmann IJ, Markusen JR (1992) Endogenous market structures in international trade (natura facit saltum). J Int Econ 32(1–2):109–129

Ito T (2013) Export-platform foreign direct investment: theory and evidence. World Econ 36 (5):563–581

Kim Y-H (2007) Impacts of regional economic integration on industrial relocation through FDI in East Asia. J Policy Model 29(1):165–180

Krugman PR (1991) Increasing returns and economic geography. J Polit Econ 99:483–499

Krugman PR (1993) On the relationship between trade theory and location theory. Rev Int Econ 1:110–122

Krugman PR, Venables A (1990) Integration and the competitiveness of peripheral industry. London (Discussion paper series / Centre for Economic Policy Research, 363)

Krugman P, Venables AJ (1995) Globalization and the inequality of nations. https://ideas.repec.org/p/hhs/iuiwop/0430.html

Markusen JR (1984) Multinationals, multi-plant, economies, and the gains from trade. University of Stockholm (Reprint series, 238), Stockholm

Markusen JR (2002) Multinational firms and the theory of international trade. MIT Press, Cambridge, MA. ISBN: 0-262-13416-0. http://search.ebscohost.com/login.aspx?direct=true&scope=site&db=nlebk&db=nlabk&AN=75013

Markusen JR, Venables AJ (1998) Multinational firms and the new trade theory. J Int Econ 46 (2):183–203

Montout S, Zitouna H (2005) Does north-south integration affect multinational firms' strategies? Rev Int Econ 13(3):485–500

Motta M (1992) Multinational firms and the tariff-jumping argument. Eur Econ Rev 36 (8):1557–1571

Motta M, Norman G (1996) Does economic integration cause foreign direct investment? Int Econ Rev 37(4):757–783 https://ideas.repec.org/a/ier/iecrev/v37y1996i4p757-83.html

Neary JP (2002) Foreign direct investment and the single market. Manchester School 70 (3):291–314 https://ideas.repec.org/a/bla/manchs/v70y2002i3p291-314.html

Neary JP (2009) Trade costs and foreign direct investment. Int Rev Econ Financ 18(2):207–218

OECD.Stat (2017) Corporate income tax rate. https://stats.oecd.org/index.aspx?DataSetCode=Table_II1. Accessed 20 Mar 2017.

Ono H, Davis C (2005) Intra-industry trade and FDI under oligopoly trade patterns and trade policies. Economic Journal of Hokkaido University 34(2005):137–160

Pomerleau K, Potosky E (2016) Corporate income tax rates around the world. https://files.taxfoundation.org/legacy/docs/TaxFoundation-FF525.pdf

Puga D, Venables AJ (1997) Preferential trading arrangements and industrial location. J Int Econ 43 (3–4):347–368

Ragoussis A, Miroudot S (2009) Vertical trade, trade costs and FDI. OECD Trade Policy Pap 89:1–48

Rowthorn RE (1992) Intra-industry trade and investment under oligopoly: the role of market size. Econ J 102(411):402

Smith A (1987) Strategic investment, multinational corporations and trade policy. Eur Econ Rev 31 (1–2):89–96 http://EconPapers.repec.org/RePEc:eee:eecrev:v:31:y:1987:i:1-2:p:89-96

The Council of the European Communities (1992) Council regulation (EEC) no 2913/92 of 12 October 1992 establishing the community customs code. http://eur-lex.europa.eu/legal-content/EN/ALL/?uri=celex%3A31992R2913

The Council of the European UN 2013 on the association of the overseas countries and territories with the European Union ('Overseas Association Decision'). http://eur-lex.europa.eu/LexUriServ/LexUriServ.do?uri=OJ:L:2013:344:0001:0118:en:PDF
The EC-Turkey Association Council (1995) Decision no 1/95 of the EC-Turkey Association Council of 22 December 1995 on implementing the final phase of the customs union (96/142/EC). http://www.avrupa.info.tr/fileadmin/Content/Downloads/PDF/Custom_Union_des_ENG.pdf
The European Economic Community and the Principality of Andorra (1990) Customs union between the European community and the principality of Andorra (L374). http://www.ab.gov.tr/files/ardb/evt/1_avrupa_birligi/1_3_antlasmalar/1_3_8_gumruk_birligi/andorra_customs_union_agreement_1990.pdf
The European Economic Community and the Republic of San Marino (1991) Agreement on cooperation and customs union between the European economic community and the Republic of San Marino. Off J Eur Communities (L 84). http://ec.europa.eu/world/agreements/downloadFile.do?fullText=yes&treatyTransId=10041
UNCTAD (1998) Trends and determinants. New York, NY: United Nations (World investment report, 1998)
UNCTAD (2003) World investment report: FDI policies for development: national and international perspectives. United Nations, New York. ISBN: 92-1-112580-4
UNCTAD (2005) Transnational corporations and the internationalization of R&D. United Nations, New York. ISBN: 92-1-112667-3
Yeaple SR (2003) The complex integration strategies of multinationals and cross country dependencies in the structure of foreign direct investment. J Int Econ 60(2):293–314

Chapter 4
Empirical Model

The previous chapter is aimed at the formulation of a theoretical model that we will empirically test in this chapter. We also present here the estimation strategy and the explanation of empirical results. Thus, the main objective of this chapter is to estimate the factors that affected FDI location in CEE.

4.1 Factors

The location of FDI is closely related to a country's comparative advantage, which in turn affects a multinational's expected profits in a host country.

The components of host country location motives could be broadly classified into two types: first, there are traditional factors, which mainly consist of market potential, production costs and macroeconomic stability; second, there exists an integration effect, which implies access to neighbouring markets. In the previous chapter, we developed an empirical model that combines traditional FDI determinants and integration factors that are expected to play an important role in attracting foreign investors.

In the empirical literature, there is no consensus on the factors of FDI that need to be included in an empirical model. In addition, determinants of FDI may vary across characteristics of industry, production factor intensity, and the nature and source of investment. However, some variables such as market size, labour costs, are represented as the traditional factors, are generally incorporated in the empirical models (see Sect. 2.3). The preferences for other less prominent determinants may vary from one empirical model to another (see Appendix B, Table 2.6). Thus, the criteria for a variable choice include ease of data availability, sound theoretical justifications, and the variable's robustness in the empirical FDI literature. All additional variables we include progressively into our empirical model.

H. Makhavikova, *Determinants of FDI in Central and Eastern Europe*, Contributions to Economics, https://doi.org/10.1007/978-3-319-91878-5_4

In the previous chapter we obtained an equation that can be estimated empirically:

$$f_{jT} = \beta_0 + \beta_1 s_{jT} + \beta_2 l_{jT} + \beta_3 \sum s_k + \beta_4 t_{jT} + \nu_{jT},\ j = 1, \ldots N,\ T = 1, \ldots \text{y} \quad (4.1)$$

where β are the estimated coefficients, s_{jT} represents the host country size, l_{jT} is the labour cost in the location country, $\sum s_k$ is the neighbouring market size, t_{jT} stays for internal trade barriers and/or international trade openness.

4.1.1 Dependent Variable

Our dependent variable, f_{jT}, is the aggregate annual FDI inflows in a country j. Because of data limitation, we do not differentiate between either the countries of origin or the location sectors or the types of FDI.

We take FDI inflows rather than accumulated FDI inward stocks because stocks are almost time invariant. That is, as long as FDI stocks are relatively large, annual changes to these stocks are likely to be negligible. Moreover, significant stocks result from past investment decisions. They, however, do not depict a present attractiveness of a country, causing an empirical model to have difficulty identifying the determinants of the dependent variable. In addition, the calculation of FDI stocks is often not homogeneous across countries (Globerman and Shapiro 2002).

We also use FDI inflows instead of net FDI flows. Since we do not observe the country of origin, we are not able to distinguish whether, for example, a positive change in net FDI flows is driven by increased inflows or reduced outflows. This also makes it difficult to select the determinants, because the inward and outward flows depend on different conditions. Moreover, the results are difficult to interpret.

In our database, we can distinguish between missing data and a flow of zero. If data is indeed missing in the original dataset, we drop missing observations from the dataset. The usage of logarithms, however, generates problems with zero and negative FDI inflows. In the literature, there are three main approaches for dealing with negative and zero values of FDI inflows: either all negative or zero values of FDI are deleted from the analysis; or they are replaced by a very small positive number; or two-stage estimation (Heckman model (Heckman 1979)) is used (it is complicated procedure, needs additional assumptions and is more effective in the case of the large number of zero flows (stocks)—for example, trade flows) (Bos and van de Laar 2004).

For negative and zero observations, we make a transformation widely used in empirical literature: $\ln(|FDI_{jt}| + 1)$. Thus, all zero flows will be zero. There are only 5 negative cases among 440 observations; we suppose, thus, that they will not significantly change our estimation results.

4.1.2 Market-Seeking Factors

Market-related factors are generally considered the most significant determining factors of FDI. There are several reasons behind this. Firms are always seeking new market opportunities for their products. Once the Iron Curtain fell, it led to the reintegration into the world economy of a relatively large market made up of 370 million inhabitants.

Firms are also attracted by current demand and a relatively low competition in the market. Thus, an investment location in CEE could be a strategic decision for multinationals looking to maintain or increase their international strategic position. In addition, the big market size allows companies to achieve economies of scale and to reach optimum scale. It also leaves room for new factories and avoids a fall of prices when total industrial productive capacity goes up.

The importance of the local market size, s_{jT}, can explain the high FDI in Poland, Romania, Ukraine and Serbia (see Figs. 2.6 and 2.9). Among all studied CEE countries, they attracted the biggest amount of investments. However, all large countries except Poland, despite their potential, attracted fewer investments because of their "stop and go transition" (Fig. 4.1). This confirms our assumption that the market size is not the single factor of FDI.

In a survey-based study, Lankes and Venables (1996) found evidence that a majority of firms that invested in transitional economies were looking for new market opportunities. The empirical evidence of the importance of market-related factors is also extensive: Altomonte (1998), Clausing and Dorobantu (2005), Carstensen and Toubal (2004). Meyer (1998) as well as Brenton (1999), Kinoshita and Campos (2003) and Faeth (2009) found that market size is the primary determinant for foreign direct investment in the CEE region.

In contrast, Holland and Pain (1998) and Asiedu (2002) declaired growth and market size as insignificant determinants of FDI flow. Indeed, market size has different implications for FDI inflows in accordance with its motive. For instance, it might be crucially important for FDI stimulated by horizontal motives, while it might offer little incentive for vertical FDI. Furthermore, a high rate of growth in the host country's market identifies a good development for the future, which suggests that a high growth rate in the host country would promote FDI inflows.

In the previous literature, several proxies were employed to measure market factors. Among them we can find total GDP, GDP per capita and population. The results of the main papers that explicitly consider market factors are presented in Appendix B, Table 2.6.

In our book, we employ GDP, which represents the host country's economic conditions and the potential demand for their output. It is an important element in FDI decision making. The figures are drawn from UNCTAD (2016c) databases. The expected relationship between the size of the market and FDI is positive.

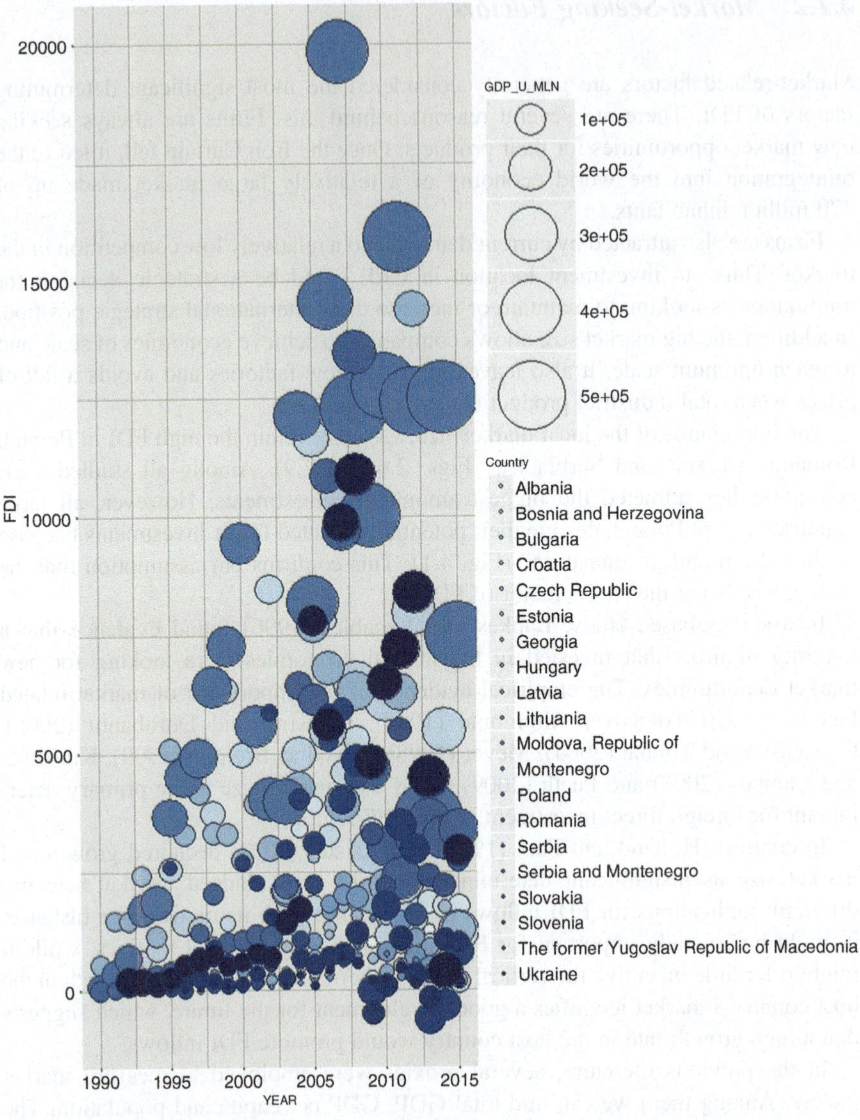

Fig. 4.1 Bubble chart. FDI inflows in million US dollars during 1990–2015 by countries and GDP size (in million US dollars). *Source*: Estimated by the author based on UNCTAD (2016c, d)

4.1.3 Resource-Seeking Factors

Labour and natural resources are the production factors which have been suggested as determinants of FDI into Central and Eastern Europe in a number of empirical studies.

The availability of low-cost skilled labour, l_{jT}, is also one of the prime attractions for a multinational, enabling them to take advantage of lower production costs. The main idea behind is very simple: firms move different stages of production process to countries with lower costs. We use the nominal wage rate as a proxy for labour cost. Our data for average wages come from UNECE databases and from ILO (2016) and ILOSTAT (2016) Databases.

We would generally expect a negative sign of the coefficient (e.g. countries with lower labour costs would attract more FDI).

However, the expected effect of low-cost labour availability cannot be established apriori. CEE might have attracted investment due to its cheap labour but once the decision was taken to locate it there, finding the cheapest possible labour within a region already characterised by low wages might not be so important. The existent differences in labour cost terms between the studied countries are not significant enough to have a strong influence on the location choice. Czech Republic, Hungary, Croatia, Slovakia and Slovenia have the highest annual compensation per employee but they received the biggest amounts of investment, while the Western Balkans and Moldova and Ukraine, which registered cheaper labour costs, received less FDI (Fig. 4.2).

CEE still has low labour costs, compared to most of the countries in the Western Europe, however, they are higher than in many Asian countries that are more preferable for the location of the resource-seeking investments.

The previous results are also rather inconclusive. Thus, Lankes and Venables (1996), Clausing and Dorobantu (2005) find no statistically significant evidence of labour costs as a determinant for FDI. Holland and Pain (1998) presented evidence of the importance of relative labour costs for the location decision within Eastern Europe and Lansbury et al. (1996) found evidence of the importance of the relatively lower wages in Eastern Europe for re-orientation of investment from other low-wage regions in Southern Europe to Eastern Europe. When also taking into account the productivity of labour, as suggested by Lankes and Venables (1996), the evidence of the importance of labour as a determinant of FDI into CEE is more extensive. Carstensen and Toubal (2004) and Bevan and Estrin (2000) found significant evidence of the productivity-adjusted labour costs' impact on FDI. As showed Bevan and Estrin (2000), not only an increase in productivity-adjusted labour deter FDI, but also the rate of growth of productivity-adjusted cost can be negatively correlated with the growth rate of FDI.

Kinoshita and Campos (2003) argue that the relationship between labour costs and inward FDI could be also positive because higher labour costs reflect a higher skill level. A more educated labour force can learn and adopt new technology faster and is generally more productive. Indeed, the influence of wage costs on FDI decisions varies among industries, depending on their factor combinations (labour or capital intensive) and investment motives (domestic or export market oriented) (Agarwal 1997). Some industries, such as computing, require high-skilled labour,

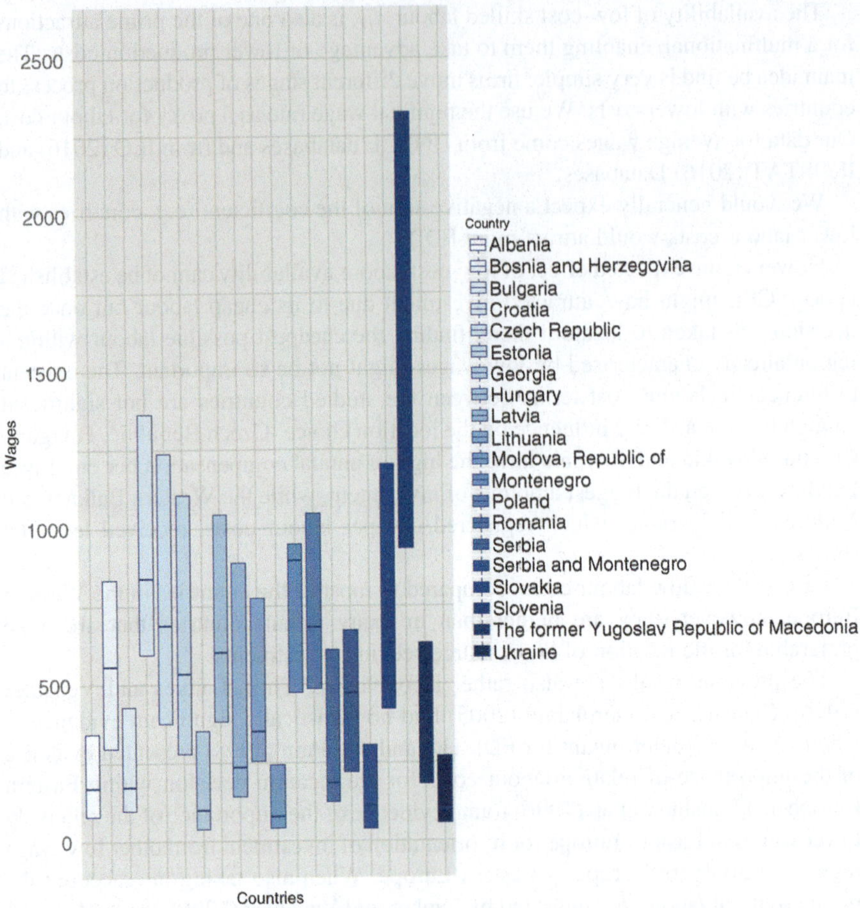

Fig. 4.2 Gross average monthly wages by countries, in US dollars. *Source*: Estimated by the author based on ILO (2016); ILOSTAT (2016); UNECE

which is often associated with high wages. Therefore the effect of labour costs on FDI might vary with the type of industry. This implies that the high-skilled labour associated with high level of wages might attract FDI in some industries instead of deterring it.

4.1.4 Integration Factors

It is natural that the sudden opening of the CEE market and its free access to the EU market, $\sum s_k$, attracted the interest of foreign investors. By locating itself in a host country with access to the EU market, an investing multinational firm gains not only an access to the local market of its host economy but importantly unlimited access to the market of 500 million consumers. Indeed, compared to other developing countries in Latin America and Asia and due to the fact that the trade barriers almost disappeared as a result of the FTAs and AAs, the dimension of the CEECs might be seen as insignificant; but their geographical and cultural proximity might have attracted a considerable number of multinationals. Immediately after opening up, the FDI inflows were low, but as the liberalisation of the market advanced the FDI inflows increased.

To measure the market potential of integration with the EU we estimate the coefficients of three variables. They are all calculated as the sum of the GDPs of all available for free-trade markets, depending on the agreements signed. They all correspond to the market potential defined in Sect. 3.4: the FTAs, AAs, and membership in the EU (see Figs. 4.3 and 4.4). The market size of the neighbouring markets has never been used in the empirical literature (see Appendix B). To estimate the effect of the integration dummy variables were commonly used. The

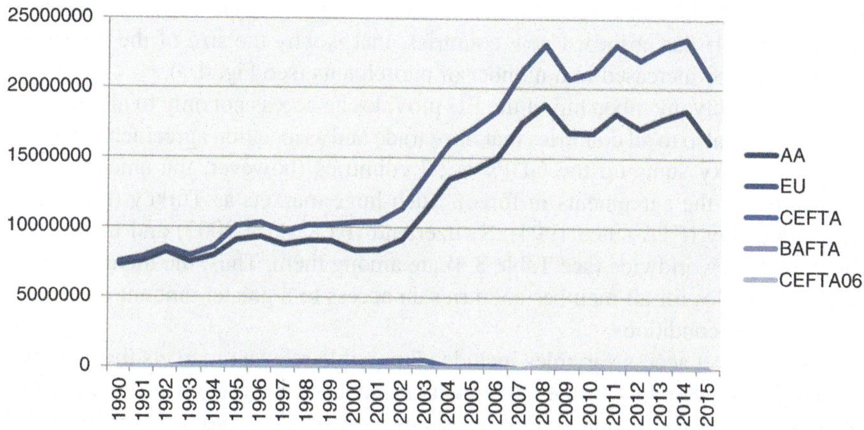

Fig. 4.3 Market potential of all regional integration agreements in CEE (the sum of all GDPs in million US dollars). *Source*: Author's calculations based on UNCTAD (2016c, d)

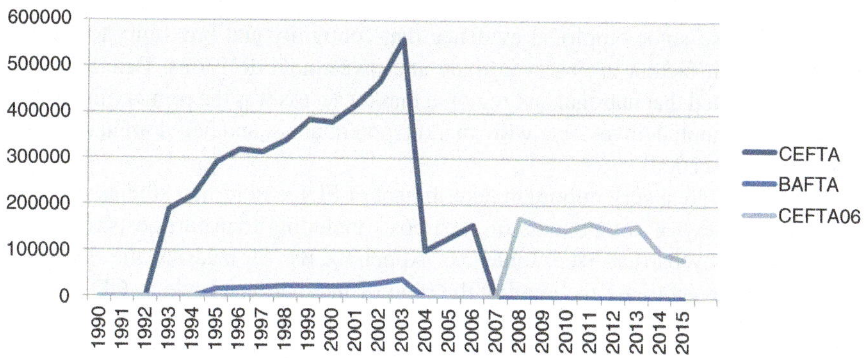

Fig. 4.4 Market potential of free trade agreements in CEE (the sum of all GDPs in million US dollars). *Source*: Author's calculations based on UNCTAD (2016c, d)

exception are some theoretical studies (e.g. Altomonte 2007) that employed the alternative measure of market accessibility initially proposed by Harris (1954). He measured GDPs with weights equal to the inverse of the distance between the host and each partner. By doing so Harris (1954) included possible transportation costs that arise between distant FDI locations. Unfortunately, we can employ only aggregate data that do not identify the source of FDI.

We also employ three independent variables to capture the integration effect instead of just one because it enables different agreements to have different degrees of impact as well as some degree of variation in term of statistical significance, in case that the regional integration agreements have non-linear impact on FDI.

The first proxy, $FTAMA_{jT}$, measures the size of the FTA market. It is the sum of the GDPs of all partner countries in the European FTAs (CEFTA, CEFTA 2006, and BAFTA).

The signing of the Association Agreement provides access to the EU market. That is why the $AAMA_{jT}$ variable measures the size of the EU's GDP. During this time horizon the EU has absorbed new countries, that is why the size of the associated market has also increased in a number of participants (see Fig. 4.3).

Consequently, membership of the EU provides an access not only to all members of the EU but also to all countries that have trade and association agreements with the EU. This proxy sums up the GDPs of 57 countries (however, the amount varies depending on the agreements in force). Such huge markets as Turkey (FTA since 1995), Norway (FTA since 1994), Switzerland (FTA since 2002) and many other large markets worldwide (see Table 3.4) are among them. Thus, the membership in the EU provides for all member-countries an access to a greater amount of markets on preferable conditions.

Thus, market access variables include all possible relevant markets that are open for free trade according to the agreements signed. Such a framework is consistent with the emergence of integration strategies, namely the export-platforms, which includes the market potential of the associated countries. For the purposes of the book, a main working hypothesis can thus be derived: the greater the degree of trade integration, the larger the increase in each market's potential and hence the higher the profits obtainable by production relocation through FDI.

There is also some empirical evidence that contiguity and proximity to the EU were important factors in observed trade and investment decisions. Benacek et al. (2000) suggested that national and regional market access was the primary factor that influenced potential investors, with market potential as another dominant factor (Benacek et al. 2000).

Trade costs are a very important determinant of FDI, and former studies take into account a variety of components of such costs including transport costs, distance, and trade policy barriers (see Table 2.6, Appendix B). To measure the degree of openness of an economy we employ the ratio of international trade to GDP. In the literature, this ratio is often used as the measure of openness of a country and is also often interpreted as a measure of trade restrictions. An alternative measure of the openness is tariff levels and revenues of duties on imports (see Table 2.6), but these data are scarce. Moreover, tariffs vary across industries. The tariffs also are different for different trade partners according to the bilateral and multilateral trade agreements signed. Finally, low tariffs do not always indicate a more open economy due to the presence of non-tariff barriers which are notoriously difficult to measure. An important element of the trade cost is the time it takes to ship products between plants. Proximity is a good variable to measure these costs. However, we do not observe sources of FDI, thus, we are not able to add these distance weights in our model.

The relation between trade openness and FDI may differ by the type of investment: FDI can substitute trade (in the case of tariff jumping), or stimulate exports (in the case of export-platforms). Holland and Pain (1998) found that trade openness should be not an important determinant for horizontal FDI, in contrast, export-oriented vertical FDI would be greatly affected export volume with positive re-action (Holland and Pain 1998). In the context of CEECs, the literature reveals a positive correlation between FDI and trade openness (see Appendix B). The countries that are more liberal in their trade approach tend to export more and this might attract foreign investors, especially ones which are export driven (Bevan and Estrin 2000). Resmini (2000) suggested that export-driven investors were mainly attracted by low labour costs (which give the possibility of reducing costs) and by the degree of openness. Kinoshita and Campos (2003) showed that trade openness is an important attractor for the less developed of the transition countries (CIS), but less relevant for the more developed ones. Most findings indicate that investors prefer countries with liberal trade regimes, located in regions with national free-trade arrangements. Therefore, we expect that openness should have a positive influence on FDI.

4.1.5 Efficiency-Seeking Factors

We include supplementary efficiency-seeking factors in our model. They are GDP growth rate, Gross Capital formation and agglomeration. These factors are used to measure macroeconomic stability and the economic effectiveness of a host country.

As anticipated, market growth (GDP growth rate) positively influences FDI. A country which has a stable macroeconomic condition with high and sustained GDP growth rates will receive more FDI inflows than a more volatile economy. Higher GDP growth indicates a potentially larger market and more promising prospects. It also implies better infrastructure, provides greater incentive for inward FDI and positively influences the business climate for inward FDI. Moreover, rapid growth may also give rise to the presence of economic rents that will encourage inward FDI (Globerman and Shapiro 1999).

We also include in our model Gross fixed capital formation (GCF). According to the World Bank definition, it includes land improvements (fences, ditches, drains, and so on); plants, machinery, and equipment purchases; and the construction of roads, railways, and the like, including schools, offices, hospitals, private residential dwellings, and commercial and industrial buildings (The World Bank 2016).

Apparently, the increase in Gross capital formation results in the improvements of infrastructure which further attracts higher FDI inflows. However, the relationship between FDI and Capital Formation is not clear observable (Krkoska 2001). For example, privatisation attracts FDI into a country; however, there can be no improvements in the infrastructure and investment climate. Thus, the possible effect of GCF can be not observed in countries in transition (Krkoska 2001).

To measure the agglomeration effect, we include in our model lagged for one period FDI inflows. The use of this variable implies the presence of dynamic effects in the model, i.e., AR(1) process in the model. There are a few motives for including this proxy in our model. Firstly, new foreign investors follow the past investment decisions of former investors about where to invest. Secondly, FDI inflows include among others reinvested earnings, thus present inflows are bound with former investment inflows. Thus, Kinoshita and Campos (2003) confirmed that the agglomeration plays a crucial role in attracting FDI in a country.

To proxy the institutional effects of the integration we include EU dummy variables in our regression model. The recent accession of the CEECs into the EU has been suggested to be a major driver of the transformation of institutions within the region. The institutional type of explanation states that countries facing the prospect of accession to the European Union had a strong incentive to establish well-functioning democracies and legal institutions. The new member states had to introduce all institutions of the *acquis communautaire*, the joint institutions of the European Union. There was strong monitoring of the progress of accession candidates in introducing the required institutions.

European Union membership also opens the possibility of a country's adopting the euro, which further harmonises the country's macroeconomic policies with those of the rest of Europe. Both effects serve to reduce investors' perceived level of country risk within CEE. By using the accession announcements made by the European Council as a measure of the accession progress of the candidate countries, Clausing and Dorobantu (2005) and Bevan and Estrin (2000) find evidence supporting the hypothesis that the EU accession process has had an impact on FDI into accession countries. The EU's commitment to accept qualified candidate countries and the recent enlargement of the EU are suggested as major sources for reducing the perceived level of risk when investing in accession countries.

Thus, we estimate the effect of membership in CEFTA or BAFTA, the signing of the Association Agreement, entry into force of the Association Agreement, application for membership, granting of candidate status, the start of negotiations, the signing of the Accession Treaty with the EU, membership in the EU, and Euro area membership (all stages are described in Sect. 2.3). The value 1 indicates that a country was approved for a particular stage of the integration before the 1st of July in a particular year, and 0 displays that the stage has not been reached yet.

To capture the effect from announcements we also employ individual proxies because of the non-linear effect of the integration. This non-linear effect can arise when multinationals and other potential investors are not very sensitive to the progress in the integration or when progress in the EU accession from a specific stage to the next contains the use of FDI-friendly instruments, such as direct subsidies and corporate tax exemption and, hence, offsets the positive effect of EU enlargement (Iwasaki and Suganuma 2009).

We expect to observe a positive effect on FDI inflows because integration into the EU results in the improvement of institutions and investment climate.

4.1.6 Completed Model

The final overview of our empirical equation is:

$$\begin{aligned} FDI_{jT} = \beta_0 + \beta_1 FDI_{jT-1} + \beta_2 GDP_{jT} + \beta_3 WAGE_{jT} + \beta_4 FTAMA_{jT} \\ + \beta_5 AAMA_{jT} + \beta_6 EUMA_{jT} + \beta_7 OPEN_{jT} + \beta_8 GCF_{jT} \\ + \beta_9 GDPGR_{jT} + \nu_{iT} \end{aligned} \tag{4.2}$$

Where β are coefficients, GDP_{jT} and $WAGE_{jT}$ are traditional factors of FDI, $FTAMA_{jT}$, $AAMA_{jT}$, $EUMA_{jT}$ represent the markets size of the markets to which countries get access after signing FTAs, AAs and Accession Treaty correspondingly, and $OPEN_{jT}$ is the overall openness of the economy. FDI_{jT-1}, GCF_{jT} and $GDPGR_{jT}$ are additional macroeconomic factors. The description of the proxies, their sources and measures are summarised in Table 4.1.

The dataset is an unbalanced panel of 19 acceding countries over the 1992–2015 period. FDI in Central and Eastern Europe was practically non-existent before 1992 and data are only available through 2015.

All values are expressed in current US dollars. Our dependent variable is the natural logarithm of the FDI flow in millions of U.S. dollars to country j at time T. Some independent variables are also measured in logarithmic values (see Table 4.1). This has two advantages: such reduces the likelihood of outliers; the coefficients can be directly interpreted as elasticities and semi-elasticities.

We additionally calculate the effect of lagged for 1 year variables because there is a clear theoretical reason to expect that the effect of an explanatory variable influences the investment decisions only with a one-period lag.

There are several other explanatory variables that could be added to the model specification. Measures of institutional factors may be also important. However, we do not have enough data to measure the effects of institutions. That is why we estimate this effect by including EU accession dummies. In doing so we rely on Berglöf and Roland (1997) who highlighted the role the European Union played as the institutional anchor for transition economies from Central and Eastern Europe. Roland and Verdier (2003) showed how the prospect of admission to the European Union served as a coordination device to introduce the rule of law in CEECs (Berglof and Bolton 2002).

Table 4.1 Description of the proxies

Code name	Definition	Measure	Expected sign	Source
FDI_{jT}	Foreign direct investment inflows	US Dollars at current prices and current exchange rates in millions, logged		UNCTAD (2016c)
GDP_{jT}	Real Gross Domestic Product	US Dollars at current prices and current exchange rates in millions, logged	+	UNCTAD (2016d)
$WAGE_{jT}$	Gross Average Annual Wages	US Dollars at current prices and current exchange rates, logged	+/−	UNECE, ILO (2016), ILOSTAT (2016)*
$FTAMA_{jT}$	Market size of all countries in a FTA with the exception of a host country	US Dollars at current prices and current exchange rates in millions, logged		UNCTAD (2016c, d)
$AAMA_{jT}$	Market size of the EU	US Dollars at current prices and current exchange rates in millions, logged		UNCTAD (2016c, d)
$EUMA_{jT}$	Market size of all countries in the EU, plus all FTAs and AAs, with the exception of a host country	US Dollars at current prices and current exchange rates in millions, logged		UNCTAD (2016c, d)
$OPEN_{jT}$	Goods and services trade openness indicators	Percentage of GDP	+	WBDI
GCF_{jT}	Gross Capital Formation	Percentage of GDP	+/−	WBDI
$GDPGR_{jT}$	GDP growth rate	Annual average growth rate	+	UNCTAD (2016d)
FTA_{JT}	Membership in BAFTA of CEFTA	Dummy variable	+	
$Aasig_{jT}$	The signing of the Association Agreement	Dummy variable	+	
$Aafor_{jT}$	Entry into force of the Association Agreement	Dummy variable	+	
$Poten_{jT}$	Application for the EU-membership	Dummy variable	+	
$Candid_{jT}$	Getting of a "candidate" status	Dummy variable	+	
$Acces_{jT}$	The start of negotiations	Dummy variable	+	
$Acced_{jT}$	The conclusion of negotiations	Dummy variable	+	
EU_{jT}	Membership in the EU	Dummy variable	+	
$Euro_{jT}$	Euro area membership	Dummy variable	+	

Source: Author's work

Note: '*' Some not available values were taken from State's Statistics Offices (State Statsistic Service of Ukraine 2016; National Statistic Office of Georgia 2016)

4.2 Robustness Check

4.2.1 Descriptive Statistics

Before proceeding the estimation of the panel data analysis, we provide descriptive statistics analysis. The outcomes of the analysis are summarized in Table 4.12. It gives the descriptive statistics both for the dependent and independent variables, namely number of the observations, means, standard deviations for each variable, as well as minimum and maximum values and rage of the variables, their skew, kurtosis and standard error.

Among descriptive statistics of explanatory variables, several points should be pointed out. The CEE markets are mostly small economies. The highest value of GDP (545795,70 million dollars) was obtained by Poland in 2014. However, Poland only had the 25th largest GDP in the world in 2016; other countries are even smaller (International Monetary Fund 2016).

The average wage in CEECs is equal to $543,19 which is much lower than in many developed European countries (see Fig. 4.5).

The lowest values were recorded in the early periods of transition: in Georgia in 1994 and 1995 with $8,5 and $9,6 average monthly wages; in 1992 average wages in Ukraine was $10,15. They were so low because in those most of the salaries were paid in coupons (National Statistic Office of Georgia; State Statistic Service of Ukraine). This payment pattern was common to all former members of the USSR.

Figures 4.9 and 4.10 in Appendix B present coefficients of pair correlation. All pair-correlation coefficients have acceptable values. Coefficients of correlation greater than 0,50 appear only between factors that represent the accession stages. Dummies FTA_{jT}, $Aafor_{jT}$ and EU_{jT} are highly correlated (at 100%) with

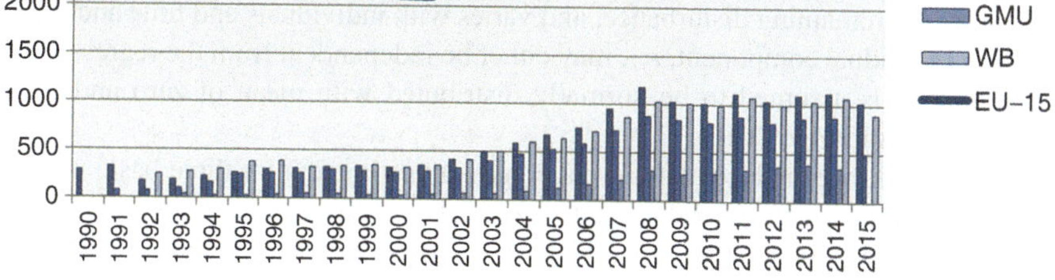

Fig. 4.5 Gross average monthly wages by subregions and year, US dollars. *Source*: Author's calculations based on the data from UNECE. *Note*: Some values are not available and added as zeroes

corresponding market access variables, $FTAMA_{jT}$, $AAMA_{jT}$, and $EUMA_{jT}$. That is why we estimate these variables in different specifications to eliminate the problem of multicollinearity.

For a regression analysis, there is an important assumption in a classical regression model, that is, the sequence must be stable. If the sequence is unstable, the test will be invalid or the regression will be false. In practice, the sequence stability test is usually completed by Dickley-Fuller (ADF) test and Phillips-Perron Unit Root Test (PP-test) (Dickey and Fuller 1979; Phillips and Perron 1988). Both unit root tests were conducted on all variables to check whether they are stationary at same level or not. The results of the unit root testing procedure are presented in Table 4.13.

All the variables were found to be stationary.

Having identified and checked the determinants of FDI, the next step is to outline the model to empirically test the level of influence of the aforementioned variables on FDI.

4.2.2 *Choice of the Model*

The basic linear panel models used in econometrics can be described through suitable restrictions of the following general model:

$$y_{jT} = \beta_0 + \beta x_{jT} + \nu_{jT}, \ j = 1, \ldots n, \ \ T = 1, \ldots Y \tag{4.3}$$

where j denotes a country, T denotes time, β_0 is an absolute term, β is a vector of the factor coefficients, x_{jT} $(x_{1,\,jT}, x_{2,\,jT}, \ldots, x_{p,\,jT})$ is a vector of explanatory variables, ν_{jT} represents the vector of the error components with:

$$\nu_{jT} = u_j + \varepsilon_{jT} \tag{4.4}$$

The error term has two separate components, one of which, u_j, is specific to a country and does not change over time. We regard u_j as a proxy of the combined effect on y_{jT} of all unobserved variables that are constant over time (Wooldridge 2010).

The error ε_{jT}, is often called the idiosyncratic error or time-varying error, because it denotes the remaining disturbance, and varies with individuals and time and affect y_{jT}. The individual component, ε_{jT}, may either be independent from the regressors or correlated. It is assumed to be normally distributed with mean of zero and finite variance (Wooldridge 2010).

In our book, we analyse and present consistent estimators for three basic models of panel data: the pooling model, the fixed effects or least squares dummy variables (LSDV) model, and the random effects or error components model. They differ mainly in the assumption of the intercept and error term.

In Appendix F, in Tables 4.14–4.18, we present ten model specifications.

The baseline specifications, namely (1) and (2), only include traditional determinants of FDI inflows (market size and production costs) but exclude the determinants of the export-platform FDI. The only difference between the first and the second one is that we use the factors lagged for one period. In specifications (3) and (4), we additionally include the variables that measure market access and openness. Further, we progressively add variables to our baseline model until Adjusted R-squared does not significantly change. In specifications (5) and (6) we add GCF; we add GDP growth rate in specifications (7) and (8).

In the last two specifications, (9) and (10), we replace the market access variables with integration dummies.

Choosing between present and lagged for 1-year values, we refer to the relative better results of the present values. On the whole, specifications (7) and (9) provide the best estimations in terms of R-squared, and expected signs.

In Table 4.2, we represent some of the results from the panel data analysis. First, we consider the OLS estimator results for both specifications. Almost all variables enter the regression with expected signs in addition to their statistical significance. The adjusted R-squared for the specifications (7) and (9) indicates that the variables included explain approximately 76,35% and 77,14% of the variation in FDI inflows in a country.

However, the estimations of the OLS estimator would give inconsistent results because of the correlation between the dependent variable and error term. Random and fixed-effects models remove the inconsistency because they include the individual effect of the countries (Wooldridge 2010).

Generally, in the panel data analysis, the fixed effects (FE) model assumes that each country differs in its intercept term, whereas the random effects (RE) model assumes that each country differs in its error term (Wooldridge 2010).

We used F-test or Chow and Wald test to compare FE and OLS estimators. The null hypothesis is that all the constants are the same (homogeneous), and, therefore, the Common constant method (OLS) is applicable (Wooldridge (2013), pp. 245–248). We decline the null hypothesis (see results in Table 4.3) and conclude that the fixed effect model is more preferable than the pooling model.

We carried out the Breusch Pagan (1980) Lagrange multiplier (LM) test to choose between pooled and random effects estimators (Greene 2003, pp. 223–225). With the large chi-squared (see Table 4.3) too much of the variance is explained by the additional explanatory variables. That is why we reject the null hypothesis in favour of the random group effect model.

Taking into the consideration the results of the tests, OLS model would generate inconsistent estimates, because the correlation between the dependent variable and error term biases the estimations of β_0 and β (Wooldridge 2013, p. 468). That is why we do not further consider it.

We need to apply tests to check whether fixed or random effects should be included in the model. Turning to the choice of deciding between fixed and random effects, the random effects model is preferred when there is no a significant correlation between the unobserved sector-specific random effects and the regressors. But if there is such a correlation, the random effects model would be inconsistently

Table 4.2 Estimation results

	(7)									(9)								
	OLS			FE			RE			OLS			FE			RE		
	Coef.	t		Coef.	t		Coef.	t		Coef.	t		Coef.	t		Coef.	t	
FDI_{jT-1}	0,5086	13,29	***	0,3686	8,14	***	0,6451	19,90	***	0,4920	12,78	***	0,3554	7,71	***	0,5696	16,33	***
GDP_{jT}	0,4270	8,45	***	0,2269	0,99		0,3324	9,48	***	0,4591	8,80	***	0,4186	1,62		0,3969	10,01	***
$WAGE_{jT}$	−0,0617	−1,18		0,3125	1,80	.	−0,1060	−3,42	***	0,0159	0,27		0,2570	1,42		−0,0227	−0,54	
$FTAMA_{jT}$	0,0063	0,60		0,0104	0,90		−0,0008	−0,09										
$AAMA_{jT}$	0,0065	1,58		0,0103	2,17	*	0,0068	2,02	*									
$EUMA_{jT}$	0,0071	1,64		0,0142	2,55	*	0,0040	1,36										
FTA_{jT}										−0,1525	−1,01		−0,0473	−0,27		−0,2531	−1,88	.
$Aasig_{jT}$										0,0559	0,32		0,0601	0,32		0,1443	0,86	
$Aafor_{jT}$										0,0742	0,29		0,0736	0,26		0,2271	0,95	
$Poten_{jT}$										0,2099	0,93		0,3158	1,29		0,1752	0,79	
$Candid_{jT}$										0,1285	0,48		0,3425	1,16		−0,0526	−0,21	
$Acces_{jT}$										0,2634	0,99		0,4751	1,57		0,2031	0,82	
$Acced_{jT}$										0,0940	0,31		0,1639	0,48		0,0546	0,19	
EU_{jT}										−0,0596	−0,36		0,3017	0,94		−0,0723	−0,64	
$Euro_{jT}$										−0,7640	−3,07	**	−0,2969	−0,76		−0,8193	−4,15	***
$OPEN_{jT}$	0,0000	0,03		−0,0012	−0,43		0,0009	1,10		0,0024	1,52		−0,0014	−0,48		0,0030	2,75	**
GCF_{jT}	0,0111	1,55		0,0142	1,68	.	0,0045	0,83		0,0116	1,61		0,0114	1,33		0,0093	1,55	
$GDPGR_{jT}$	0,0353	4,37	***	0,0392	4,48	***	0,0308	4,08	***	0,0332	4,12	***	0,0400	4,52	***	0,0321	4,19	***
F-statistics	132,33		***	57,06		***	1777,90		***	81,68		***	34,72		***	435,03		***
Total sum of squares	919,68			479,41			11006,00			919,68			479,41			4258,10		
Residual sum of squares	217,54			194,64			248,08			210,21			191,05			224,39		
R-squared	0,7635			0,5940			0,9775			0,7714			0,6015			0,9473		
Adj, R-squared	0,7433			0,5501			0,9517			0,7389			0,5475			0,9073		
Hausman test				2,2951			0,0021						1,9223		0,0136			

Source: Author's calculations

Note: Signif. codes: 0 '***' 0,001 '**' 0,01 '*' 0,05 '.' 0,1 ' ' 1

Table 4.3 The results of the tests

	(7)				(9)			
	F	Chisq	p-Value		F	Chisq	p-Value	
Chow F-test	2,2951		0,0021	**	1,9223		0,0136	*
Wald test	2,5307	45,553	0,0006/ 0,0003	***	2,5799	46,438	0,0004/ 0,0003	***
Breusch and Pagan Lagrangian Multiplier test		49,406	0,0000	***		30,147	0,0000	***
Hausman test		143,19	0,0000	***		55,165	0,0000	***

Source: Author's calculations
Note: Signif. codes: 0 '***' 0,001 '**' 0,01 '*' 0,05 '.' 0,1 ' ' 1

estimated and the fixed effects model would be the model of choice (Clark et al. 2010).

Therefore, standard restriction tests should be carried out so that an appropriate statistical model can be chosen.

We performed the specification test to choose between the fixed and random effect model (Wooldridge 2013, pp. 495–496). According to Ahn and Moon (2002), the Hausman statistic is viewed as a distance measure between the fixed effects and the random effects estimators. The null hypothesis of Hausman test is that time-invariant error u_j is not correlated with any explanatory variable in all time periods. If the null hypothesis is rejected, then the fixed effect model should be used. Whereas, if the null hypothesis is accepted, the random effect model should be used (Wooldridge 2013, pp. 495–496).

The result of the test clearly rejects the null hypothesis assumption (Table 4.3). Under alternative hypothesis, the fixed effects estimator is still consistent, but the random effects is inconsistent. We conclude that endogeneity is a problem for the random effects estimator and we should use the fixed effects estimator.

In principle, by including country fixed effects, we are controlling for the average differences across countries in any observable or unobservable predictors. This greatly reduces the threat of omitted variable bias.

The results of all conducted tests are reported in Table 4.3.

4.2.3 *Robustness Tests*

The estimates in the previous section may not account for several important patterns in the model residuals. In the following discussion, we identify some of these problems and consider how they might be addressed.

According to the Gauss-Markov theorem (Greene 2003, pp. 10–17), the estimator is BLUE (Best Linear Unbiased Estimator) when the expectation of errors is zero, given any values of the independent variables:

$$E(v|x_1, x_2, \quad \ldots, x_k) = 0 \tag{4.5}$$

they are uncorrelated:

$$Cov(v_i, v_j) = 0 \, for \, all \, i \neq j \tag{4.6}$$

and have equal variances:

$$Var(v|x_1, x_2, \quad \ldots, x_k) = \sigma^2 \tag{4.7}$$

The errors do not need to be normal, nor do they need to independent and identically distributed.

In this part, we test the pooling and fixed effect models of the specifications (7) and (9) that are the baseline models in our research. The issues we consider are non-linearity, cross panel heteroskedasticity and sectoral correlation, multicollinearity, and endogeneity.

4.2.3.1 Non-linearity and Influential Data

Violations of linearity or additivity are extremely serious: if a linear model includes data which is nonlinearly or nonadditively related, the predictions are likely to be seriously in error.

We tested our data for normal distribution, unusualness of independent variables and for outliers of the independent variables.

First, we constructed the Q-Q plot (see Appendix G, Figs. 4.11 and 4.12). The Q-Q plot, (quantile-quantile plot), is a graphical tool to assess whether the data is normally distributed. It plots two sets of quantiles against one another. If both sets of quantiles came from the same distribution, they form a symmetrical shape around the mean. From the plot we see that our sample data is not skewed. We can identify light tails; thus, we can conclude that the residuals are normally distributed.

However, the Q-Q plot is only a visual check and somewhat subjective, but it allows for the identification of the presence of general problems and whether our assumptions are plausible (Atkinson 1987; Fox and Weisberg 2011).

In multiple regression models, nonlinearity or nonadditivity may also be revealed by systematic patterns in the plots of the residuals versus individual independent variables (see Appendix G, Fig. 4.14). Added variable plots help to project multidimensional data in the two-dimensional world. They identify the presence of outliers that determine the slope (Fox and Weisberg 2011).

The added-variable plot (partial-regression leverage plot) depicts the relationship between dependent and one independent variable, adjusting for the effects of other independent variables (Fox and Weisberg 2011).

High leverage observations are shown in added variable plots as points horizontally distant from the rest of the data. Figure 4.14 suggests a problem in determining the coefficient of $GDPGR_{jT}$, GDP_{jT}, and FDI_{jT-1} because of the points on the bottom of the plot.

Leverage plots also help to identify the "unusualness" of independent variables (see Appendix G, Fig. 4.13). An observation that has an extreme value on a predictor variable—i.e. it is far from the independent variable's mean—has leverage on (i.e. the potential to influence) the regression line (Fox and Weisberg 2011; Cook and Weisberg 1999).

High leverage does not necessarily mean that it influences the regression coefficients. In our case $GDPGR_{jT}$, GDP_{jT}, and FDI_{jT-1} have high leverages and yet follow straight in line with the pattern of the rest of the data.

Our plots reveal also some "abnormal" observations on $WAGE_{jT}$. We have identified a "doubtful" observation that reveals very low wages in Ukraine and Georgia in the early 1990s. This observation contains valuable information about the process under investigation. We conclude that our outlier does not indicate incorrectly measured or recorded data. In this situation, it is not legitimate to simply drop it.

Moreover, Cook's distance confirms that all observations lie within the acceptable range (see Appendix G, Fig. 4.15).

A threshold level of the Cook's distance is calculated as $4/N$ or $4/(N-k-1)$, where N is the number of observations and k the number of explanatory variables (Cook and Weisberg 1999; Fox and Weisberg 2011). The latter formula should yield a threshold around 0,09. An observation with a Cook's distance larger than three times the mean might be an outlier. In our case the values do not exceed value of 0,20 (see Appendix G, Fig. 4.15).

4.2.3.2 Heteroskedasticity and Autocorrelation

The third condition of the Gauss-Markov theorem is that the variance of the error term is homoskedastic, the error v has the same variance given any values of the explanatory variables. If the error terms do not have constant variance, they are said to be heteroskedastic.

In other words:

$$Var(v|x_1, x_2, \quad \ldots, x_k) = \sigma^2 \tag{4.8}$$

If this assumption fails, then the model exhibits heteroskedasticity. This means that the variance in the error term, v, conditional on the explanatory variables, is the same for all combinations of outcomes of the explanatory variables. If Var(u|x) is not constant, OLS is no longer BLUE. That is why the violation of this assumption makes the estimators of β_j biased. Since the OLS standard errors are directly based on these variances, they are no longer valid for constructing confidence intervals and t statistics. Similarly, F statistics are no longer F distributed, and the LM statistic no longer has an asymptotic chi-square distribution (Wooldridge 2013, pp. 268–271).

It is important to mention that heteroskedasticity does not cause bias or inconsistency in the OLS estimators of the β_j, whereas the omitting of an important variable would have this effect.

Heteroskedasticity may occur with the quantitative change of independent variables. In this case we assume that there are modelling errors and some important variables not included in the model. Measurement errors can also cause heteroskedasticity. Some respondents might provide more accurate responses than others. Heteroskedasticity can also appear if there are subpopulation differences or other interaction effects. This problem also can be eliminated by incorporating such differences into the model (Wooldridge 2013, pp. 268–271).

The plots on the Figs. 4.16 and 4.17 in Appendix H show that there is a possible heterogeneity across countries. Thus, the including of the country-specific effect (FE) may eliminate this problem. The heterogeneity across years seems to not be a problem in our analysis.

There are a great number of tests for heteroskedasticity. Some of them are able to detect heteroskedasticity, however, they do not directly test the assumption that the variance of the error does not depend upon the independent variables (Wooldridge 2013, p. 268). Apart these tests we also employ tests which detect the kind of heteroskedasticity.

Firstly, we carried out Score Test for Non-Constant Error Variance in the pool and fixed effect model for both specifications. This test checks at the hypothesis of constant error variance against the alternative that the error variance changes with the level of the response. This test is often called the Breusch-Pagan test; it was independently suggested with some extension by Cook and Weisberg (1999) (Wooldridge 2013, pp. 275–278; Greene 2003, pp. 222–225). The test rejected the null hypothesis of constant variance or homoskedastic standard errors and indicated the presence of heteroskedastic standard errors in both specifications (see Table 4.4).

We conduct two additional test to identify the non-homoskedastic errors. The Goldfeld–Quandt test compares the variances of two submodels divided by a specified breakpoint and rejects null hypothesis if the variances differ, and, hence, the test is sometimes called a two-group test. If the null hypothesis is rejected there is ground to suppose that the standard deviation of errors is proportional to some

Table 4.4 Tests for heteroskedasticity

	(7)				(9)			
Test	OLS		FE		OLS		FE	
Breusch-Pagan/ Cook-Weisberg test	BP = 18,974	p-value = 0,0254	BP = 43,597	p-value = 0,0400	BP = 28,642	p-value = 0,0179	BP = 49,748	p-value = 0,0505
Goldfeld-Quadt test	GQ = 0,0505	p-value = 0,0000	GQ = 1,6064	p-value = 0,0015	GQ = 1,9836	p-value = 0,0000	GQ = 1,592	p-value = 0,0000
Harrison-McCabe test	HMC = 0,3372	p-value = 0,0000	HMC = 0,3383	p-value = 0,0000	HMC = 0,2919	p-value = 0,0000	HMC = 0,3757	p-value = 0,0000
RESET test	RESET = 0,3961	p-value = 0,6732	RESET = 0,4052	p-value = 0,6672	RESET = 0,4781	p-value = 0,6203	RESET = 0,4459	p-value = 0,6406

Source: Author's calculations

variable (Greene 2003, pp. 223–224). In our case Goldfeld-Quandt test against heteroskedasticity rejected the null hypothesis and showed that the variances differ into subgroups (Table 4.4).

The Harrison–McCabe test is similar to the Goldfeld-Quand test. Its statistic is the fraction of the residual sum of squares that relates to the fraction of the data before the breakpoint. Under null hypothesis the test statistic should be close to the size of this fraction, e.g. in the default case close to 0,5 (Harrison and McCabe 1979). In our case, the null hypothesis is rejected because the statistic is too small (Table 4.4).

Both tests confirmed the presence of heteroskedasticity.

Unfortunately, the Goldfeld–Quandt and the Harrison–McCabe tests are not very robust to specification errors. They detect non-homoskedastic errors but cannot distinguish between heteroskedastic error structure and an underlying specification problem such as an incorrect functional form or an omitted variable. Jerry G. Thursby proposed a modification of the Goldfeld–Quandt test using a variation of the Ramsey RESET test in order to provide some measure of robustness (Thursby 1982).

The Ramsey Regression Equation Specification Error Test (RESET) test is a general specification test for the linear regression model. It tests whether non-linear combinations of the explanatory variables have any power in explaining the response variable. More specifically, it tests whether non-linear combinations of the fitted values help explain the response variable (Wooldridge 2013, pp. 306–307). To implement RESET, we must decide how many functions of the fitted values to include in an expanded regression. There is no right answer to this question, but the squared and cubed terms have proven to be useful in most applications (Wooldridge 2013, pp. 306–307). In our test, we use quadratic influence of the fitted response.

RESET test shows the correctness of the structure of our model both for specification (7) and (9) for OLS and FE estimators.

Some tests reveal the presence of cross-panel heteroskedasticity in our models, which can significantly influence standard errors and therefore affect hypothesis testing.

Apart from groupwise heteroskedasticity, panel data might also suffer from serial correlation. Serial correlation occurs in time-series studies when the errors associated with a given time period carry over into future time periods. The errors should fulfil the next condition:

$$cov(\varepsilon_j, \varepsilon_k) = 0, \quad for\ all\ j \neq k \tag{4.9}$$

The consequences of autocorrelation are similar to heteroskedasticity, but the problems caused by the latter are usually more severe. Autocorrelation of errors violates the ordinary least squares (OLS) assumption that the error terms are uncorrelated, meaning that the Gauss Markov theorem does not apply, and that OLS estimators are no longer the Best Linear Unbiased Estimators (BLUE) (Wooldridge 2013, pp. 353–354).

Models with lagged values of dependent variables as factors should be carefully tested for the presence of autocorrelation because the autocorrelation of idiosyncratic errors may lead to biased and inconsistent estimates.

We apply several tests for residual autocorrelation. Lagrange multiplier test developed by Baltagi and Li (1995) (Greene 2003, pp. 270–271) and a "corrected" versions of the standard LM test developed by Bera et al. (2001) are used to test for first-order serial correlation in residuals (Croissant and Millo 2008). The results of our tests (see Table 4.5) reveal the presence of serial correlation in OLS models, but taking into account the country-specific factors (FE) eliminates this problem.

Secondly, we applied the Breusch-Godfrey/Wooldridge test. It is a Lagrange multiplier test on the residuals, which should be serially uncorrelated under the null hypothesis. This test allows for lagged dependent variables (Wooldridge 2013, p. 422). The Breusch-Godfrey/Wooldridge test for serial correlation also does not reveal the presence of autocorrelation in FE models.

A Wooldridge test for autocorrelation in in fixed-effects panel models confirms the null hypothesis of no first-order serial correlation (Table 4.5). FE coefficient estimates are consistent, unbiased and asymptotically efficient (Wooldridge 2010, pp. 310–312).

A popular test for serial correlation is the Durbin-Watson statistic. The DW statistic lies in the 0–4 range, with a value near two indicating no first-order serial correlation. Positive serial correlation is associated with DW values below 2 and

Table 4.5 Tests for autoregression

	(7)				(9)			
Test	OLS		FE		OLS		FE	
Baltagi and Li two-sided LM test	chisq = 5,1032	p-value = 0,0238	chisq = 2,2284	p-value = 0,1355	chisq = 7,4125	p-value = 0,0065	chisq = 1,3794	p-value = 0,2402
Bera, Sosa-Escudero and Yoon locally robust test	chisq = 11,451	p-value = 0,0007	chisq = 2,492	p-value = 0,1144	chisq = 8,8634	p-value = 0,0029	chisq = 1,2594	p-value = 0,2618
Breusch-Godfrey/ Wooldridge test for serial correlation in panel models	chisq = 35,693	p-value = 0,0000	chisq = 1,8682	p-value = 0,9814	chisq = 17,192	p-value = 0,0086	chisq = 1,7259	p-value = 0,9431
Wooldridge's test for serial correlation in FE panels			chisq = 1,1064	p-value = 0,2929			chisq = 0,51798	p-value = 0,4717
Durbin-Watson test for serial correlation in panel models	DW = 2,2486	p-value = 0,981	DW = 2,2113	p-value = 0,9667	DW = 2,2574	p-value = 0,9763	DW = 2,1813	p-value = 0,9182

Source: Author's calculations

negative serial correlation with DW values above 2 (Greene 2003, p. 270; Wooldridge 2013, pp. 418–419). This test also confirms the robustness of the results (Table 4.5).

The tests revealed the presence of heteroskedasticity in OLS and FE models, and autocorrelation in OLS models. We can easily eliminate the problem of autocorrelation by including country specific effects (FE). In order to account for heteroskedasticity within panels we can employ White-corrected standard errors (see Appendix I).

4.2.3.3 Multicollinearity

Multicollinearity is a high (but not perfect) correlation between independent variables. Correlation among regressors is quite common in time-series data and even extreme multicollinearity (so long as it is not perfect) does not affect the stability of the model. OLS estimates are still unbiased and BLUE. Nevertheless, the greater is the multicollinearity, the greater are the standard errors because it affects calculations regarding individual predictors (Greene 2003, pp. 56–59). To reduce the negative effects of the multicollinerity, each explanatory variable was progressively added (Appendix F, Tables 4.14–4.18).

We have already mentioned multicollinearity issues in Sect. 4.2.1. The potential multicorrelation problems include correlation between integration variables. The matter of fact, they represent the gradual process in which some stages appear only once the agreements were achieved on the previous stages.

The only problem that can arise is only in pairs of dummies and market access variables. The pair correlation coefficients are 100%. That is why we consider them in different specifications (specification (7) and (8); (9) and (10)).

Formal tests for multicollinearity (Variance Inflation Factor ($VIF = 1/1-R^2$)) is not clearly applicable to panel data (Greene 2003, pp. 56–59). The result for the proxies are reported in Table 4.6 and confirm that none of the variables are highly correlated, as none of VIF's are excessively high based on rule of $VIF > 4$ for the existence of problematic multicollinearity. The correlation coefficients between the explanatory variables are also not alarming high ($R^2 > 0{,}80$ or $R^2 > 0{,}90$), as can be seen from the correlation matrix presented in Appendix E, Fig. 4.9.

4.2.3.4 Endogeneity

One of the most important assumptions of the regression models is that factors are exogenous. The violation of this condition leads to a significant deterioration of the estimates. Endogeneity, or two-ways causality, occurs when some of the explanatory variables are wholly or partly influenced by the dependant variable. This may cause problems not only in inference but also for estimations as the independent variable is potentially correlated with the variation in the dependent variable that is relegated to the error term.

Table 4.6 Variance inflation factors test

	(7)			(9)		
	GVIF	Df	GVIF^(1/(2×Df))	GVIF	Df	GVIF^(1/(2×Df))
FDI_{jT-1}	2,7049	1	1,6447	2,7841	1	1,6686
GDP_{jT}	2,9094	1	1,7057	3,1586	1	1,7772
$WAGE_{jT}$	1,8599	1	1,3638	2,4871	1	1,5771
$FTAMA_{jT}$	2,2793	1	1,5097			
$AAMA_{jT}$	2,1049	1	1,4508			
$EUMA_{jT}$	2,0189	1	1,4209			
FTA_{jT}				3,5206	1	1,8763
$Aasig_{jT}$				2,2410	1	1,4970
$Aafor_{jT}$				9,3863	1	3,0637
$Poten_{jT}$				3,0049	1	1,7335
$Candid_{jT}$				3,0816	1	1,7555
$Acces_{jT}$				5,3608	1	2,3153
$Acced_{jT}$				2,9199	1	1,7088
EU_{jT}				3,3106	1	1,8195
$Euro_{jT}$				2,2226	1	1,4908
$OPEN_{jT}$	1,3130	1	1,1459	1,6759	1	1,2946
GCF_{jT}	1,1971	1	1,0941	1,2174	1	1,1034
$GDPGR_{jT}$	1,1686	1	1,0810	1,1860	1	1,0890

Source: Author's calculations

Endogeneity is often described as having three sources: omitted variables, measurement error, and simultaneity. All the sources of the endogeneity may appear simultaneously, they can compensate or strengthen one another.

In our model, the relation between FDI and GDP attracts special attention. The correlation between FDI and GDP could arise from an endogenous determination of GDP, that is, GDP itself may be influenced by wages, GCF or integration. In these circumstances there would exist a correlation between GDP and the country-specific error term, which would bias the estimated coefficients.

Moreover, as a matter of fact, high market potential attracts more FDI. Foreign investors add capital stock in the host country, what in the issue stimulates the economic growth. Moreover, domestic investment financed by FDI is included in the definition of GDP. These and other potential endogeneity problems with GDP are non-trivial, and have prompted several studies to move the GDP level to the left-hand side, estimating FDI as a share of GDP.

Therefore, in order to gauge the magnitude of the potential endogeneity problems, we employ the Granger causality tests. "Granger causality" is a term for a specific notion of causality in time-series analysis. Its main idea of this test is to evaluate two models with and without doubtful factors and compare them. Evaluations are made in both directions with lagged values of dependent variables (see Table 4.7) (Greene 2003, p. 592).

Table 4.7 Basic Granger causality tests

Granger test		
$FDI_{jT} \sim FDI_{jT-1} + GDP_{jT-1}$	F = 22,722	Pr(>F) = 0,0000***
$GDP_{jT} \sim FDI_{jT-1} + GDP_{jT-1}$	F = 22,493	Pr(>F) = 0,0000***

Source: Author's calculations
Note: Signif. codes: 0 '***' 0.001 '**' 0.01 '*' 0.05 '.' 0.1 ' ' 1

Table 4.8 Granger causality with FE

	Estimate	t-Value		Estimate	t-Value	
	$GDP_{jT} \sim FDI_{jT-1} + GDP_{jT-1} + factor$ *(Country)*			$GDP_{jT} \sim GDP_{jT-1} + factor$ *(Country)*		
FDI_{jT-1}	0,049668	7,653	***			
GDP_{jT-1}	0,880358	57,349	***	0,958768	76,271	***
Analysis of Var.	F = 26,985	Pr(>F) = 0,0000	***			
	$FDI_{jT} \sim FDI_{jT-1} + GDP_{jT-1} + factor$ *(Country)*			$FDI_{jT} \sim FDI_{jT-1} + factor$ *(Country)*		
FDI_{jT-1}	0,584983	14,882	***	0,65873	21,580	***
GDP_{jT-1}	0,271816	2,936	**			
Analysis of Var.	F = 8,6213	Pr(>F) = 0,0035	**			

Source: Author's calculations
Note: Signif. codes: 0 '***' 0.001 '**' 0.01 '*' 0.05 '.' 0.1 ' ' 1

The results are shown in Table 4.7 and suggest that there is causality between FDI and GDP. This suggests that endogeneity may be a significant problem in our sample.

As far as I know, the Granger causality test in panel data is not generally used because it does not account for country differences. Thus, we estimate equations adding county dummies and compare models by ANOVA (see Table 4.8).

Furthermore, we have made previous references to the extensive literature that has established a robust positive relationship between FDI on the left-hand side and market size.

In this section, we conducted the basic tests for non-linearity, heteroskedasticity and autoregression, multicollinearity and endogeneity. The baseline models showed no evidence for unmanageable multicollinearity and autocorrelation, but confirmed the presence of heteroskedasticity and endogeneity.

The endogeneity and unobserved heterogeneity often refer to the same thing. Endogeneity comes, for example, from omitted variables; unobserved heterogeneity is caused by the same problem. Thus, the elimination of endogeneity will automatically eliminate heteroskedasticity (Wooldridge 2012).

In next section we will try to account for these problems by running fixed-effect instrumental variables estimator.

4.2.4 Instrumental Variables (IV) Estimators

In our book, we use dynamic panel data methods to examine the determinants of FDI in the Central and Eastern European countries. There are several dynamic model estimators for panel data, such as 2SLS and GMM, that have been developed in the econometric literature to solve the problem of endogeneity. For our estimations we employ 2SLS and GMM with fixed effects.

A common problem for this type of analysis is coming up with a set of instruments that have to be correlated with the endogenous regressors but must not be correlated with the time-varying error term:

$$Cov(y_{1\,jt}, z_{1\,jt}) \neq 0 \tag{4.10}$$

and

$$Cov(z_{1\,jt}, \varepsilon_{jt}) = 0 \tag{4.11}$$

The choice of instrumental variables in the literature is arbitrary and there is no consensus on a set of variables that are widely used (Wooldridge 2010, pp. 83–84).

In our case, the instrument choice is rather obvious. We use population as an alternative proxy for market size. It is highly correlated with GDP, and has lower correlation with FDI. Moreover, it does not cause much difference in the estimation results. We also dummy for years as an instrumental variable.

Thus, we have two exogenous instruments that are not included in the model: natural logarithm value of population, and a factor of year. Lagged for one period value of FDI inflows, wages, market access and openness proxies, as well as GCF, and GDP growth are used as endogenous instrumental variables.

In Table 4.11, we reported results from the 2SLS fixed effect model and GMM fixed effects model.

The overall validity of instruments is checked by Sargan test. Sargan test statistics (1988) is generally used to detect the correlation between instrumental variables and error term. Weak correlation between instrumental variables and endogenous variables lead to the problem of identification of equations (Kleiber and Zeileis 2008; Wooldridge 2010, pp. 122–124). As Sargan test in Table 4.9 indicates, the null hypothesis that the instruments are valid instruments is not rejected for both models. In other words, the instruments are not correlated with the error term and the choice of instruments is appropriate.

In addition, Sargan and Basmann tests evaluate whether the equation is misspecified and whether one or more of the excluded exogenous variables should in fact be included in the structural equation (structural model is heteroskedastic). Both tests assume that the errors are independent and identically distributed random variables. The estimations are invalid when this condition is not fulfilled (Kleiber and Zeileis 2008). This seems not to be true. Sargan statistic is valid at 0,1% level, though we do reject the hypothesis that our instruments are invalid or our model is incorrectly specified.

Table 4.9 2SLS Diagnostic tests

	(7)					(9)				
	Df1	Df2	Statistic	p-Value		Df1	Df2	Statistic	p-Value	
Weak instruments	25	326	13,951	0,0000	***	25	320	9,657	0,0000	***
Wu-Hausman	1	349	4,185	0,0415	*	1	343	5,835	0,0162	*
Durbin	1		4,47866	0,0343	***	1		6,32317	0,0119	***
Sargan	24		69,362	0,0000	***	24		71,983	0,0000	***
Bamann	24		73,2634	0,0000	***	24		75,2724	0,0000	***

Source: Author's calculations
Note: Signif. codes: 0 '***' 0.001 '**' 0.01 '*' 0.05 '.' 0.1 ' ' 1

The results of above mentioned test show that the elimination of endogeneity also accounted the problem of heterogeneity as was assumed in Sect. 4.2.3 *Heterogeneity and Autocorrelation.*

Wu-Hausman F and Durbin-Wu-Hausman tests are commonly used to estimate the quality of instruments. These tests compare the evaluation results before and applying the instruments. They determine whether the instruments are endogenous. The null hypothesis of the Durbin and Wu–Hausman tests is that the variable under consideration can be treated as exogenous. If the endogenous regressors are in fact exogenous, then the OLS estimator is more efficient (Wooldridge 2010, pp. 118–122). As Wu-Hausman F Test and Durbin-Wu-Hausman test in Table 4.9 indicate that the exogeneity of the variable FDI is clearly rejected. Both estimates of the error variance are consistent.

To test for weak instruments we implement F test of the first stage regression proposed Cragg-Donald (1993) and Kleibergen and Paap (2002) LM test to provide further model evaluation. Stock and Yogo (2005) completed this test by calculating critical values to measure relative bias of 2SLS; they also provided critical values for worst-case rejection rates (Wooldridge 2010, pp. 92–94). Overall, Crag-Donald F statistic is just below the Stock and Yogo 1% critical value (see Table 4.9). Hence, the instruments are strong and lead to relatively small biases in 2SLS with FE.

Generalised Method of Moments (GMM) is another estimator for ARDL models. This estimator was developed by Arellano and Bond (1991) to get asymptotically efficient estimators. This estimator is designed for datasets with many panels and periods, and it requires that there be no autocorrelation in the idiosyncratic errors (see Table 4.11).

To estimate the validity of instruments in our GMM model we employ the Hansen's J test which is analogous to Sagran and Basmann tests. Hansen test is used to check the correlation between an endogenous variable and time-varying error term. The null hypothesis is that instrumental variables are exogenous. The alternative hypothesis is that some of the instrumental variables are not exogenous or are correlated with the time error term (Greene 2003, pp. 154–155). Table 4.10 shows that J test rejects the hypothesis of the overidentifying restriction in both specifications.

The results reported in Table 4.11 are robust to heteroskedasticity and autocorrelation (HAC).

Table 4.10 GMM diagnostic test, specification (7) and (9)

	(7)				(9)			
	Df1	Statistic	p-Value		Df1	Statistic	p-Value	
J-Test	24	73,6400	0,0000	***	24	64,8430	0,0000	***

Source: Author's calculations
Note: Signif. codes: 0 '***' 0.001 '**' 0.01 '*' 0.05 '.' 0.1 ' ' 1

Table 4.11 Results of 2SLS and GMM with fixed effects estimations, specification (7) and (9)

	(7)						(9)					
	2SLS			GMM			2SLS			GMM		
	Coef.	t		Coef.	t		Coef.	t		Coef.	t	
FDI_{jT-1}	0,3557	7,71	***	0,3212	4,60	***	0,3405	7,21	***	0,2707	4,39	***
GDP_{jT}	0,6771	2,12	*	0,7871	3,17	**	1,1354	2,84	**	1,0225	3,20	**
$WAGE_{jT}$	0,0236	0,10		−0,0871	−0,52		−0,1523	−0,61		−0,1496	−0,73	
$FTAMA_{jT}$	0,0100	0,86		0,0037	0,36							
$AAMA_{jT}$	0,0105	2,20	*	0,0106	2,38	*						
$EUMA_{jT}$	0,0118	2,05	*	0,0094	1,62							
FTA_{JT}							−0,1547	−0,85		−0,1009	−0,70	
$Aasig_{jT}$							0,0480	0,25		−0,0161	−0,10	
$Aafor_{jT}$							0,0469	0,16		0,0439	0,18	
$Poten_{jT}$							0,3084	1,24		0,5252	2,53	*
$Candid_{jT}$							0,3593	1,20		0,4619	1,72	
$Acces_{jT}$							0,4528	1,48		0,7356	2,81	*
$Acced_{jT}$							0,0445	0,13		0,2660	0,88	
EU_{jT}							−0,0825	−0,23		0,4122	1,44	
$Euro_{jT}$							−0,7540	−1,71	.	−0,0811	−0,18	
$OPEN_{jT}$	−0,0033	−1,13		−0,0030	−1,23		−0,0032	−1,08		−0,0059	−2,44	*
GCF_{jT}	0,0116	1,35		0,0345	4,76	***	0,0067	0,75		0,0250	2,99	**
$GDPGR_{jT}$	0,0438	4,79	***	0,0691	5,79	***	0,0460	4,92	***	0,0670	6,02	***
Residual standard error	0,7498						0,7534					
Multiple R-squared	0,7853						0,7870					
Adjusted R-squared	0,7688						0,7666					
Wald test	1288		0				1284					

Source: Author's calculations
Note: Signif. codes: 0 '***' 0,001 '**' 0,01 '*' 0,05 '.' 0,1 ' ' 1

4.3 Empirical Results

In this section, we analyse the empirical results obtained from the previous section. The results (Table 4.11) show that regression model with FDI as a dependent variable fits well with independent variables, since value of adjusted R-Squared is high (0,77). The R-square (0,79) shows the proportion of variance in FDI inflows which can be predicted by independent variables.

The empirical results also support our hypotheses, as although some are not significant, all the explanatory variables have shown signs as expected. The estimations of 2SLS and GMM are similar, but some necessary points should be mentioned.

4.3.1 Traditional Determinants of FDI

According to the results presented in Table 4.11, GDP is found to be a fundamental factor of attraction for multinationals, even accounting for endogeneity in the model. The coefficient indicates that a 1% increase in GDP is associated with a proportional increase from 0,69% to 1,13% of FDI inflow (2SLS and GMM estimations of the specification (7) and (9)).

The coefficient of GDP accurately reflects theoretical expectations (Table 4.1). Flows are expected to be greater in larger economies with well-built markets. As investing in a given countries implies large fixed costs, multinationals are most likely interested in capturing a greater share of the market when expanding to the CEE countries.

Unfortunately, we do not clearly observe the motives of FDI in CEE: whether FDI in the region is market-seeking (tariff-jumping motive prevail) or resource-seeking (off-shoring and export-platform motives also exist) (see Dunning 1973). Still, the analysis of the sector structure can shed additional light upon this question. Most FDI has been domestic-market seeking in traditional services such as finance, tourism and trading, or in industries such as electricity, water or telecommunications. This largely reflects the non-tradable nature of these sectors. They are non-storable and transportable and hence need to be produced when and where they are consumed.

Section 2.2 shows that in the largest host countries of the CEE region, the industry composition of inward FDI gradually shifted from manufacturing in the 1990s towards services in the early 2000s, and within services, from privatised network industries in earlier years towards business services (UNCTAD 2004). In the Czech Republic, Hungary and Poland, services already became dominant in terms of FDI in the late 1990s. Generally, in the early 2000s the countries of CEE were characterised by substantial FDI penetration in infrastructure services (e.g. banking, telecommunications, water, electricity) (UNCTAD 2004).

Thus, significant FDI in the service attributed market-seeking FDI inflows in Poland, Hungary, the Czech Republic, Romania and Ukraine in the 2000s (see Sects. 2.2.3 and Sect. 2.2.4). Further, some evidence of a negative relationship between FDI and tariff rates confirms the presence of a tariff-jumping motive (see Table 4.11).

These results suggest also that countries with a smaller market size may have problems in attracting foreign investors, all other factors being equal. Countries such as Albania, Macedonia, and Moldova may become less desirable for foreign investors seeking high purchasing-power and demand, but trade agreements with the EU (preferential or association agreements) may affect market size, one of the key determinants of FDI. As trade blocs and regional links grow, the significance of national markets thus diminishes.

The importance of market size was also supported by a survey analysis undertaken by Altzinger and Bellak (1999). They questioned more than 150 Austrian firms investing in the CEECs, and found that market potential is the most important factor. According to Savary (1997), 22 surveyed French industrial firms that invested in the CEECs also mentioned market size as being among the most important factors. Thus, they found Poland more attractive than most South-East European countries. However, market size was found to be slightly less important than factor costs in other smaller countries of the region (Savary 1997).

In our model, the value of the labour cost coefficient implies that a decrease in average monthly wages by 1% would generally lead to an up to 0,15% increase in the magnitude of FDI flow.

Thus, high levels of FDI were expected to flow into the CEECs, mainly due to low wages and open access to EU markets. As the output from resource-seeking FDI is typically intended for export, and intermediate goods are imported from outside the host economy, the reduction of trade barriers will ease international trade and, thus, will increase the level of FDI in low-wage countries. The presence of export-platforms also can be further confirmed by sector analysis. Besides market-seeking FDI in services, the CEE countries attracted FDI in the automobile industry which is typically export-oriented (see Sect. 2.2). There are plenty of examples of resource-seeking FDI in the region. As mentioned previously, these include; Toyota and VW/Skoda in the Czech Republic; Suzuki and Audi in Hungary; Fiat, GM/Opel, Daewoo, VW in Poland; PSA/Peugeot and VW in Slovakia; and Renault in Slovenia (see UNCTAD 2003, p. 61).

According to our estimations (see Fig. 4.5), average wages in the new EU member states are still on average 60% lower than the EU-15 average. The results prove the further potential for installation of export platforms in the integrating countries. We can also conclude that the countries with the lowest average wages in the region such as the countries in the Western Balkans, Georgia, Moldova and Ukraine that have just begun integrating with the EU will attract more FDI from both outside and inside of the EU. We can even observe in the future, the reallocation of production not only from the EU-15 but also from new EU members.

However, we should also point out that the coefficient of labour cost is insignificant. The issue of whether labour costs affect the decision to invest in the transition economies is an important one, and the subject of some debate due to the inconclusive results (See Appendix F)—it appears both with positive and negative signs. The explanation was given by Rolfe and Woodward (2004) who pointed out that once the decision to locate in a low wage area—as Eastern Europe—has been taken, "finding the cheapest possible labour within an already low wage region may or may not be an important consideration" (Rolfe and Woodward 2004). Elsewhere, labour cost advantage was viewed as less important than market access (Janssens and Konings 1996; Savary 1997; Altzinger and Bellak 1999).

4.3.2 Macroeconomic Variables

The pattern of FDI may be different among countries with similar market size and production costs. The location choices of multinationals between countries are increasingly related to advantages arising from other factors that influence the supply capacities of host countries, such as scale economies (particularly in the manufacturing sector) and clustering (agglomeration economies), as well as institutional and policy variables. The investors address this as "business climate", which comprises many individual factors.

The positive and statistically significant effect (at up to 0,1% level) of Gross capital formation (or gross domestic investment) in relation to FDI, indicates that the improvement of infrastructure positively affects FDI inflow in the CEE countries. From the results, it is clear that physical infrastructure (ports, roads, power, telecommunications), knowledge infrastructure (universities, technology parks, etc.) and business infrastructure (EPZs, clusters, etc.) increase the attractiveness of a country.

Agglomeration also exhibits a high degree of statistical significance, and has a large and positive impact on the location of FDI. This also confirms the importance of infrastructure and firm concentration. Firms benefit from locating close to other firms, to markets and factors of production, and from the availability of specialised skills, developed production factor markets, and well-built supply chains.

In Sect. 3.1, we mentioned NEG studies (Fujita et al. 1999; Puga and Venables 1997; etc.) that identified the importance of agglomeration for industrial structures and international trade. Head and Mayer (2004) studied the factors that influence the location of Japanese firms within Europe. They found that that firms prefer to locate "where the markets are." (Head and Mayer 2004).

In addition, the presence of other foreign firms in the region reduces the risk of TNCs by demonstration effect, wherein, multinationals tend to place more trust in locations where other multinationals are present. Thus, Kinoshita and Campos (2003) found that the existence of agglomeration economies has a positive and statistically significant effect on FDI, especially in non-CIS countries. It appears because a country's environment is not well explored. That is why foreign investors may view the investment decisions of others as a good signal for favourable conditions, and invest there too to reduce uncertainty (Kinoshita and Campos 2003).

The reasons for the importance of agglomeration and gross domestic investment for location decisions are not difficult to find. Foreign firms want to place their subsidiaries close to centres of corporate, political and financial decision-making, high levels of income, access to technology and, especially, innovative activities, universities, institutions and modern infrastructure (including easy access to international air transport) and quality of life.

The coefficient for GDP growth is positive and highly significant in our specifications. This proxy enters both specifications estimated by IV with coefficient up to 0,06% and 0,1% level of significance. The results show that the strong economic growth of new integrating countries and their favourable growth prospects are very attractive for market-seeking investors. Indeed, the real GDP growth rate in CEE is more than double the EU-15 average (UNCTAD 2016d).

There are several reasons why foreign investors might prefer faster-growing markets. Firstly, higher growth rates signal higher rates of return on investment. Thus, investment in countries with rapid economic development promises growing profits. Secondly, GDP growth rate also measures the increasing market size (Blonigen et al. 2007; Vernon 1966; Carstensen and Toubal 2004). Therefore, investors are attracted by better production opportunities and increasing demand.

4.3.3 Integration Effect

We also want to analyse how FDI inflows are affected when countries start building integration unions. For this purpose, we analyse trade openness and access to foreign markets.

The negative sign of the trade openness confirms the presence of tariff-jumping FDI motives. Indeed, the existence of tariff and non-tariff barriers could affect location choice with respect to servicing markets. The results show that more open economies are attractive for export strategies; whereas the presence of trade barriers stimulates more FDI as a supply opportunity. Thus, some host countries and member-countries of regional trade blocs can intentionally use tariffs, quotas, and local standards to encourage direct investment. However, a proxy for openness is significant only for 2SLS estimation of specification (9).

The variable $FTAMA_{jt}$ appears with negative and insignificant coefficient (specification (7)). Indeed, membership of CEFTA and BAFTA did not significantly improve the market size of the economies (see Fig. 4.5). Moreover, members of CEFTA or BAFTA got access only to the countries of a similar economy and demand structure (see Sect. 2.3.3). Thus, foreign firms did not get the advantage of installing an export-platform within the European FTAs.

These results are in line with the estimations of specification (9). The FTA dummy variable has a negative sign. One explanation for the negative sign is that both FTAs (the Baltic Free Trade Area (BAFTA) and the Central European Free Trade Agreement (CEFTA) were created to favour the development of intra-regional trade and competition in these countries. This is why FTAs are an important determinant of economic trade, since they institute free trade among a number of nations.

The further results show that integration agreements with the EU have significant and positive effects on attraction of FDI. $AAMA_{jt}$, and $EUMA_{jt}$ variables appear with 0,011%, and 0,012% coefficients in 2SLS; and 0,012% and 0,010% in GMM, correspondingly.

The Association Agreements form a free-trade area with the EU, remove trade barriers, and allow free access to the EU market. Thus, in the early 1990s, when the AAs with the CEE countries were signed, the countries were afforded access to a market with a population of 380 million, and $7711 billion GDP. Current AAs provide access to a market of already 506 million people and $17868 billion GDP (UNCTAD 2016d). Foreign investors cannot but use the opportunity to supply such a huge and significant market.

Access to the EU market has the stronger effect according to the t-value. Thereby, the reduction of internal trade costs associated with regional integration affected volumes and patterns of FDI both into and within the integrated area. This made the CEECs more attractive to foreign investors from the US and Japan that wanted to bypass the EU's external trade barriers so as to gain access to the whole European market. Moreover, reduced trade barriers stimulated a shift of EU production towards countries with relatively low production costs (negative sign of WAGE supports this statement). A decrease in tariff barriers pushes FDI in the CEECs which confirms off-shoring and export-platform motives. However, we do not observe the sources of FDI, and that is why we are not able to conclude whether inflows from inside or outside of the region dominate in CEE.

According to the t-value, the effect of market access after becoming an EU member-country is weaker than the effect after signing the AAs. The reason behind is that CEE enjoyed free access to the EU market for many years before their accession to the EU. Companies that wanted to benefit from it had invested in these countries long before they became full EU members. Moreover, newly accessible markets are usually distant lands. As previous literature suggests, proximity plays an important role both for FDI and trade flows (Altononte and Guagliano 2003; Carstensen and Toubal 2004). Taking labour cost differences into account also, CEE countries are most unlikely to become export-platforms for Asian, African, Latin American and Oceania countries. Therefore, significant changes in FDI inflow around or following accession to the EU are not to be expected.

These results have important implications for understanding the determinants of FDI. European integration expands the determinants of FDI from the level of the country to the level of the whole region. As a result, the complete set of FDI determinants includes both country and neighbourhood characteristics.

Another aspect of European integration is the ongoing transformation of the countries in CEE to market economies (institutional transformation). Thus, the signing of the AAs indicates a favourable investment climate, as it guarantees investors the country's adherence to certain economic standards, as well as the adoption of regulations designed to harmonise its business and legal environment with that of the EU. However, the effect of AAs dummies is not significant. We can conclude that in the case of the AAs, the effect of market access is stronger than the effect of institutional reforms.

Nevertheless, we found the effects of EU accession from the application for membership onwards are positive and statistically significant (specification (9)). The processes determining EU membership are based on an evaluation of progress in transition, which is a determining factor of FDI. Integrating countries became more attractive to foreign investors as their economic systems and regulatory frameworks became more similar to those of the Union, and as the dynamic effects of the association agreements began to manifest themselves. The admission into the Union raises the likelihood of free trade with the EU member states and the adoption of EU law.

The accession countries also developed the institutional framework to administer and properly channel the variety of funds available from European Community sources for assisting economic development. In their search for international competitiveness under EU membership, some accession countries are also lowering their corporate taxes. This combination of factors, combined with a favourable business climate, highly skilled workforce and free access to the rest of the EU market, made the accession countries attractive locations for FDI. This applied particularly to efficiency-seeking FDI.

Thus, we also observe the confirmation of our hypothesis—the greater the degree of trade integration, the larger the increase in each market's potential, hence the higher the obtainable profits are by relocation production through FDI. While the European Agreements have implied an opening up of the markets only for trade, capital and factor movements, the EU accession has involved an economic and political change within the candidate countries. This has an impact on inward FDI into CEE.

On average, CEECs are predicted to receive about 0,58% more FDI after they apply for membership, 0,51% after they are granted candidate status and 0,76% after membership negotiations with the EU start. The effect is even more apparent if we advert to specification (10) with lagged variable values (See Table 4.22). Four variables appear with a significant coefficient. We may conclude that the effects resulting from the EU announcements are stronger with time.

In constructing a linear chart on coefficients of specification (8), where the nine dummy variables are designed to measure the effect of the EU announcements, we proved that this effect increases over time. The significant result of the variables supports the hypothesis that even deeper EU integration of the CEE countries contributes to a greater increase in FDI inflows (see Fig. 4.6). The empirical results reinforce the assumptions provided in Sect. 2.4.

From Fig. 4.6 we can also conclude that the EU accession negotiation process and the FDI inflows are not a simple monotonic relationship. Hence, we assume that the positive effect of the integration diminishes as a country becomes a full member of the EU than at the accession negotiation stage mostly because membership in the EU does not imply further economy transformations.

Thus, the countries that have successfully implemented transition policies join the EU relatively quickly, which further accelerates FDI and generates more growth and development. In contrast, countries that are less successful in implementing transition policies gain less FDI because they are less attractive for investors in this context, and also, because in the near future they will not become full members of the EU and be able to enjoy the advantages of membership.

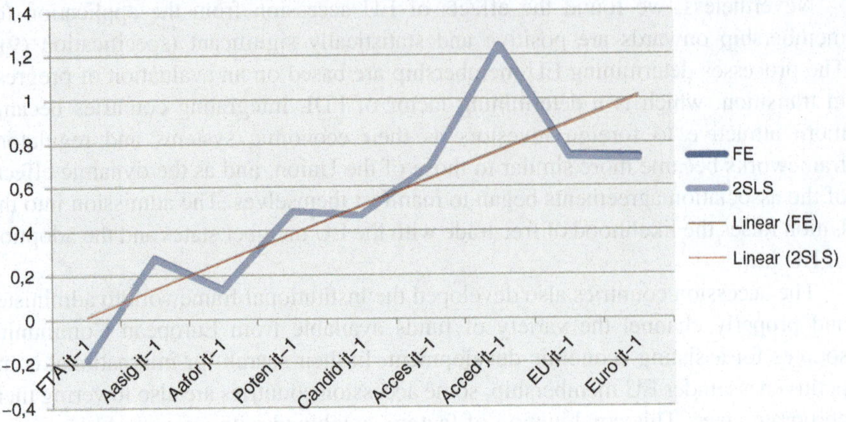

Fig. 4.6 The coefficients of the integration stages. *Source*: Author's calculations. *Note*: Complete estimations are in Tables 4.18 and 4.21

In spite of the fact that we used other proxies to estimate the effect of EU integration, we obtained results in line with the previous findings. Bevan and Estrin (2004) concluded that EU announcements about potential accession have significant independent effects on FDI flows to transition countries.

Clausing and Dorobantu (2005) showed that future EU members receive more foreign direct investment. Results indicate that the Copenhagen announcement is associated with positive and statistically significant effects on foreign direct investment, and after the release of *Agenda 2000*, both first and second wave countries experienced continued simulative effects regarding foreign direct investment.

4.3.4 Future FDI Flows

We now turn to the question of whether FDI inflows in the CEECs are close to their "normal" levels, or whether they are overestimated or underestimated by investors in some countries. For this purpose, we compare fitted and observed values of inward FDI.

We use the estimated by 2SLS coefficients of the specification (7) to calculate the expected FDI levels for the period 1992–2015. Although these countries have seen differing progress in terms of integration and stabilisation, they follow the same transition and integration strategies.

Appendix H reports the expected and actual annual FDI inflows. The expected levels of inflow fit well with the observed values of inward FDI in CEE, with only minor differences between them. However, as can be seen from Fig. 4.18 in Appendix K, the early periods of transition are characterised by shortfalls in FDI inflow. In the mid-1990s FDI inflows reached the corresponding amounts. Thus, both good macroeconomic performance and integration have contributed to the growth of FDI in the transition economies.

We can also identify a period of economic boom, 2005–2009, when the observed values surpassed the estimated values. Indeed, this period is characterised by excessive investor activity in the CEECs (see Sect. 2.2.3).

Further, we mark out a dramatic drop in FDI. This supports our conclusions in Sect. 2.2.4, that the FDI inflows in CEE overestimated the consequences of the economic crisis. During this period, considerable differences between estimated and real values are observed in Lithuania, Latvia, and Slovenia. The empirical results confirm our observations that these countries experienced the strongest reduction in FDI inflow among all CEE countries what amounted decline by 2–4 times.

We can conclude that our model performs well. Our findings suggest that a large part of the FDI inflows to these countries can be attributed to macroeconomic performance and integration progress, including the positive effects of increased market access. Moreover, since we employ FE estimators, we also account for the effect of each country's economic characteristics on FDI inflow. In this regard, the starting conditions of transformation are also covered by our estimations.

Therefore, from our findings, FDI inflows in CEE can be forecasted and evaluated based on these countries' macroeconomic characteristics and the trade agreements signed.

In this part, we also want to estimate the amount of FDI adjusted to the integration effect. Figure 4.7 accounts for the effect of the AAs and EU membership on FDI inflows. Since FDI inflows are volatile, the effect of EU integration is not good observable.

That is why we also constructed the difference plot to show the additional FDI inflows generated under influence of EU integration (Fig. 4.8). Our estimations show that integration with the EU has brought an additional $215,52 billion to the region since 1992.

On the whole, the effect of improved access to neighbouring markets had a continuous and significant effects upon countries' attractiveness for multinationals.

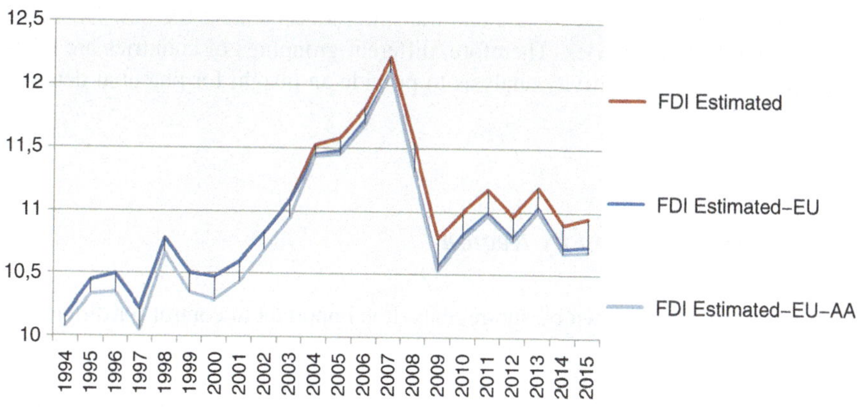

Fig. 4.7 FDI inflows in CEE less integration effect. *Source*: Author's calculations. *Note*: Based of the 2SLS FE estimations

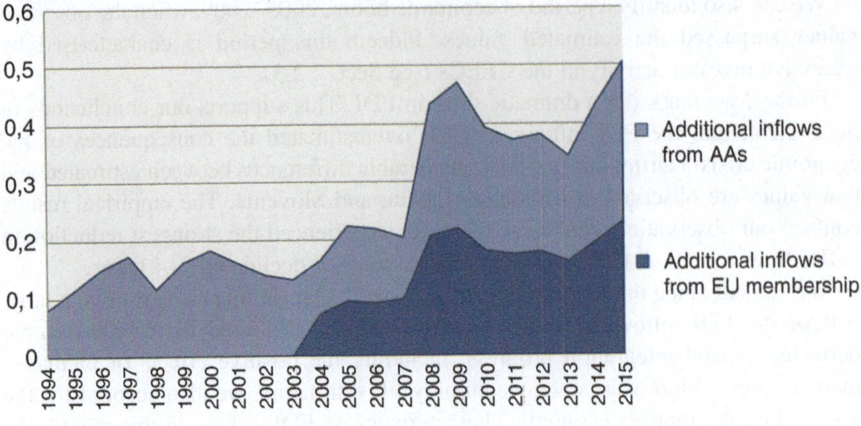

Fig. 4.8 Estimated effect of integration. *Source*: Author's calculations. *Note*: Based of the 2SLS FE estimations

4.4 Subtests

Although our results appear to be economically sound, there remains some possibility that the reported coefficients may be subject to bias given that the panel regression explores FDI determinants across CEE countries at different stages of transition and integration. In this section, we attempt various decompositions of our sample, namely by geographic region and time periods. This is to determine whether our aggregate results dissemble some important sub-trends. In addition, the estimates of this section will serve as extra tests to assess the robustness of the aggregate relationship between European integration and FDI in the smaller sub-samples.

As stated in the literature, the empirical results are most sensitive to the selected sample and selected time period (Heckman 1979). The existing sample exhibits large discrepancies in terms of economic and transition levels among the new EU members and candidate countries. Therefore, different groupings of countries are taken into account for the sensitivity analysis to provide an insight for potential determinants of FDI.

4.4.1 Decomposition by Region

We begin with a breakdown by sub-regions. It is important to control for differences across the main European regions because such differences may influence FDI inflows.

Firstly, we follow the procedure employed by Holland and Pain (1998) and test for common parameters using four country groups. Groups are formed on the basis of their inclusion in the accession process:

- Eight Central European (CE) countries (the Czech Republic, Estonia, Hungary, Latvia, Lithuania, Poland, Slovakia, and Slovenia) that joined the EU in 2004;

- South-East European (SEE) countries (Bulgaria, Romania, Croatia), the first two countries joined the EU in 2007. Croatia became the 28th member state of the EU on the 1st of July, 2013;
- Three former members of the Soviet Union that signed the Accession Agreements in 2014, namely Georgia, the Republic of Moldova, and Ukraine (GMU);
- The Western Balkans (WB) (Serbia, Bosnia and Herzegovina, Montenegro, Macedonia and Albania), the future members of the EU, that are at their different stages of integration with the EU (see Table 2.3).

The results of these tests also can be compared with the previous studies that estimated the effects of integration in smaller samples (see Table 2.1).

We re-estimate Eq. (4.2) allowing for separate slope parameters in each of the distinct country groups. The OLS and FE estimates of the baseline model (7) and (9) are shown in Appendix L. Both the coefficient values and their significance levels are not too different from the reference specification.

The coefficients on market size (GDP) are somewhat larger for GMU than in the reference model, and significant at 0,1%. That indicates that from three countries in the subregion, Ukraine, the largest country, attracted significantly more FDI mostly thanks to its market size. The strongest effect of GDP growth rate was also observed in CE. Indeed, Poland and the Czech Republic, the fastest growing economies in the region, were the leading recipients of FDI.

Wages appear with positive sign and 10% level of significance in CE. Probably, the reason for this is that FDI is attracted in sectors where high-skill labour is required. Indeed, the CE countries possess a higher level of knowledge in comparison to other countries of the region. This assumption is confirmed by the agglomeration effect. The agglomeration effect is present for the non-CE countries, but not in the CE countries. The greater importance of agglomeration in the non-CE countries is consistent with greater externalities in the manufacturing sector and positive externalities arising from specialized and low-cost labour.

Thus, the different FDI motives explain different patterns in non-CE and CE countries. In the non-CE countries that receive FDI mostly in the manufacturing sector, institutions and agglomeration are the main considerations for investors (Kinoshita and Campos 2003). Moreover, the significant evaluation for agglomeration shows investors are more likely to invest in markets that have been explored by others.

The effect of the integration is not uniform among CEE sub-regions. The FTAs have a negative influence for FDI inflows. In the GMU, the membership in FTA costs −0,05% decrease in FDI inflow; similarly in the WB it results in −0,06% decrease of FDI inflows. Signing of the Association Agreements is statistically significant in SEE and in CE. This effect appears because we estimate countries in different stages of integration: CE and SEE had more time to enjoy the positive contribution of EU integration towards FDI inflow, whereas the inclusion of the WB and GMU countries lasts only for a few years.

The role of EU membership in CE was the most evident and important among other regions. Results show that membership of the European Union brought CE countries a 0,015% rise in FDI inflow what is higher than average region value.

These findings are in line with Brenton et al. 1998) who made the distinction between first-round EU candidates (Poland, Hungary, Czech Republic), second-round candidates (Slovakia, Bulgaria, Romania) and CIS. They proved that the first-round EU candidates always take in the highest value of FDI from Europe and Finland, followed by the second-round and then by CIS.

Altomonte and Guagliano (2001) also discovered a greater capacity of CE in the attraction of FDI flow with respect to the Mediterranean countries due to the higher degree of integration achieved among the CE countries.

The coefficients of the macroeconomic factors in specification (9) are similar to the specifications (7). However, some important findings need to be mentioned.

We found potential candidate, candidate and accession status to have positive and statistically significant effects in the CE and SEE countries. However, the impact of the announcements was stronger in SEE. These findings are in line with findings of Clausing and Dorobantu (2005) that the release of the Agenda 2000 in July 1997 affected foreign direct investment in the first wave and second wave countries differently. The announcements had a large and statistically significant in the second wave countries, but positive and less significant effects in the first wave countries.

The difference in the strength of the effect lies in the intensity and speed of the reforms associated with European integration. The SEE countries were a relatively long time in AAs with the EU before they were recognised as candidate countries. Therefore, they implemented the most changes during that period. This is confirmed by the positive and significant effect of the AAs. On the contrary, the CE countries quickly adopted all necessary reforms and were immediately granted candidate status (Clausing and Dorobantu 2005).

4.4.2 Decomposition by Time Periods

Next, we turn to breaking down a full sample into separate time periods. We want to test whether European integration has a stronger or weaker effect on the inflow of FDI during different steps of the integration and transition process. Thus, we divide the investment experience of the CEE countries into four shorter periods: 1992–1998, 1999–2004, 2005–2008, 2009–2015, in accordance with the announcements and integration waves. The results of these experiments are summarised in Appendix M.

The first group includes 1992–1998 years. Policy changes in the countries of Central and Eastern Europe were very dramatic. During this time agglomeration appears to be the most important determinant of net FDI inflows. In early 1990s there were many uncertainties in the region, which is why FDI mostly presented itself in the reliable countries which opened up shortly before the collapse of the Soviet Union (Czechoslovakia, Poland and Hungary). As the result, most of the countries of the region became quite attractive for foreign investors because of large domestic markets with relatively high purchasing power. Stern (1997) also examined the patterns of FDI during the first 6 years of transition, and found that FDI was much stronger in countries with macroeconomic stability and stronger reforms (Stern 1997).

We do not find evidence for the presence of correlation between European integration and net FDI inflow during the 1990s. As the economic and political situation was not always stable and clear, the market-seeking motives dominated in the region during that period of time.

Focusing on the latter part of the 1990s, and early years of the new millennium, the motives of foreign investors have changed. The estimated coefficients for this sample are shown in Table 4.28.

The EU accession and acceding countries became more attractive to foreign investors as their economic systems and regulatory frameworks became more similar to those of the Union, and as the dynamic effects of the association agreements begin to manifest themselves. This integration stage increased FDI inflows by 0,64%.

In the third examined period (2005–2008), inflow in CEE grew substantially. 8+2 CEE countries that joined the EU adopted the EU law. The accession countries developed an institutional framework to administer and properly channel the variety of funds available from European Community sources for assisting economic development. Bulgaria, Romania and Croatia also undertook reforms related to judicial independence, accountability, fighting corruption, and tackling of organised crime. All these measures improved the business climate for investors.

Association and partnership agreements also shaped FDI-related policies in various countries such as Albania, Bosnia and Herzegovina, Serbia and Montenegro. EU reforms brought infrastructure investments and gave regulatory stability to the EU single market, but the economic and social costs of adjustment were also high.

The financial and credit crisis significantly impacted the volume of FDI inflows in the fourth period (2009–2015), because it added new uncertainties and risks to the world economy. During the economic and financial crisis, investment flows all over the world dropped due to the reduction of economic activity and loss of confidence in the existing economic and financial system, as a result, many investment plans were cancelled or postponed.

Over this period, we observe the extremely high importance of EU market access and EU-membership dummy variables in comparison to other variables. Neither GDP, nor agglomeration, nor wages interested foreign investors as attraction factors. This supports our assumption that EU membership played a leading hand. This is especially true for periods, when the overall economic decline is observed.

Decomposing the results by sub-regions and time-periods reveals very interesting and important results. This confirms that despite many similar trends in the whole sample there are some specific sub-sample traits that attract investors.

The decomposition results must be, however, considered with a great concern, because of the small sample sizes which affect the reliability of test statistics and limit the variation in dependent and independent variables, therefore preventing efficient estimation.

4.5 Appendix

4.5.1 Appendix D

Table 4.12 Descriptive statistics

	n	Mean	SD	Min	Max	Range	Skew	Kurtosis	SE
Year	520	2002,50	7,51	1990,00	2015,00	25,00	0,00	−1,21	0,33
FDI_{jT}	440	6,42	1,87	0,00	9,90	9,90	−0,88	1,37	0,09
FDI_{jT-1}	421	6,40	1,89	0,00	9,90	9,90	−0,87	1,27	0,09
GDP_{jT}	448	10,03	1,35	7,07	13,21	6,14	0,05	−0,66	0,06
GDP_{jT-1}	430	10,01	1,35	7,07	13,21	6,14	0,05	−0,66	0,07
$WAGE_{jT}$	447	8,30	1,11	4,65	10,77	6,13	−0,66	−0,07	0,05
$WAGE_{jT-1}$	431	8,27	1,11	4,65	10,32	5,68	−0,65	−0,13	0,05
$FTAMA_{jT}$	520	3,47	5,36	0,00	13,17	13,17	0,92	−1,10	0,23
$FTAMA_{jT-1}$	520	3,34	5,31	0,00	13,17	13,17	0,98	−0,98	0,23
$AAMA_{jT}$	520	7,06	12,76	0,00	30,60	30,60	1,25	−0,44	0,56
$AAMA_{jT-1}$	520	6,77	12,57	0,00	30,60	30,60	1,31	−0,27	0,55
$EUMA_{jT}$	520	5,43	11,73	0,00	30,84	30,84	1,69	0,85	0,51
$EUMA_{jT-1}$	520	5,08	11,42	0,00	30,84	30,84	1,80	1,23	0,50
$OPEN_{jT}$	442	98,61	32,40	23,22	185,16	161,95	0,40	−0,25	1,54
$OPEN_{jT-1}$	425	97,63	32,09	23,22	183,43	160,21	0,41	−0,22	1,56
GCF_{jT}	444	24,68	6,72	0,30	59,77	59,47	0,47	2,83	0,32
GCF_{jT-1}	429	24,74	6,77	0,30	59,77	59,47	0,45	2,81	0,33
$GDPGR_{jT}$	433	2,56	6,84	−30,92	54,20	85,12	−0,22	12,65	0,33
$GDPGR_{jT-1}$	414	2,58	6,96	−30,92	54,20	85,12	−0,21	12,21	0,34
FTA_{jT}	512	0,30	0,46	0,00	1,00	1,00	0,86	−1,27	0,02

FTA_{JT-1}	513	0,29	0,45	0,00	1,00	1,00	0,92	−1,15	0,02
$Aasig_{jT}$	512	0,10	0,30	0,00	1,00	1,00	2,63	4,93	0,01
$Aasig_{jT} - 1$	513	0,10	0,29	0,00	1,00	1,00	2,74	5,54	0,01
$Aafor_{jT}$	512	0,24	0,43	0,00	1,00	1,00	1,23	−0,50	0,02
$Aafor_{jT} - 1$	513	0,23	0,42	0,00	1,00	1,00	1,29	−0,33	0,02
$Poten_{jT}$	512	0,07	0,26	0,00	1,00	1,00	3,24	8,51	0,01
$Poten_{jT-1}$	513	0,07	0,26	0,00	1,00	1,00	3,24	8,53	0,01
$Candid_{jT}$	512	0,05	0,22	0,00	1,00	1,00	3,99	13,95	0,01
$Candid_{jT-1}$	513	0,05	0,22	0,00	1,00	1,00	4,18	15,50	0,01
$Acces_{jT}$	512	0,10	0,30	0,00	1,00	1,00	2,67	5,12	0,01
$Acces_{jT-1}$	513	0,10	0,30	0,00	1,00	1,00	2,67	5,14	0,01
$Acced_{jT}$	512	0,04	0,19	0,00	1,00	1,00	4,88	21,89	0,01
$Acced_{jT-1}$	513	0,03	0,18	0,00	1,00	1,00	5,20	25,10	0,01
EU_{jT}	512	0,18	0,38	0,00	1,00	1,00	1,66	0,77	0,02
EU_{jT-1}	513	0,17	0,37	0,00	1,00	1,00	1,77	1,15	0,02
$Euro_{jT}$	512	0,05	0,21	0,00	1,00	1,00	4,27	16,31	0,01
$Euro_{jT-1}$	513	0,04	0,19	0,00	1,00	1,00	4,89	21,94	0,01

Source: Author's calculations, data sources for variables are mentioned in Table 3.1

Note: Values for FDI_{jT}, GDP_{jT}, $WAGE_{jT}$, $FTAMA_{jT}$, $AAMA_{jT}$ and $EUMA_{jT}$ are given in ln; $OPEN_{jT}$, $GDPGR_{jT}$ and GCF_{jT} are provided in %; FTA_{jT}, $Aasig_{jT}$, $Aafor_{jT}$, $Poten_{jT}$, $Candid_{jT}$, $Acces_{jT}$, $Acced_{jT}$, EU_{jT}, $Euro_{jT}$are dummies (either 0 or 1 values)

Table 4.13 Stability tests

	Dickey-Fuller		PP-test	
	Estimate	p-Value	Estimate	p-Value
FDI_{jT}	−7,9799	0,0000	−109,48	0,0000
FDI_{jT-1}	−7,9715	0,0000	−108,2	0,0000
GDP_{jT}	−3,6596	0,02717	−32,423	0,0000
GDP_{jT-1}	−32,423	0,02184	−32,861	0,0000
$WAGE_{jT}$	−6,036	0,0000	−69,519	0,0000
$WAGE_{jT-1}$	−6,0173	0,0000	−69,029	0,0000
$FTAMA_{jT}$	−6,576	0,0000	−98,6	0,0000
$FTAMA_{jT-1}$	−6,6625	0,0000	−101,57	0,0000
$AAMA_{jT}$	−6,9875	0,0000	−98, 6	0,0000
$AAMA_{jT-1}$	−6,8566	0,0000	−100,1	0,0000
$EUMA_{jT}$	−6,3764	0,0000	−87,392	0,0000
$EUMA_{jT-1}$	−6,5599	0,0000	−92,136	0,0000
$OPEN_{jT}$	−5,9349	0,0000	−59,156	0,0000
$OPEN_{jT-1}$	−5,9831	0,0000	−57,294	0,0000
GCF_{jT}	−7,8687	0,0000	−112,88	0,0000
GCF_{jT-1}	−7,7374	0,0000	−109,33	0,0000
$GDPGR_{jT}$	−12,166	0,0000	−205,27	0,0000
$GDPGR_{jT-1}$	−11,929	0,0000	−192,88	0,0000
FTA_{JT}	−6,5992	0,0000	−98,734	0,0000
FTA_{JT-1}	−6,6795	0,0000	−101,61	0,0000
$Aasig_{jT}$	−11,021	0,0000	−185,98	0,0000
$Aasig_{jT} - 1$	−11,409	0,0000	−198,37	0,0000
$Aafor_{jT}$	−6,9287	0,0000	−100,43	0,0000
$Aafor_{jT} - 1$	−6,7993	0,0000	−98,773	0,0000
$Poten_{jT}$	−11,739	0,0000	−191,91	0,0000
$Poten_{jT-1}$	−11,749	0,0000	−192,27	0,0000
$Candid_{jT}$	−11,185	0,0000	−196,7	0,0000
$Candid_{jT-1}$	−11,728	0,0000	−214,75	0,0000
$Acces_{jT}$	−9,169	0,0000	−143,16	0,0000
$Acces_{jT-1}$	−9,1759	0,0000	−143,4	0,0000
$Acced_{jT}$	−16,738	0,0000	−342,57	0,0000
$Acced_{jT-1}$	−17,123	0,0000	−347,89	0,0000
EU_{jT}	−6,3462	0,0000	−86,433	0,0000
EU_{jT-1}	−6,529	0,0000	−91,178	0,0000
$Euro_{jT}$	−7,9947	0,0000	−121,52	0,0000
$Euro_{jT-1}$	−8,0059	0,0000	−121,92	0,0000

Source: Author's calculations

Note: Fisher-type unit-root test based on augmented Dickey-Fuller test and Philipps-Perron tests on each panel

The dummy variables are stationary by construction because it is bounded and can't follow a random walk (Giles 2011)

4.5.2 Appendix E

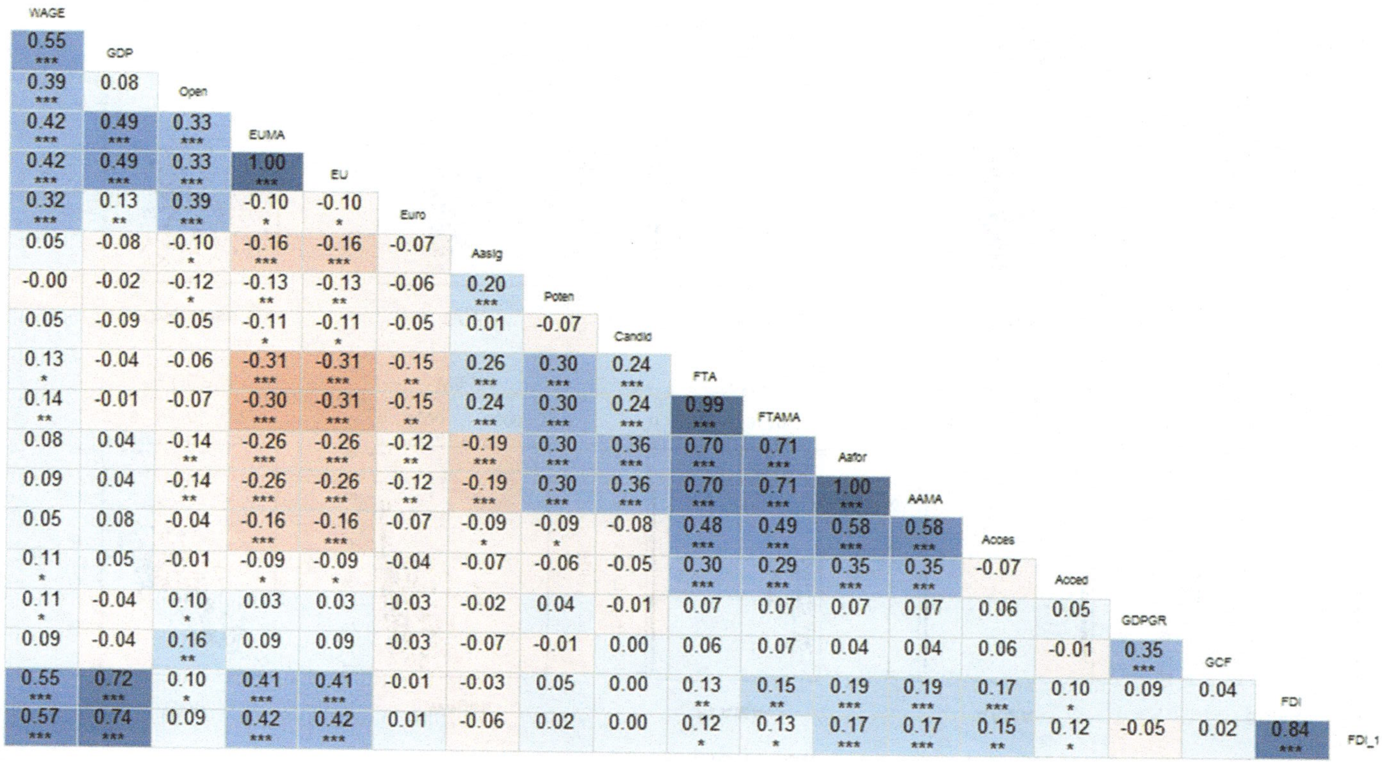

Fig. 4.9 Correlation matrix. *Source*: Author's calculations. *Note*: Signif. codes: 0 '***' 0,001 '**' 0,01 '*' 0,05 '.' 0,1 ' ' 1

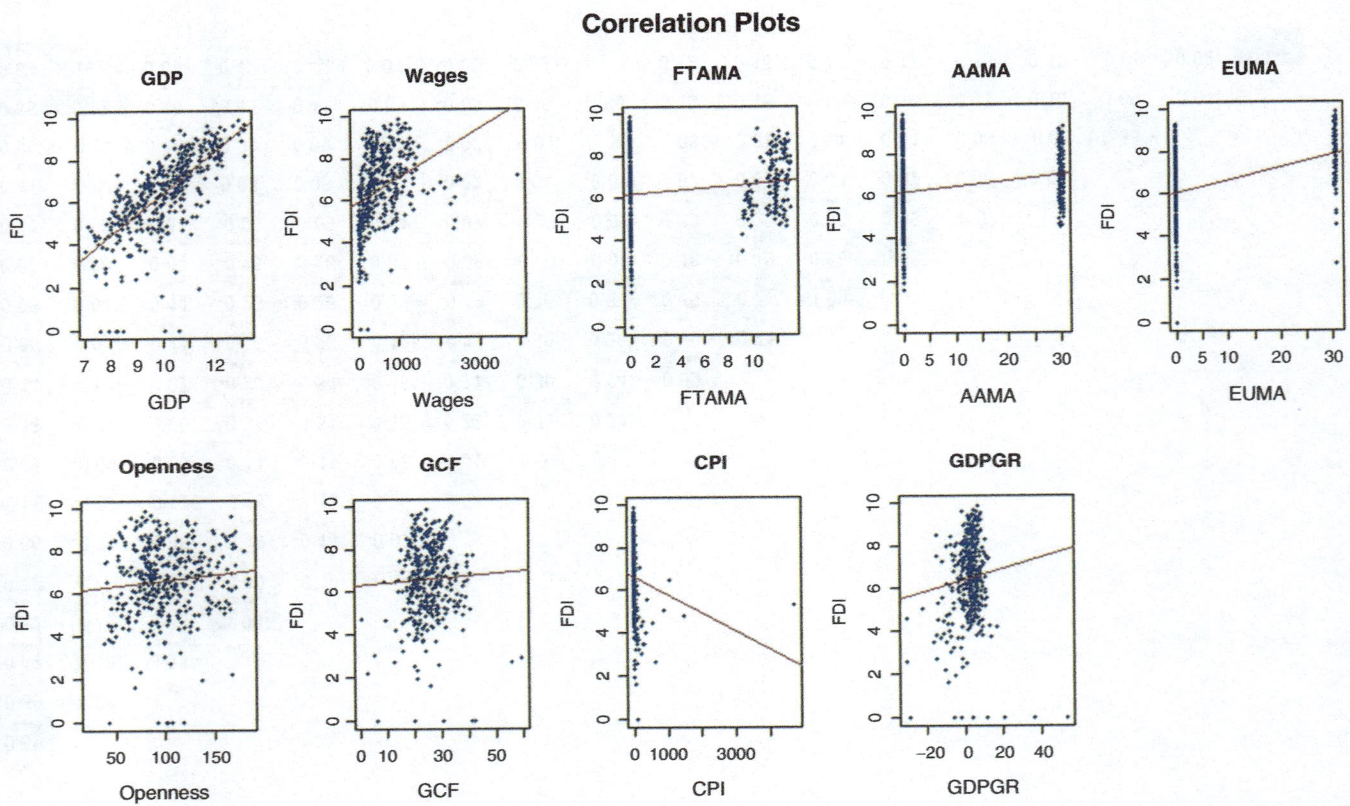

Fig. 4.10 Pair correlations. *Source*: Author's calculation based on UNCTAD (2016c). *Note*: Red line is trend line

4.5.3 Appendix F

Table 4.14 Estimation results, specification (1) and (2)

	(1)									(2)								
	OLS			FE			RE			OLS			FE			RE		
	Coef.	t		Coef.	t		Coef.	t		Coef.	t		Coef.	t		Coef.	t	
FDI_{jT-1}	0,5461	14,62	***	0,4044	9,42	***	0,7459	−0,61	***	0,5660	13,94	***	0,3791	−3,69	***	0,6370	10,14	***
GDP_{jT}	0,3582	7,19	***	−0,2261	−1,27		0,2350	28,02	***									
GDP_{jT-1}	0,0599	1,20		0,7353	4,85	***	−0,0591	9,21	**									
$WAGE_{jT}$										0,3129	6,04	***	−0,6252	6,43	***	0,3037	4,22	***
$WAGE_{jT-1}$										0,0338	0,68		0,9502	−3,69	***	0,0196	0,18	
F-statistics	354,69		***	157,99		***	NA	NA		297,93		***	121,09		***		354,69	
Total sum of squares	1093,60			597,43			NA			1015,90			522,15			NA	1093,60	
Residual sum of squares	301,49			268,16			347,79			315,18			267,98			177,14	301,49	
R-squared	0,7243			0,5511			NA			0,6898			0,4868			NA	0,7243	
Adj, R-squared	0,7172			0,5202			NA			0,6830			0,4592			NA	0,7172	
Hausman test				2,5247		0,0005							21,298		0			

Source: Author's calculations

Note: Signif. codes: 0 '***' 0,001 '**' 0,01 '*' 0,05 '.' 0,1 ' ' 1

In RE NaNs are produced

Table 4.15 Estimation results, specification (3) and (4)

	(3)									(4)								
	OLS			FE			RE			OLS			FE			RE		
	Coef.	t		Coef.	t		Coef.	t		Coef.	t		Coef.	t		Coef.	t	
FDI_{jT-1}	0,5155	13,11	***	0,3872	8,22	***	0,6719	21,24	***	0,5221	11,70	***	0,3754	7,37	***	0,6488	14,08	***
GDP_{jT}	0,3774	7,40	***	−0,0013	−0,01		0,2705	8,49	***									
GDP_{jT-1}	−0,0404	−0,75		0,4281	2,39	*	−0,0658	−2,34	*									
$WAGE_{jT}$										0,3639	6,61	***	−0,5821	−2,48	*	0,3640	6,03	***
$WAGE_{jT-1}$										−0,0195	−0,35		0,9203	4,63	***	−0,1606	−3,23	**
$FTAMA_{jT}$	0,0074	0,69		0,0135	1,12		0,0040	0,44										
$AAMA_{jT}$	0,0076	1,81	.	0,0122	2,48	*	0,0055	1,68	.									
$EUMA_{jT}$	0,0093	2,11	*	0,0175	3,08	**	0,0059	2,10	*									
$OPEN_{jT}$	0,0003	0,22		0,0013	0,48		0,0001	0,19										
$FTAMA_{jT-1}$										0,0035	0,32		−0,0022	−0,17		−0,0052	−0,43	
$AAMA_{jT-1}$										0,0073	1,69	.	0,0109	2,18	*	0,0038	0,85	
$EUMA_{jT-1}$										−0,0001	−0,01		0,0045	0,74		−0,0031	−0,78	
$OPEN_{jT-1}$										−0,0008	−0,50		−0,0006	−0,20		−0,0005	−0,44	
F-statistics	155,11		***	62,80		***	3948,05		***	120,58		***	39,72		***		155,11	
Total sum of squares	919,76			479,49			20178,00			813,51			390,66			NA	919,76	
Residual sum of squares	234,71			213,88			268,00			245,12			216,59			220,37	234,71	
R-squared	0,7448			0,5539			0,9867			0,6987			0,4456			NA	0,7448	
Adj, R-squared	0,7291			0,5160			0,9660			0,6837			0,4144			NA	0,7291	
Hausman test				1,9158		0,01							2,5322		0,00			

Source: Author's calculations
Note: Signif. codes: 0 '***' 0,001 '**' 0,01 '*' 0,05 '.' 0,1 ' ' 1

Table 4.16 Estimation results, specification (5) and (6)

	(5)									(7)								
	OLS			FE			RE			OLS			FE			RE		
	Coef.	t		Coef.	t		Coef.	t		Coef.	t		Coef.	t		Coef.	t	
FDI_{jT-1}	0,5022	12,82	***	0,3808	8,21	***	0,6496	19,89	***	0,5173	11,36	***	0,3552	6,85	***	0,5994	11,96	***
GDP_{jT}	0,4099	7,94	***	−0,0445	−0,20		0,3005	8,70	***									
GDP_{jT-1}	−0,0497	−0,93		0,4351	2,47	*	−0,0766	−2,54	*									
$WAGE_{jT}$										0,3706	6,56	***	−0,6577	−2,77	**	0,3829	6,37	***
$WAGE_{jT-1}$										−0,0199	−0,35		0,9875	4,91	***	−0,1413	−2,84	**
$FTAMA_{jT}$	0,0064	0,60		0,0107	0,90		0,0034	0,37										
$AAMA_{jT}$	0,0073	1,74	.	0,0107	2,21	*	0,0058	1,74	.									
$EUMA_{jT}$	0,0076	1,71	.	0,0142	2,47	*	0,0060	2,03	*									
$OPEN_{jT}$	0,0002	0,13		0,0026	0,98		0,0001	0,11										
$FTAMA_{jT-1}$										0,0032	0,29		−0,0041	−0,33		−0,0073	−0,61	
$AAMA_{jT-1}$										0,0073	1,70	.	0,0107	2,15	*	0,0037	0,82	
$EUMA_{jT-1}$										−0,0003	−0,07		0,0034	0,56		−0,0038	−0,99	
$OPEN_{jT-1}$										−0,0009	−0,53		−0,0001	−0,03		−0,0016	−1,28	
GCF_{jT}	0,0215	3,09	**	0,0295	3,72	***	0,0100	1,93	.									
GCF_{jT-1}										0,0040	0,55		0,0157	1,91	.	0,0222	2,41	*
F-statistics	139,65		***	58,53		***	2307,69		***	105,34		***	35,49		***	NA	139,65	
Total sum of squares	919,68			479,41			13298,00			813,51			390,66			NA	919,68	
Residual sum of squares	228,81			205,75			261,27			244,92			214,31			214,91	228,81	
R-squared	0,7512			0,5708			0,9804			0,6989			0,4514			NA	0,7512	
Adj, R-squared	0,7334			0,5302			0,9571			0,6820			0,4186			NA	0,7334	
Hausman test				2,1924		0,00							2,7374		0,00			

Source: Author's calculations

Note: Signif. codes: 0 '***' 0,001 '**' 0,01 '*' 0,05 '.' 0,1 ' ' 1

Table 4.17 Estimation results, specification (7) and (8)

	(7)									(8)								
	OLS			FE			RE			OLS			FE			RE		
	Coef.	t		Coef.	t		Coef.	t		Coef.	t		Coef.	t		Coef.	t	
FDI_{jT-1}	0,5086	13,29	***	0,3686	8,14	***	0,6451	19,90	***	0,4780	10,34	***	0,3164	6,01	***	0,6579	14,15	***
GDP_{jT}	0,4270	8,45	***	0,2269	0,99		0,3324	9,48	***									
GDP_{jT-1}	−0,0617	−1,18		0,3125	1,80	.	−0,1060	−3,42	***									
$WAGE_{jT}$										0,4370	7,44	***	−0,6082	−2,04	*	0,3458	6,30	***
$WAGE_{jT-1}$										−0,0527	−0,92		1,0582	4,30	***	−0,1372	−3,28	**
$FTAMA_{jT}$	0,0063	0,60		0,0104	0,90		−0,0008	−0,09										
$AAMA_{jT}$	0,0065	1,58		0,0103	2,17	*	0,0068	2,02	*									
$EUMA_{jT}$	0,0071	1,64		0,0142	2,55	*	0,0040	1,36										
$OPEN_{jT}$	0,0000	0,03		−0,0012	−0,43		0,0009	1,10										
$FTAMA_{jT-1}$										0,0030	0,27		−0,0053	−0,43		−0,0107	−0,90	
$AAMA_{jT-1}$										0,0078	1,78	.	0,0115	2,29	*	0,0052	1,27	
$EUMA_{jT-1}$										0,0003	0,06		0,0047	0,78		−0,0037	−1,21	
$OPEN_{jT-1}$										−0,0010	−0,61		−0,0029	−0,99		−0,0012	−1,32	
GCF_{jT}	0,0111	1,55		0,0142	1,68	.	0,0045	0,83										
GCF_{jT-1}										−0,0020	−0,27		0,0035	0,39		0,0169	2,07	*
GCF_{jT}	0,0353	4,37	***	0,0392	4,48	***	0,0308	4,08	***									
GCF_{jT-1}										0,0266	3,06	**	0,0301	3,15	**	0,0202	1,80	.
F-statistics	132,33		***	57,06		***	1777,90		***	96,88		***	32,32		***	NA	132,33	
Total sum of squares	919,68			479,41			11006,00			809,30			383,02			NA	919,68	
Residual sum of squares	217,54			194,64			248,08			235,58			206,44			220,69	217,54	
R-squared	0,7635			0,5940			0,9775			0,7089			0,4610			NA	0,7635	
Adj, R-squared	0,7433			0,5501			0,9517			0,6897			0,4260			NA	0,7433	
Hausman test				2,2951		0,0021							2,6662		0,00			

Source: Author's calculations

Note: Signif. codes: 0 '***' 0,001 '**' 0,01 '*' 0,05 '.' 0,1 ' ' 1

Table 4.18 Estimation results, specification (9) and (10)

	(9)									(10)								
	OLS			FE			RE			OLS			FE			RE		
	Coef.	t		Coef.	t		Coef.	t		Coef.	t		Coef.	t		Coef.	t	
FDI_{jT-1}	0,4920	12,78	***	0,3554	7,71	***	0,5696	16,33	***	0,4675	9,91	***	0,3100	5,86	***	0,5635	10,88	***
GDP_{jT}	0,4591	8,80	***	0,4186	1,62		0,3969	10,01	***									
GDP_{jT-1}	0,0159	0,27		0,2570	1,42		−0,0227	−0,54										
$WAGE_{jT}$										0,4466	7,28	***	−0,9706	−2,87	**	0,4276	7,07	***
$WAGE_{jT-1}$										−0,0467	−0,72		1,2392	4,89	***	−0,1982	−3,19	**
FTA_{JT}	−0,1525	−1,01		−0,0473	−0,27		−0,2531	−1,88	.									
$Aasig_{jT}$	0,0559	0,32		0,0601	0,32		0,1443	0,86										
$Aafor_{jT}$	0,0742	0,29		0,0736	0,26		0,2271	0,95										
$Poten_{jT}$	0,2099	0,93		0,3158	1,29		0,1752	0,79										
$Candid_{jT}$	0,1285	0,48		0,3425	1,16		−0,0526	−0,21										
$Acces_{jT}$	0,2634	0,99		0,4751	1,57		0,2031	0,82										
$Acced_{jT}$	0,0940	0,31		0,1639	0,48		0,0546	0,19										
EU_{jT}	−0,0596	−0,36		0,3017	0,94		−0,0723	−0,64										
$Euro_{jT}$	−0,7640	−3,07	**	−0,2969	−0,76		−0,8193	−4,15	***									
$OPEN_{jT}$	0,0024	1,52		−0,0014	−0,48		0,0030	2,75	**									
FTA_{JT-1}										−0,1956	−1,20		−0,1816	−1,01		−0,6441	−3,28	**
$Aasig_{jT-1}$										0,2017	1,04		0,2790	1,34		0,9843	3,45	***
$Aafor_{jT-1}$										0,1649	0,60		0,1394	0,46		0,8242	2,44	*
$Poten_{jT-1}$										0,2427	1,00		0,4895	1,91	.	−0,2428	−0,83	
$Candid_{jT-1}$										0,0995	0,35		0,4726	1,52		−0,3851	−1,11	
$Acces_{jT-1}$										0,2373	0,83		0,6971	2,23	*	−0,1276	−0,42	
$Acced_{jT-1}$										0,6957	2,09	*	1,2427	3,48	***	0,4681	1,23	
EU_{jT-1}										−0,0284	−0,16		0,7461	2,23	*	−0,1175	−1,16	
$Euro_{jT-1}$										−0,2531	−0,91		0,7401	1,77	.	−0,2996	−1,44	
$OPEN_{jT-1}$										0,0002	0,13		−0,0040	−1,33		0,0025	1,84	.
GCF_{jT}	0,0116	1,61		0,0114	1,33		0,0093	1,55										

(continued)

Table 4.18 (continued)

	(9)									(10)								
	OLS			FE			RE			OLS			FE			RE		
	Coef.	t		Coef.	t		Coef.	t		Coef.	t		Coef.	t		Coef.	t	
GCF_{jT-1}										−0,0003	−0,04		0,0062	0,69		0,0272	3,30	**
GCF_{jT}	0,0332	4,12	***	0,0400	4,52	***	0,0321	4,19	***									
GCF_{jT-1}										0,0245	2,82	**	0,0267	2,79	**	0,0138	1,24	
F-statistics	81,68		***	34,72		***	435,03		***	59,35		***	20,93		***	NA		NA
Total sum of squares	919,68			479,41			4258,10			809,30			383,02			NA		
Residual sum of squares	210,21			191,05			224,39			229,33			197,42			204,72		
R-squared	0,7714			0,6015			0,9473			0,7166			0,4846			NA		
Adj, R-squared	0,7389			0,5475			0,9073			0,6855			0,4398			NA		
Hausman test				1,9223		0,0136							78,5120	0,00				

Source: Author's calculations
Note: Signif. codes: 0 '***' 0,001 '**' 0,01 '*' 0,05 '.' 0,1 ' ' 1

4.5.4 Appendix G

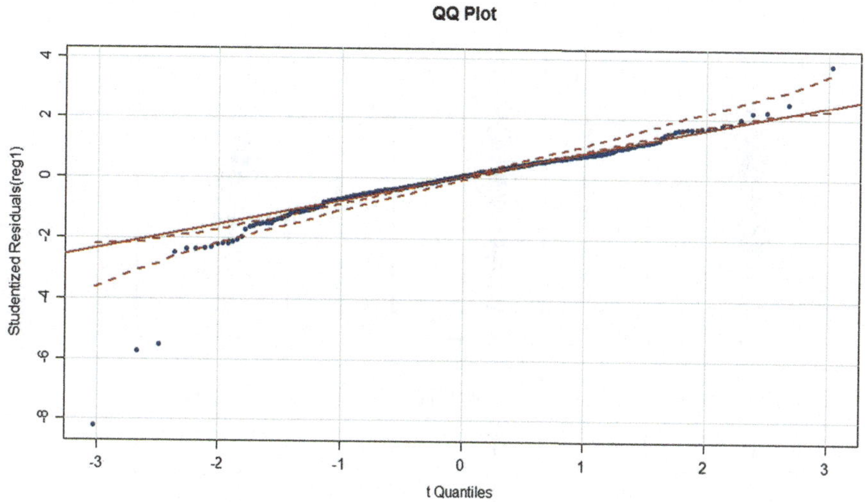

Fig. 4.11 QQ-plot for specification (7) with FE. *Source*: Author's calculations

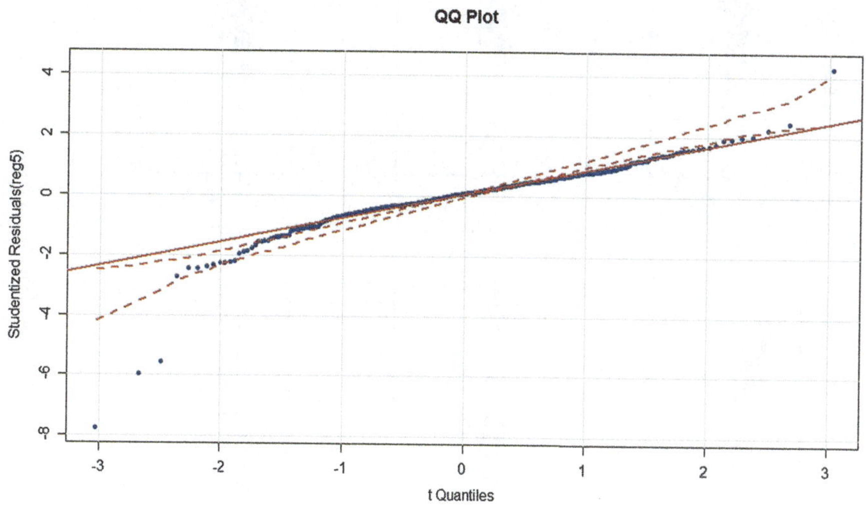

Fig. 4.12 QQ-plot for specification (9) with FE. *Source*: Author's calculations

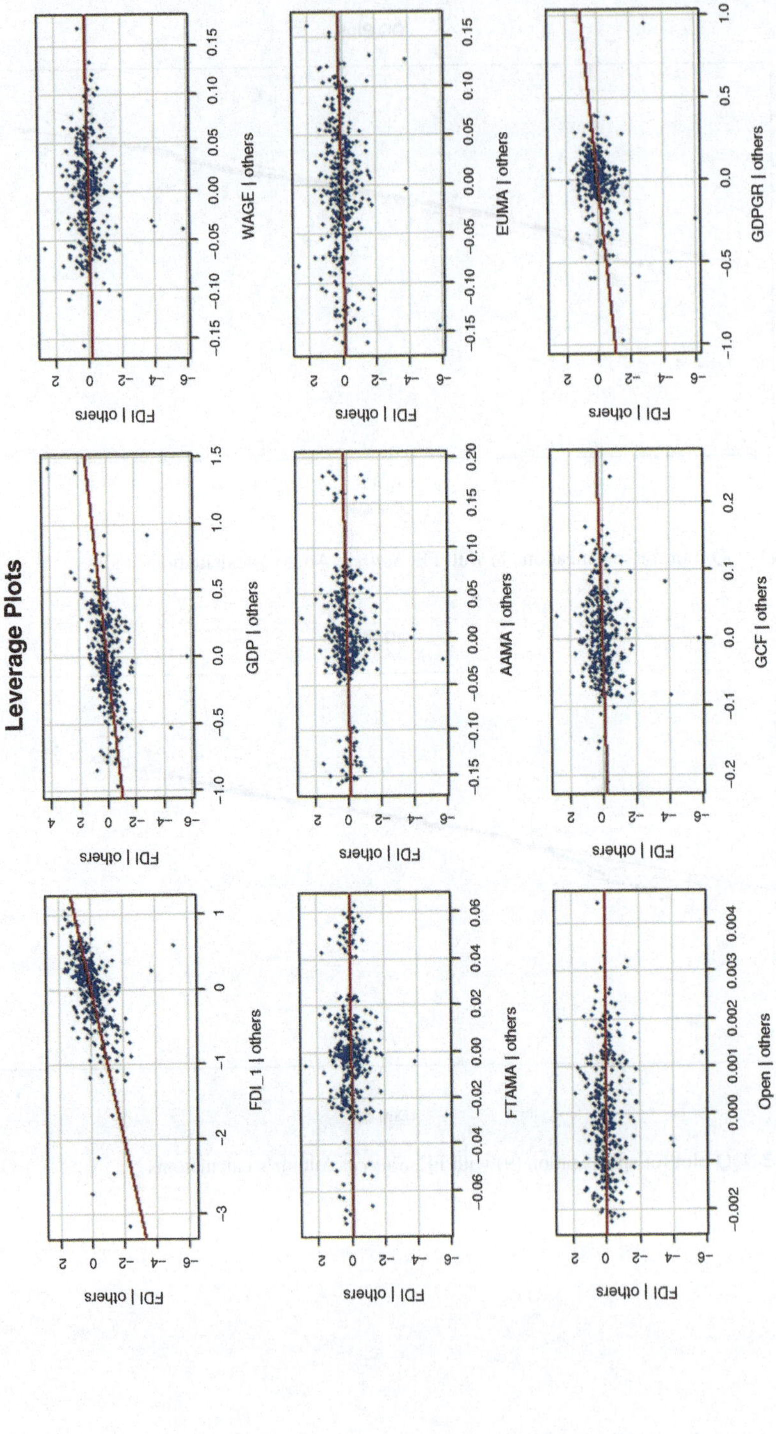

Fig. 4.13 Leverage plots. *Source:* Author's calculations

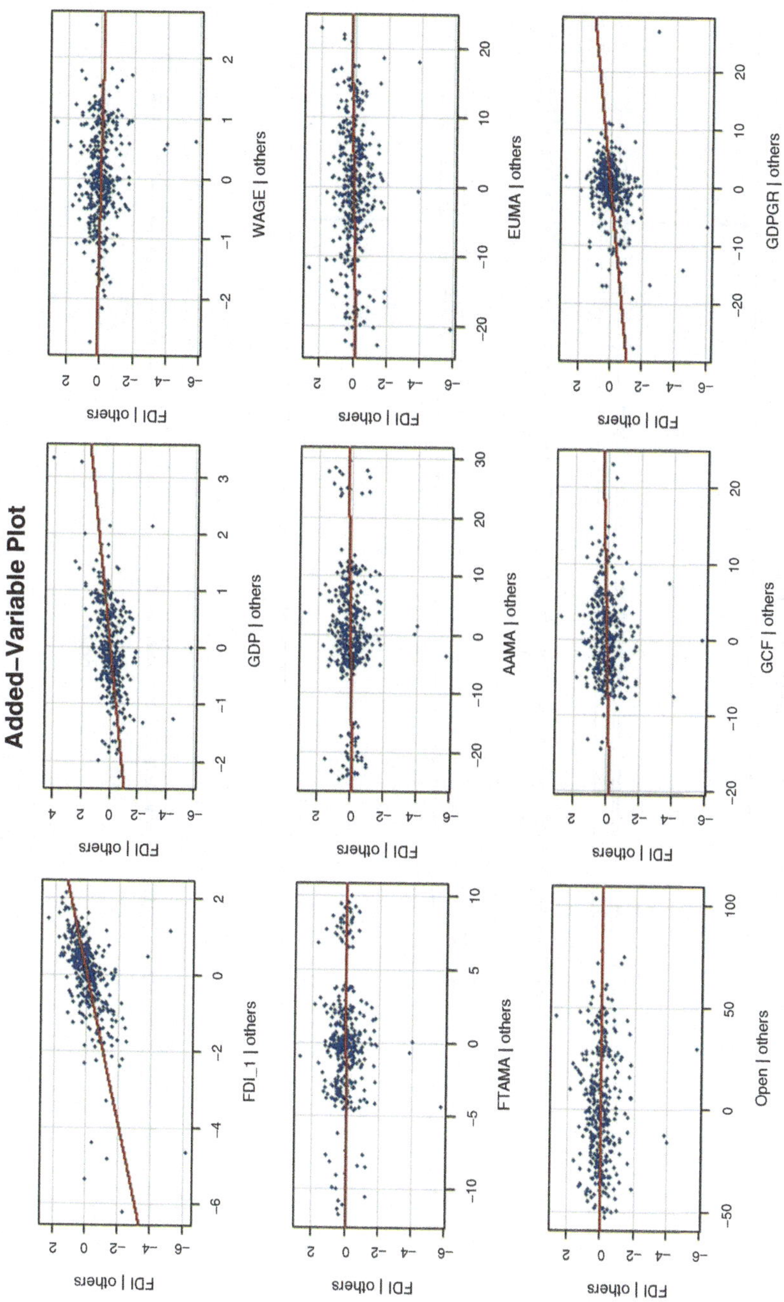

Fig. 4.14 Added-variable plots. *Source*: Author's calculations

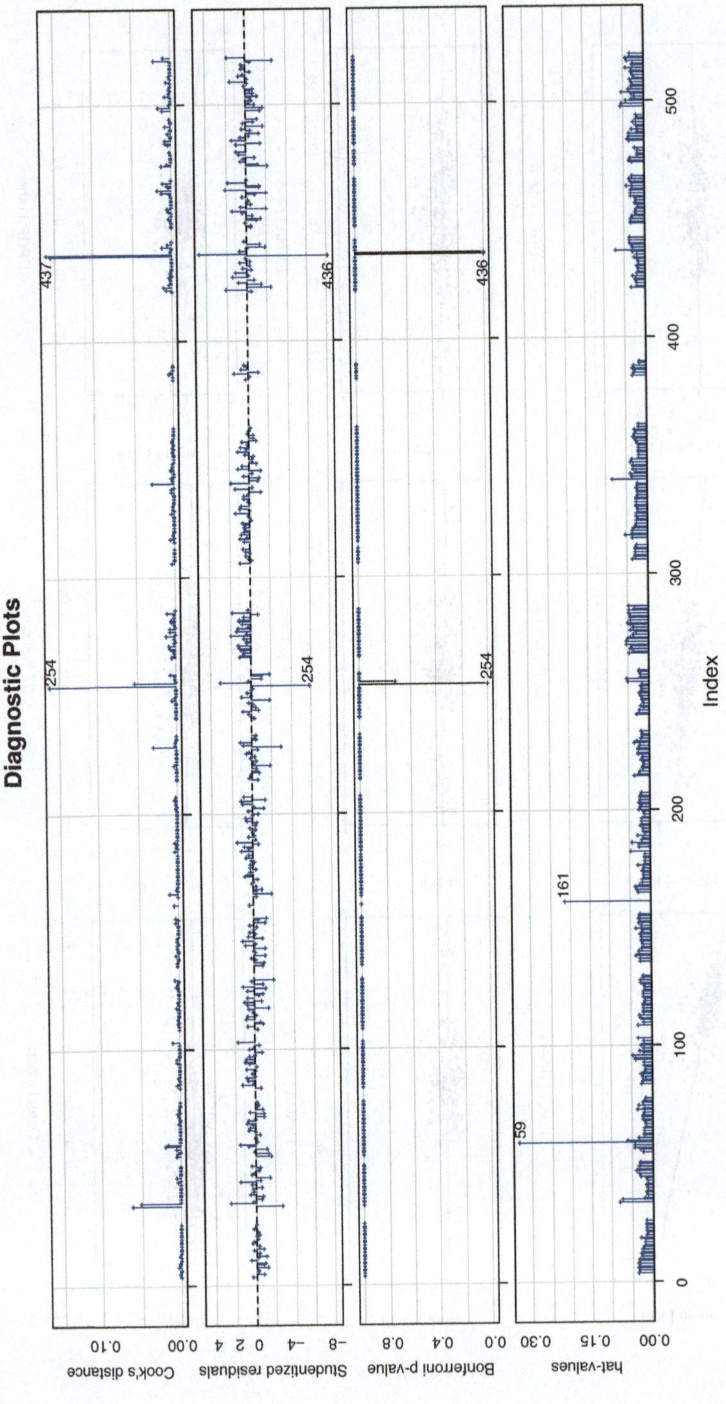

Fig. 4.15 Diagnostics plots. *Source*: Author's calculations

4.5.5 Appendix H

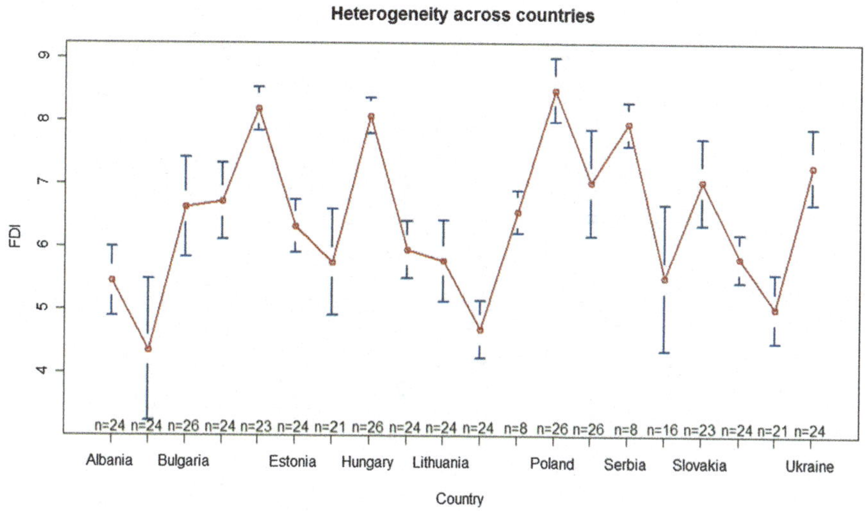

Fig. 4.16 Plot group means and confidence intervals, by countries. *Source*: Author's calculations

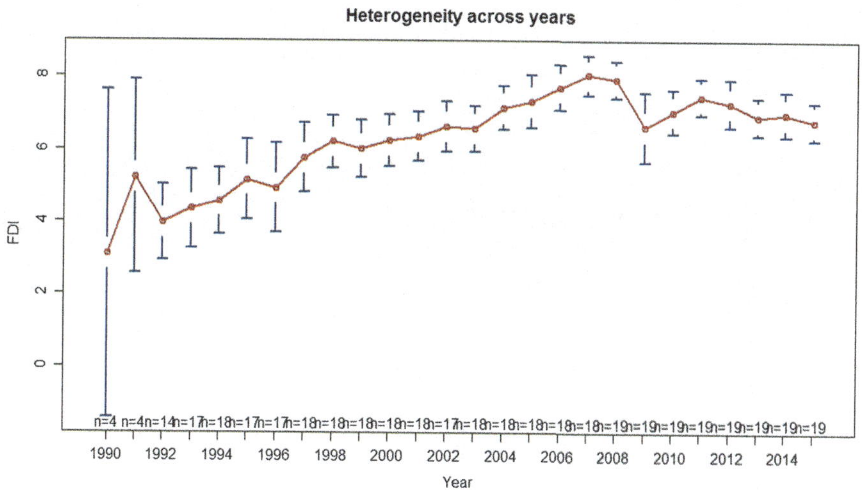

Fig. 4.17 Plot group means and confidence intervals, by years. *Source*: Author's calculations

4.5.6 Appendix I

Table 4.19 Heteroskedasticity consistent coefficients, specification (7) and (9)

	(7)						(9)					
	OLS			FE			OLS			FE		
	Coef.	t		Coef.	t		Coef.	t		Coef.	t	
FDI_{jT-1}	0,5086	6,92	***	0,3686	3,55	***	0,4920	6,00	***	0,3554	3,36	***
GDP_{jT}	0,4270	5,99	***	0,2269	1,08		0,4591	5,66	***	0,4186	1,53	
$WAGE_{jT}$	−0,0617	−1,10		0,3125	1,42		0,0159	0,24		0,2570	1,12	
$FTAMA_{jT}$	0,0063	0,64		0,0104	0,85							
$AAMA_{jT}$	0,0065	2,17	*	0,0103	2,19	*						
$EUMA_{jT}$	0,0071	1,21		0,0142	1,72	.						
FTA_{JT}							−0,1525	−1,74	.	−0,0473	−0,30	
$Aasig_{jT}$							0,0559	0,43		0,0601	0,37	
$Aafor_{jT}$							0,0742	0,34		0,0736	0,30	
$Poten_{jT}$							0,2099	1,10		0,3158	1,59	
$Candid_{jT}$							0,1285	0,63		0,3425	1,32	
$Acces_{jT}$							0,2634	0,99		0,4751	1,76	.
$Acced_{jT}$							0,0940	0,27		0,1639	0,48	
EU_{jT}							−0,0596	−0,45		0,3017	0,70	
$Euro_{jT}$							−0,7640	−2,84	**	−0,2969	−0,50	
$OPEN_{jT}$	0,0000	0,04		−0,0012	−0,65		0,0024	2,72	**	−0,0014	−0,57	
GCF_{jT}	0,0111	1,75	.	0,0142	1,69	.	0,0116	1,95	.	0,0114	1,27	
$GDPGR_{jT}$	0,0353	2,72	**	0,0392	2,43	*	0,0332	2,46	*	0,0400	2,45	*

Source: Author's calculations
Note: Signif. codes: 0 '***' 0,001 '**' 0,01 '*' 0,05 '.' 0,1 ' ' 1

Table 4.20 Heteroskedasticity consistent coefficients (Arellano), specification (7) and (9)

	(7)						(9)					
	OLS			FE			OLS			FE		
	Coef.	t		Coef.	t		Coef.	t		Coef.	t	
FDI_{jT-1}	0,5086	4,89	***	0,3686	3,55	***	0,4920	4,65	***	0,3554	3,36	***
GDP_{jT}	0,4270	2,03	*	0,2269	1,08		0,4591	1,68	.	0,4186	1,53	
$WAGE_{jT}$	−0,0617	−0,28		0,3125	1,42		0,0159	0,07		0,2570	1,12	
$FTAMA_{jT}$	0,0063	0,51		0,0104	0,85							
$AAMA_{jT}$	0,0065	1,37		0,0103	2,19	*						
$EUMA_{jT}$	0,0071	0,85		0,0142	1,72	.						
FTA_{JT}							−0,1525	−0,96		−0,0473	−0,30	
$Aasig_{jT}$							0,0559	0,34		0,0601	0,37	
$Aafor_{jT}$							0,0742	0,30		0,0736	0,30	
$Poten_{jT}$							0,2099	1,06		0,3158	1,59	
$Candid_{jT}$							0,1285	0,50		0,3425	1,32	
$Acces_{jT}$							0,2634	0,98		0,4751	1,76	.
$Acced_{jT}$							0,0940	0,27		0,1639	0,48	
EU_{jT}							−0,0596	−0,14		0,3017	0,70	
$Euro_{jT}$							−0,7640	−1,29		−0,2969	−0,50	
$OPEN_{jT}$	0,0000	0,02		−0,0012	−0,65		0,0024	1,03		−0,0014	−0,57	
GCF_{jT}	0,0111	1,33		0,0142	1,69	.	0,0116	1,29		0,0114	1,27	
$GDPGR_{jT}$	0,0353	2,19	*	0,0392	2,43	*	0,0332	2,03	*	0,0400	2,45	*

Source: Author's calculations
Note: Signif. codes: 0 '***' 0,001 '**' 0,01 '*' 0,05 '.' 0,1 ' ' 1

4.5.7 Appendix J

Table 4.21 2SLS and GMM estimations, specification (7) and (9)

	(7)						(9)					
	2SLS			GMM			2SLS			GMM		
	Coef.	t		Coef.	t		Coef.	t		Coef.	t	
FDI_{jT-1}	0,3557	7,71	***	0,3212	4,60	***	0,3405	7,21	***	0,2707	4,39	***
GDP_{jT}	0,6771	2,12	*	0,7871	3,17	**	1,1354	2,84	**	1,0225	3,20	**
$WAGE_{jT}$	0,0236	0,10		−0,0871	−0,52		−0,1523	−0,61		−0,1496	−0,73	
$FTAMA_{jT}$	0,0100	0,86		0,0037	0,36							
$AAMA_{jT}$	0,0105	2,20	*	0,0106	2,38	*						
$EUMA_{jT}$	0,0118	2,05	*	0,0094	1,62							
FTA_{JT}							−0,1547	−0,85		−0,1009	−0,70	
$Aasig_{jT}$							0,0480	0,25		−0,0161	−0,10	
$Aafor_{jT}$							0,0469	0,16		0,0439	0,18	
$Poten_{jT}$							0,3084	1,24		0,5252	2,53	*
$Candid_{jT}$							0,3593	1,20		0,4619	1,72	
$Acces_{jT}$							0,4528	1,48		0,7356	2,81	*
$Acced_{jT}$							0,0445	0,13		0,2660	0,88	
EU_{jT}							−0,0825	−0,23		0,4122	1,44	
$Euro_{jT}$							−0,7540	−1,71	.	−0,0811	−0,18	
$OPEN_{jT}$	−0,0033	−1,13		−0,0030	−1,23		−0,0032	−1,08		−0,0059	−2,44	*
GCF_{jT}	0,0116	1,35		0,0345	4,76	***	0,0067	0,75		0,0250	2,99	**
$GDPGR_{jT}$	0,0438	4,79	***	0,0691	5,79	***	0,0460	4,92	***	0,0670	6,02	***
Residual standard error	0,7498						0,7534					

Multiple R-squared	0,7853						0,7870					
Adjusted R-squared	0,7688						0,7666					
Wald test	1288		0				1284					

Source: Author's calculations

Note: Signif. codes: 0 '***' 0,001 '**' 0,01 '*' 0,05 '.' 0,1 ' ' 1

GMM is calculated by twoStep method, with Quadratic Spectral Kernel (with bw = 2.30337 for Specification (7) and bw = 2.03927 for Specification (9))

Table 4.22 2SLS and GMM estimations, specification (8) and (10)

	(8)						(10)					
	2SLS			GMM			2SLS			GMM		
	Coef.	t		Coef.	t		Coef.	t		Coef.	t	
FDI_{jT-1}	0,3089	5,79	***	0,5360	8,56	***	0,3097	5,78	***	0,5759	9,23	***
GDP_{jT-1}	0,0780	0,16		0,5159	1,21		−0,9435	−1,44		−0,1813	−0,35	
$WAGE_{jT-1}$	0,5420	1,41		−0,1701	−0,51		1,2214	2,70	**	0,3567	0,99	
$FTAMA_{jT-1}$	−0,0043	−0,35		−0,0077	−0,74							
$AAMA_{jT-1}$	0,0116	2,28	*	0,0170	3,84	***						
$EUMA_{jT-1}$	0,0020	0,32		0,0183	2,78	***						
FTA_{jT-1}							−0,1828	−0,99		−0,2256	−1,84	.
$Aasig_{jT-1}$							0,2763	1,30		0,2333	1,57	
$Aafor_{jT-1}$							0,1358	0,44		0,4549	1,88	.
$Poten_{jT-1}$							0,4906	1,91	.	0,3434	1,62	
$Candid_{jT-1}$							0,4746	1,52		−0,0383	−0,17	
$Acces_{jT-1}$							0,6973	2,22	*	0,0296	0,12	
$Acced_{jT-1}$							1,2392	3,36	***	0,6805	2,45	*
EU_{jT-1}							0,7362	1,76	.	0,5976	1,84	.
$Euro_{jT-1}$							0,7272	1,40		−0,3489	−0,61	
$OPEN_{jT-1}$	−0,0049	−1,54		−0,0064	−2,50	*	−0,0041	−1,31		−0,0014	−0,47	
GCF_{jT-1}	−0,0009	−0,10		−0,0041	−0,51		0,0060	0,62		0,0001	0,01	
$GDPGR_{jT-1}$	0,0363	3,53	***	0,0377	4,44	***	0,0268	2,54	*	0,0282	2,96	*
Residual standard error	0,7864						0,7700					
Multiple R-squared	0,7405						0,7556					
Adjusted R-squared	0,7198						0,7314					
Wald test	968,5		0				1024		0			

Source: Author's calculations
Note: Signif. codes: 0 '***' 0,001 '**' 0,01 '*' 0,05 '.' 0,1 ' ' 1
GMM is calculated by twoStep method, with Quadratic Spectral Kernel (with bw = 2.08167 for Specification (8) and bw = 2.29798 for Specification (10))

4.5.8 Appendix K

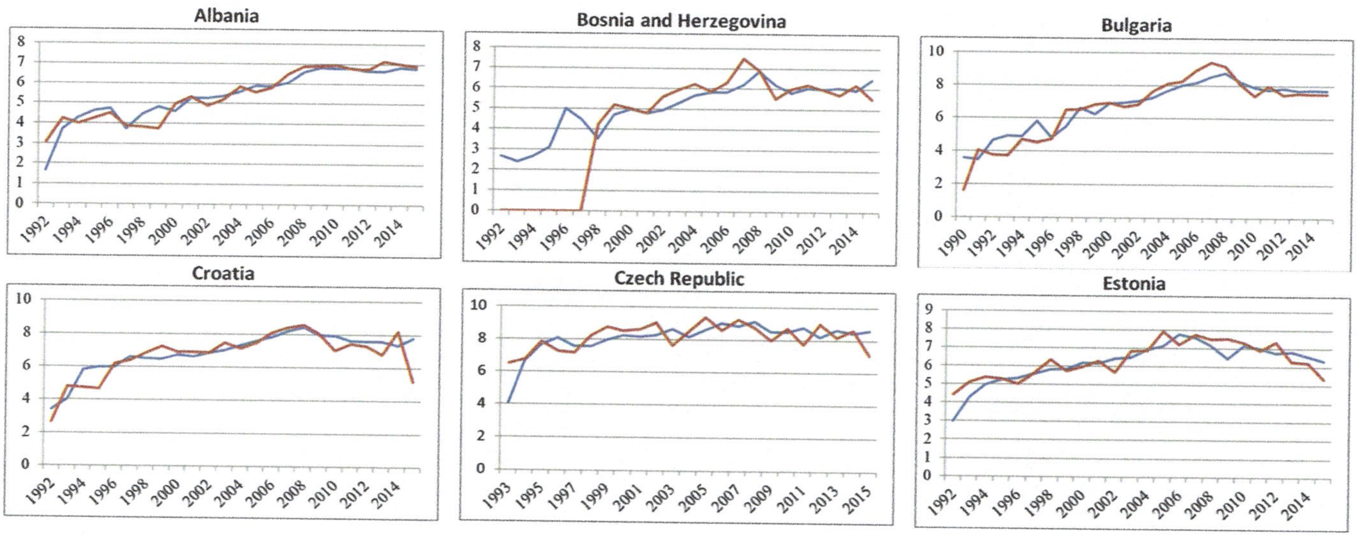

Fig. 4.18 Fitted FDI inflows vs. observed values based on 2SLS FE estimations. *Source*: Author's calculations. *Note*: Blue line is for estimated values (2SLS FE), red one is for observed values of FDI inflows. The data for The former Yugoslav Republic of Macedonia 2002 and Georgia 1995–1996 are not available

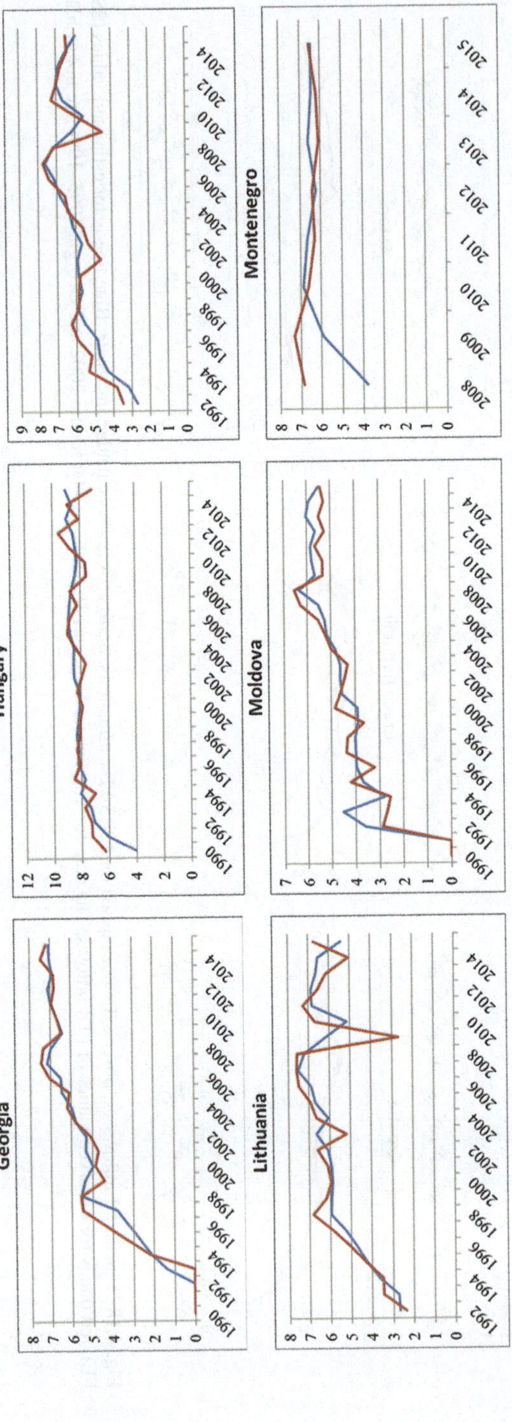

Fig. 4.18 (continued)

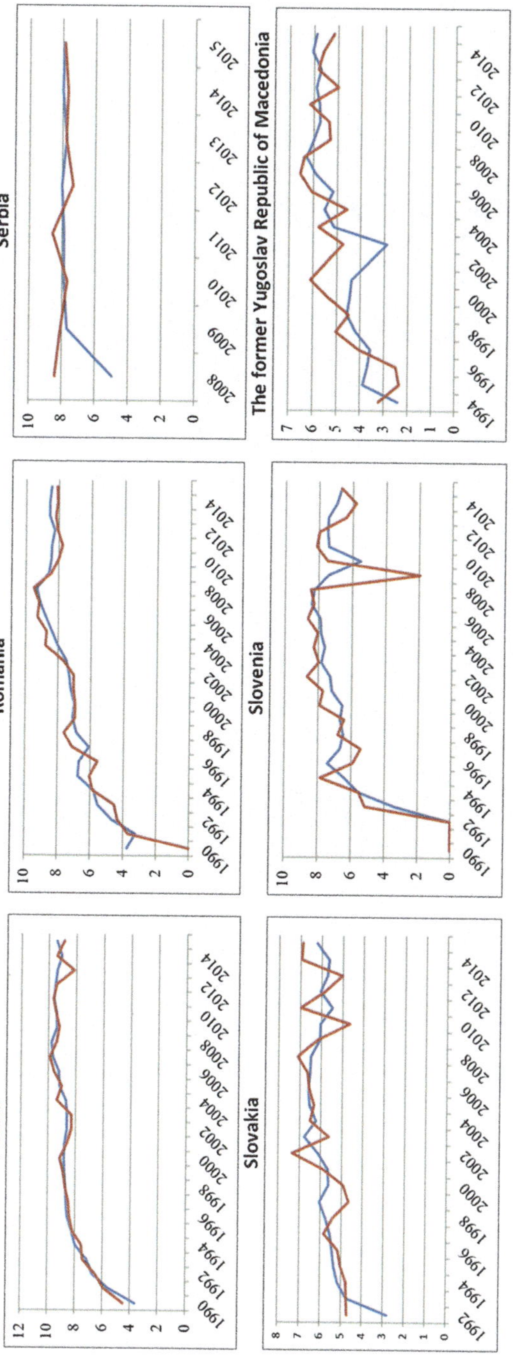

Fig. 4.18 (continued)

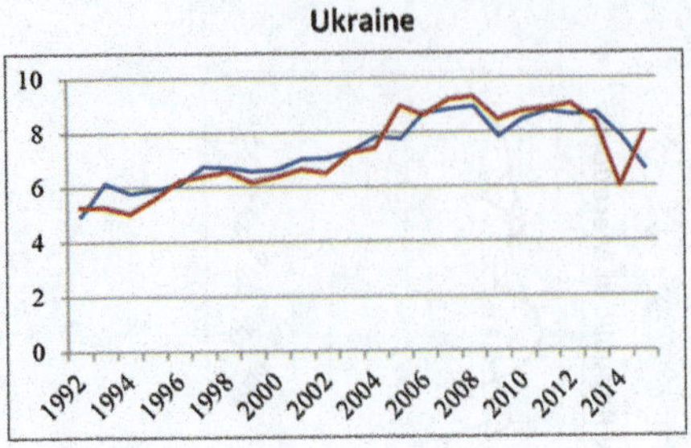

Fig. 4.18 (continued)

4.5.9 Appendix L

Table 4.23 Estimation results for CE subregion, specification (7) and (9)

	(7)						(9)					
	OLS			FE			OLS			FE		
CE	Coef.	t		Coef.	t		Coef.	t		Coef.	t	
FDI_{jT-1}	0,2140	2,89	**	0,1093	1,49		0,2293	3,06	**	0,0952	1,28	
GDP_{jT-1}	0,8375	7,34	***	−0,5651	−1,06		0,8114	6,86	***	−0,6377	−1,11	
$WAGE_{jT-1}$	−0,4586	−2,75	**	0,9642	1,91	.	−0,3046	−1,52		1,0183	2,00	*
$FTAMA_{jT-1}$	0,0008	0,03		−0,0224	−0,76							
$AAMA_{jT-1}$	0,0098	1,15		0,0151	1,82	.						
$EUMA_{jT-1}$	0,0151	2,08	*	0,0208	2,83	**						
FTA_{JT-1}							−0,8038	−1,34		−0,0343	−0,06	
$Aasig_{jT-1}$							−0,1731	−0,25		−0,5520	−0,84	
$Aafor_{jT-1}$							0,1372	0,18		−0,4807	−0,66	
$Poten_{jT-1}$							−0,0521	−0,13		0,2500	0,67	
$Candid_{jT-1}$							0,1354	0,25		0,8086	1,51	
$Acces_{jT-1}$							0,1034	0,23		0,7841	1,75	.
$Acced_{jT-1}$							−0,5095	−0,94		0,2746	0,50	
EU_{jT-1}							−0,6612	−0,91		0,6785	0,85	
$Euro_{jT-1}$							−1,2844	−1,67	.	0,1529	0,18	
$OPEN_{jT-1}$	0,0025	0,98		−0,0010	−0,24		0,0037	1,36		−0,0046	−0,99	
GCF_{jT-1}	0,0352	2,29	*	0,0157	0,78		0,0312	2,01	*	0,0070	0,35	
$GDPGR_{jT-1}$	0,0469	2,67	**	0,0819	4,04	***	0,0597	3,22	**	0,0936	4,43	***
Total sum of squares	349,3			158,9			349,3			158,9		
Residual sum of squares	116,48			96,563			111,88			91,96		

(continued)

Table 4.23 (continued)

	(7)						(9)					
	OLS			FE			OLS			FE		
CE	Coef.	t		Coef.	t		Coef.	t		Coef.	t	
R-squared	0,6665			0,3923			0,6797			0,4213		
Adj, R-squared	0,6282			0,3540			0,6172			0,3656		
F-statistic				4,6259		0,0000				4,6725		0,0000

Source: Author's calculations

Note: Signif. codes: 0 '***' 0,001 '**' 0,01 '*' 0,05 '.' 0,1 ' ' 1

Essentially perfect fit for the RE estimations, summary is unreliable that is why it is not included into the consideration

Table 4.24 Estimation results for GMU subregion, specification (7) and (9)

	(7)						(9)					
	OLS			FE			OLS			FE		
GMU	Coef.	t		Coef.	t		Coef.	t		Coef.	t	
FDI_{jT-1}	0,2817	2,85	**	0,2781	2,51	*	0,2475	2,42	*	0,2472	2,15	*
GDP_{jT-1}	0,5290	6,36	***	0,8003	2,72	**	0,5405	6,49	***	0,7372	2,45	*
$WAGE_{jT-1}$	0,3013	2,77	**	0,1710	0,88		0,3763	3,03	**	0,2744	1,25	
$FTAMA_{jT-1}$	−0,0502	−2,29	*	−0,0596	−2,46	*						
$AAMA_{jT-1}$												
$EUMA_{jT-1}$												
FTA_{JT-1}							−0,5891	−2,29	*	−0,6719	−2,33	*
$Aasig_{jT-1}$							−0,3201	−1,23		−0,2725	−0,99	
$Aafor_{jT-1}$												
$Poten_{jT-1}$												
$Candid_{jT-1}$												
$Acces_{jT-1}$												
$Acced_{jT-1}$												
EU_{jT-1}												
$Euro_{jT-1}$												
$OPEN_{jT-1}$	0,0005	0,14		−0,0007	−0,13		0,0002	0,06		−0,0008	−0,15	
GCF_{jT-1}	0,0150	1,28		0,0124	0,98		0,0132	1,12		0,0113	0,89	
$GDPGR_{jT-1}$	0,0469	4,37	***	0,0490	4,09	***	0,0449	4,15	***	0,0469	3,86	***
Total sum of squares	150,40			87,48			150,40			87,48		
Residual sum of squares	14,03			13,79			13,65			13,52		
R-squared	0,9067			0,8423			0,9093			0,8454		
Adj. R-squared	0,7916			0,7086			0,7794			0,6978		
F-statistic	0,4643		0,6311				0,2341		0,7921			

Source: Author's calculations

Note: Signif. codes: 0 '***' 0,001 '**' 0,01 '*' 0,05 '.' 0,1 ' ' 1

Essentially perfect fit for the RE estimations, summary is unreliable that is why it is not included into the consideration

Table 4.25 Estimation results for SEE subregion, specification (7) and (9)

	(7)						(9)					
	OLS			FE			OLS			FE		
SEE	Coef.	t		Coef.	t		Coef.	t		Coef.	t	
FDI_{jT-1}	0,4885	5,96	***	0,4830	5,48	***	0,4624	5,32	***	0,4696	5,14	***
GDP_{jT-1}	0,1571	0,74		0,1587	0,20		0,1329	0,56		0,6903	0,76	
$WAGE_{jT-1}$	0,1220	1,09		0,2074	0,27		0,0768	0,62		−0,3418	−0,41	
$FTAMA_{jT-1}$	0,0060	0,33		0,0041	0,21							
$AAMA_{jT-1}$	0,0174	1,98	.	0,0166	1,76	.						
$EUMA_{jT-1}$	0,0163	1,16		0,0127	0,71							
FTA_{jT-1}							−0,0019	−0,01		0,0413	0,11	
$Aasig_{jT-1}$							−0,4256	−1,37		−0,4922	−1,48	
$Aafor_{jT-1}$							−0,3018	−0,62		−0,4410	−0,83	
$Poten_{jT-1}$							0,7974	1,93	.	0,8730	2,00	.
$Candid_{jT-1}$							0,7896	1,69	.	0,8449	1,72	.
$Acces_{jT-1}$							0,8565	1,47		0,8632	1,43	
$Acced_{jT-1}$							1,0292	1,52		0,9692	1,36	
EU_{jT-1}							0,5990	1,14		0,4453	0,63	
$Euro_{jT-1}$												
$OPEN_{jT-1}$	0,0009	0,17		−0,0005	−0,07		0,0001	0,01		−0,0013	−0,19	
GCF_{jT-1}	0,0329	2,15	*	0,0326	1,88	.	0,0294	1,80	.	0,0240	1,28	
$GDPGR_{jT-1}$	0,0333	1,99	.	0,0331	1,92	.	0,0392	2,24	*	0,0415	2,28	*
Total sum of squares	133,48			132,05			133,48			132,05		
Residual sum of squares	17,692			17,653			16,228			16,085		
R-squared	0,8675			0,8663			0,8784			0,8782		
Adj. R-squared	0,7399			0,7134			0,6847			0,6586		
F-statistic	0,0614	0,9405					0,2277	0,7972				

Source: Author's calculations

Note: Signif. codes: 0 '***' 0,001 '**' 0,01 '*' 0,05 '.' 0,1 ' ' 1

Essentially perfect fit for the RE estimations, summary is unreliable that is why it is not included into the consideration

Table 4.26 Estimation results for WB subregion, specification (7) and (9)

	(7)						(9)					
	OLS			FE			OLS			FE		
WB	Coef.	t		Coef.	t		Coef.	t		Coef.	t	
FDI_{jT-1}	0,6797	7,20	***	0,3941	3,64	***	0,6359	6,52	***	0,3843	3,36	**
GDP_{jT-1}	0,2951	1,81	.	−0,0022	0,00		0,3049	1,79	.	0,0028	0,00	
$WAGE_{jT-1}$	−0,0608	−0,29		1,1588	2,02	*	−0,1656	−0,71		1,0439	1,60	
$FTAMA_{jT-1}$	−0,0167	−0,70		−0,0597	−2,48	*						
$AAMA_{jT-1}$	0,0000	−0,01		−0,0130	−1,34							
$EUMA_{jT-1}$												
FTA_{jT-1}							−0,4290	−1,36		−0,7972	−2,43	*
$Aasig_{jT-1}$							0,4600	1,24		0,2557	0,69	
$Aafor_{jT-1}$							0,0365	0,08		−0,1104	−0,17	
$Poten_{jT-1}$							0,4891	1,21		0,0978	0,18	
$Candid_{jT-1}$							0,1829	0,43		−0,0986	−0,17	
$Acces_{jT-1}$							0,5675	0,84		−0,3152	−0,32	
$Acced_{jT-1}$							0,7450	1,30		0,0072	0,01	
EU_{jT-1}												
$Euro_{jT-1}$												
$OPEN_{jT-1}$	0,0100	1,55		0,0248	3,39	**	0,0122	1,77	.	0,0257	3,32	**
GCF_{jT-1}	0,0078	0,61		−0,0333	−1,87	.	0,0105	0,79		−0,0314	−1,68	.
$GDPGR_{jT-1}$	−0,0118	−0,61		−0,0273	−1,35		−0,0135	−0,68		−0,0299	−1,39	
Total sum of squares	145,69			100,99			145,69			100,99		
Residual sum of squares	30,741			23,491			28,327			22,806		
R-squared	0,7890			0,7674			0,8056			0,7742		
Adj. R-squared	0,6930			0,6326			0,6532			0,5859		
Hausmann				4,706		0,0022				3,3891		0,0149

Source: Author's calculations

Note: Signif. codes: 0 '***' 0,001 '**' 0,01 '*' 0,05 '.' 0,1 ' ' 1

Essentially perfect fit for the RE estimations, summary is unreliable that is why it is not included into the consideration

4.5.10 Appendix M

Table 4.27 Estimation results for 1990–1998 time period, specification (7) and (9)

	(7)									(9)								
	OLS			FE			RE			OLS			FE			RE		
P1	Coef.	t		Coef.	t		Coef.	t		Coef.	t		Coef.	t		Coef.	t	
FDI_{jT-1}	0,5221	7,22	***	0,3610	2,90	**	0,5503	8,10	***	0,5129	6,89	***	0,3555	2,63	*	0,5202	7,11	***
GDP_{jT-1}	0,3381	3,04	**	0,5376	0,56		0,3082	3,22	**	0,3802	3,16	**	0,4569	0,44		0,3699	3,20	**
$WAGE_{jT-1}$	0,0715	0,51		0,9246	1,44		0,0720	0,57		0,0447	0,31		0,8219	1,23		0,0449	0,32	
$FTAMA_{jT-1}$	0,0243	1,05		0,0156	0,33		0,0248	1,18										
$AAMA_{jT-1}$	0,0115	1,52		0,0090	0,75		0,0110	1,57										
$EUMA_{jT-1}$																		
FTA_{JT-1}										0,3853	1,26		0,2885	0,49		0,3881	1,31	
$Aasig_{jT-1}$										−0,1376	−0,46		−0,1577	−0,30		−0,1327	−0,46	
$Aafor_{jT-1}$										0,1286	0,31		−0,1387	−0,19		0,1464	0,37	
$Poten_{jT-1}$										0,0401	0,13		0,2099	0,57		0,0289	0,09	
$Candid_{jT-1}$										0,4052	0,85		0,7420	1,25		0,3694	0,78	
$Acces_{jT-1}$										0,2140	0,46		0,4116	0,73		0,1972	0,42	
$Acced_{jT-1}$																0,0007	0,20	
EU_{jT-1}																0,3881	1,31	
$Euro_{jT-1}$																−0,1327	−0,46	
$OPEN_{jT-1}$	0,0012	0,32		0,0066	0,85		−0,0002	−0,06		0,0011	0,28	0	0,0056	0,67		0,1464	0,37	
GCF_{jT-1}	−0,0159	−1,31		−0,0330	−1,39		−0,0094	−0,88		−0,0191	−1,43		−0,0374	−1,35		−0,0173	−1,34	
$GDPGR_{jT-1}$	−0,0040	−0,29		−0,0116	−0,59		−0,0047	−0,35		−0,0021	−0,14		−0,0072	−0,34		−0,0023	−0,16	
Total sum of squares	234,52			63,34			545,27			234,52			63,34			283,15		
Residual sum of squares	41,08			33,24			44,297			40,18			32,14			40,991		

R-squared	0,8248			0,4752			0,9188			0,8287			0,4926			0,8552		
Adj. R-squared	0,7364			0,3338			0,8203			0,7004			0,3225			0,7229		
F statistic	0,8702		0,6							0,8595		0,7						
Breusch-Pagan							5,069		0,02							5,71		0,02

Source: Author's calculations

Note: Signif. codes: 0 '***' 0,001 '**' 0,01 '*' 0,05 '.' 0,1 ' ' 1

Table 4.28 Estimation results for 1999–2004 time period, specification (7) and (9)

	(7)									(9)								
	OLS			FE			RE			OLS			FE			RE		
P2	Coef.	t		Coef.	t		Coef.	t		Coef.	t		Coef.	t		Coef.	t	
FDI_{jT-1}	0,5519	5,15	***	0,0936	0,64		0.5519	5.15		0,5602	5,37	***	0,1029	0,72		0.5602	5.37	***
GDP_{jT-1}	0,3734	2,86	**	0,5101	0,41		0.3733	2.86		0,4147	3,41	**	0,5395	0,45		0.4147	3.41	***
$WAGE_{jT-1}$	−0,0028	−0,03		0,5414	0,55		−0.0028	−0.03		−0,0168	−0,18		0,6355	0,62		−0.0168	−0.18	
$FTAMA_{jT-1}$	0,0868	1,21		0,8069	0,65		0.0868	1.21										
$AAMA_{jT-1}$	−0,0340	−1,24		−2,5221	−1,47		−0.0340	−1.24	*									
$EUMA_{jT-1}$							NA	NA										
FTA_{jT-1}										−0,5152	−1,82	.	−2,2212	−1,88		−0.1022	−0.33	.
$Aasig_{jT-1}$										0,4850	1,10		0,3535	0,79		0.4850	1.10	
$Aafor_{jT-1}$										NA	NA		NA	NA		NA	NA	
$Poten_{jT-1}$										−0,0153	−0,02		−0,2127	−0,30		−0.0153	−0.02	
$Candid_{jT-1}$										0,4130	1,09		0,4259	0,93		NA	NA	
$Acces_{jT-1}$										0,6380	2,80	**	0,6675	2,45		0.2249	0.74	*
$Acced_{jT-1}$										NA	NA		NA	NA		−0.4130	−1.09	
EU_{jT-1}																		
$Euro_{jT-1}$																		
$OPEN_{jT-1}$	0,0026	0,87		0,0022	0,25		0.00257	0.87	**	0,0034	1,17		0,0033	0,38		0.0034	1.17	
GCF_{jT-1}	0,0168	1,23		0,0230	0,95		0.0168	1.23	.	0,0194	1,47		0,0157	0,65		0.0194	1.47	*
$GDPGR_{jT-1}$	−0,0085	−0,36		−0,0168	−0,68		−0.0085	−0.36	.	−0,0080	−0,33		−0,0153	−0,59		−0.0078	−0.33	
Total sum of squares	154,81			19,48														
Residual sum of squares	26,33			16,55														
R-squared	0,8299			0,1505			0,8397			0,8575			0,9030			0.8575		
Adj. R-squared	0,7399			0,1051						0,8354			0,8580					
F statistic				1,8745					0,04	1,7519		0,1						
Hausman				30,02		0,00							49,45	0,00				

Source: Author's calculations

Note: Signif. codes: 0 '***' 0,001 '**' 0,01 '*' 0,05 '.' 0,1 ' ' 1

Some coefficients are not defined because of singularities

Table 4.29 Estimation results for 2005–2008 time period, specification (7) and (9)

	(7)									(9)								
	OLS			FE			RE			OLS			FE			RE		
P3	Coef.	t		Coef.	t		Coef.	t		Coef.	t		Coef.	t		Coef.	t	
FDI_{jT-1}	0,4450	5,33	***	−0,2319	−1,90	.	0,6976	13,93	***	0,0004	0,00		−0,2140	−1,77	.	0,4733	5,59	***
GDP_{jT-1}	0,5742	5,54	***	0,0350	0,06		0,3055	5,32	***	0,0004	0,00		−0,2935	−0,48		0,4947	4,61	***
$WAGE_{jT-1}$	−0,2838	−3,23	**	1,3642	2,58	*	−0,2080	−4,31	***	0,0004	0,00		1,5899	3,05	**	−0,2263	−2,21	*
$FTAMA_{jT-1}$	0,0054	0,34		0,0129	0,81		0,0054	0,45										
$AAMA_{jT-1}$	0,0118	2,09	*	0,0146	1,41		0,0070	2,27	*									
$EUMA_{jT-1}$	0,0049	1,03		0,0072	0,81		0,0036	1,39										
FTA_{JT-1}										−0,0539	−0,24		0,1065	0,50		−0,0655	−0,29	
$Aasig_{jT-1}$										−0,0603	−0,22		0,0838	0,31		−0,0607	−0,22	
$Aafor_{jT-1}$										0,5468	0,97		0,2714	0,48		0,5539	0,99	
$Poten_{jT-1}$										−0,9388	−1,45		−1,5634	−1,93	.	−0,9545	−1,48	
$Candid_{jT-1}$										−0,2348	−0,47		−0,7946	−1,04		−0,2384	−0,48	
$Acces_{jT-1}$										0,0160	0,03		−0,1279	−0,13		0,0188	0,03	
$Acced_{jT-1}$										−0,0970	−0,16		−0,0456	−0,05		−0,0892	−0,15	
EU_{jT-1}										0,1141	0,60		0,1161	0,16		0,1234	0,69	
$Euro_{jT-1}$										−0,2520	−0,59		0,1217	0,15		−0,2477	−0,59	
$OPEN_{jT-1}$	0,0022	1,05		0,0025	0,48		0,0012	1,21		0,0017	0,78		−0,0005	−0,09		0,0017	0,82	
GCF_{jT-1}	0,0139	1,29		0,0430	2,14	*	0,0032	0,58		0,0079	0,66		0,0360	1,78	.	0,0058	0,50	
$GDPGR_{jT-1}$	0,0209	1,19		0,0271	1,56		0,0198	1,32		0,0219	1,24		0,0275	1,61		0,0221	1,26	
Total sum of squares	136,56			18,96			784.77			136,56						163.3		
Residual sum of squares	13,82			7,33			17.264			12,63						12.885		
R-squared	0,8988			0,6131			0.978			0,9075			0,9534			0.9211		
Adj. R-squared	0,7931			0,4255			0,8629			0,7367			0,9275			0,7477		

(continued)

Table 4.29 (continued)

	(7)									(9)								
	OLS			FE			RE			OLS			FE			RE		
P3	Coef.	t		Coef.	t		Coef.	t		Coef.	t		Coef.	t		Coef.	t	
F statistic				3,2594		0,00							6,2662		0,00			
Hausman test				42,824		0,00							26,149		0,02			

Source: Author's calculations

Note: Signif. codes: 0 '***' 0,001 '**' 0,01 '*' 0,05 '.' 0,1 ' ' 1

Table 4.30 Estimation results for 2009–2015 time period, specification (7) and (9)

	(7)									(9)								
	OLS			FE			RE			OLS			FE			RE		
P4	Coef.	t		Coef.	t		Coef.	t		Coef.	t		Coef.	t		Coef.	t	
FDI_{jT-1}	0,2554	2,95	**	−0,1133	−1,32		0,2554	2,95	**	0,1324	1,54		−0,1444	−1,62	.	0,1324	1,54	
GDP_{jT-1}	0,5391	4,67	***	−0,2526	−0,29		0,5391	4,67	***	0,6089	5,50	***	−0,5426	−0,60		0,6089	5,50	***
$WAGE_{jT-1}$	−0,1625	−1,03		−0,1497	−0,43		−0,1625	−1,03		0,0490	0,23		0,0347	0,09		0,0490	0,23	
$FTAMA_{jT-1}$	0,0061	0,23		0,0837	0,92		0,0061	0,23										
$AAMA_{jT-1}$	0,0041	0,42		−0,0109	−0,69		0,0041	0,42										
$EUMA_{jT-1}$	0,0083	1,16		0,0478	2,83	**	0,0083	1,16										
FTA_{JT-1}										−0,7829	−2,05	*	8,2354	1,05		−0,7829	−2,05	*
$Aasig_{jT-1}$										0,0539	0,14		−0,6313	−1,52		0,0539	0,14	
$Aafor_{jT-1}$										−0,8038	−1,32		−0,9170	−1,06		−0,8038	−1,32	
$Poten_{jT-1}$										1,5111	2,93	**	−0,5935	−0,69		1,5111	2,93	**
$Candid_{jT-1}$										0,7012	1,30		−0,5660	−0,65		0,7012	1,30	
$Acces_{jT-1}$										1,8064	2,40	*	−0,4811	−0,44		1,8064	2,40	*
$Acced_{jT-1}$										1,5589	2,27	*	−0,7878	−0,75		1,5589	2,27	*
EU_{jT-1}										−0,4103	−1,10		7,4295	0,95		−0,4103	−1,10	
$Euro_{jT-1}$										−1,3339	−2,63	**	5,9189	0,75		−1,3339	−2,63	**
$OPEN_{jT-1}$	−0,0061	−1,94	.	0,0105	1,40		−0,0061	−1,94		−0,0006	−0,19		0,0142	1,77	.	−0,0006	−0,19	
GCF_{jT-1}	0,0100	0,44		0,0911	2,79	**	0,0100	0,44		0,0308	1,30		0,0947	2,68	**	0,0308	1,30	
$GDPGR_{jT-1}$	0,0796	3,76	***	0,0434	1,82	.	0,0796	3,76	***	0,0725	3,53	***	0,0352	1,35		0,0725	3,53	***
Total sum of squares	221,87			74,78						221,87								
Residual sum of squares	99,86			54,06						83,43								
R-squared	0,5499			0,2772			0,5499			0,6240			0,9920			0,6240		
Adj. R-squared	0,5066			0,2161						0,5454			0,9891					
F statistic				5		0,00							3		0,00			
Hausman				−1311,70		0,00							−2684,25		0,00			

Source: Author's calculations
Note: Signif. codes: 0 '***' 0,001 '**' 0,01 '*' 0,05 '.' 0,1 ' ' 1

References

Agarwal JP (1997) European integration and German FDI: implications for domestic investment and Central European economies. Natl Inst Econ Rev 160:100–111 http://www.freepatentsonline.com/article/National-Institute-Economic-Review/56908891.html

Ahn SC, Moon H (2002) Large-N and large-T properties of panel data estimators and the Hausman test. http://EconPapers.repec.org/RePEc:cpd:pd2002:a6-2

Altomonte C (1998) FDI in the CEEC's and the theory of real options: an empirical assessment. https://ideas.repec.org/p/lic/licosd/7698.html

Altomonte C (2007) Regional economic integration and the location of multinational firms. Rev World Econ 143(2):277–305

Altomonte C, Guagliano C (2001) Competing locations? Market potential and FDI in Central and Eastern Europe vs the Mediterranean. https://ideas.repec.org/p/lic/licosd/10801.html

Altomonte C, Guagliano C (2003) Comparative study of FDI in Central and Eastern Europe and the Mediterranean. Econ Syst 27(2):223–246

Altzinger W, Bellak C (1999) Direct versus indirect FDI: impact on home country exports an employment—Empirical evidence for Austrian FDI in CEECs. Globalisation 1999:131–154

Arellano M, Bond S (1991) Some tests of specification for panel data. Monte Carlo evidence and an application to employment equations. In: The review of economic studies, vol 194, pp 277–297

Asiedu E (2002) On the determinants of foreign direct investment to developing countries: is Africa different? World Dev 30(1):107–119

Atkinson AC (1987) Plots, transformations, and regression: an introduction to graphical methods of diagnostic regression analysis. Clarendon Pr, Oxford. ISBN: 0198533713

Baltagi BH, Li Q (1995) Testing AR(1) against MA(1) disturbances in an error component model. J Econ 68(1):133–151. https://doi.org/10.1016/0304-4076(94)01646-H

Benacek V, Gronicki M, Holland D, Sass M (2000) The determinants and impact of foreign direct investment in Central and Eastern Europe: a comparison of survey and econometric evidence. Transl Corp 9(3):163–212 http://pure.iiasa.ac.at/5953/

Bera AK, Walter SE, Yoon MJ (2001) Tests for the error component model in the presence of local misspecification. J Econ 101(1):1–23

Berglof E, Bolton P (2002) The great divide and beyond: financial architecture in transition. J Econ Perspect 16(1):77–100

Berglöf E, Roland G (1997) The EU as an "outside anchor" for transition reforms. SITE working paper

Bevan AA, Estrin S (2000) The determinants of foreign direct investment in transition economies, 2638

Bevan AA, Estrin S (2004) The determinants of foreign direct investment into European transition economies. J Comp Econ 32(4):775–787

Blonigen BA, Davies RB, Waddell GR, Naughton HT (2007) FDI in space. Spatial autoregressive relationships in foreign direct investment. Eur Econ Rev 51(5):1303–1325

Bos J, van de Laar M (2004) Explaining foreign direct investment in Central and Eastern Europe: an extended gravity approach, 8

Brenton P (1999) Removing obstacles to deeper economic integration in the broad European trade area: Report of the CEPS working party on trade and investment in an enlarging Europe. CEPS, Brussels. ISBN: 9290792574

Brenton P, DiMauro F, Lücke M (1998) Economic integration and FDI: an empirical analysis of foreign investment in the EU and in Central and Eastern Europe. http://EconPapers.repec.org/RePEc:kie:kieliw:890

Carstensen K, Toubal F (2004) Foreign direct investment in Central and Eastern European countries: a dynamic panel analysis. J Comp Econ 32(1):3–22

Clark P, Crawford C, Steele F, Vignoles A (2010) The choice between fixed and random effects models: some considerations for educational research. CMPO, Bristol

Clausing K, Dorobantu C (2005) Re-entering Europe: does European Union candidacy boost foreign direct investment? Econ Transit 13(1):77–103 http://EconPapers.repec.org/RePEc:bla:etrans:v:13:y:2005:i:1:p:77-103

Cook RD, Weisberg S (1999) Applied regression including computing and graphics. Wiley, New York, NY. ISBN: 9780471317111. http://www.loc.gov/catdir/description/wiley037/99017200.html

Cragg JG, Donald SG (1993) Testing identifiability and specification in instrumental variable models. Econ Theory 9:222

Croissant Y, Millo G (2008) Panel data econometrics in R: the plm package. J Stat Softw 27(2)

Dickey DA, Fuller WA (1979) Distribution of the estimators for autoregressive time series with a unit root. J Am Stat Assoc 74(366):427

Dunning JH (1973) The determinants of international production. Oxf Econ Pap 25(3):289–336 http://EconPapers.repec.org/RePEc:oup:oxecpp:v:25:y:1973:i:3:p:289-336

Faeth I (2009) Determinants of foreign direct investment—A tale of nine theoretical models. J Econ Surv 23(1):165–196

Fox J, Weisberg S (2011) An R companion to applied regression. SAGE, Los Angeles. ISBN: 141297514X

Fujita, M, Venables, A, Krugman, PR (1999) The spatial economy. Cities, regions and international trade. Cambridge, Mass: MIT Press. Online verfügbar unter http://search.ebscohost.com/login.aspx?direct=true&scope=site&db=nlebk&db=nlabk&AN=9243.

Giles D (2011) Dummies for dummies. http://davegiles.blogspot.de/2011/03/dummies-for-dummies.html. Accessed Mar 2017

Globerman S, Shapiro DM (1999) The impact of government policies on foreign direct investment: the Canadian experience. J Int Bus Stud 30(3):513–532

Globerman S, Shapiro D (2002) Global foreign direct investment flows: the role of governance infrastructure. World Dev 30(11):1899–1919

Greene WH (2003) Econometric analysis. Prentice-Hall, Upper Saddle River, NJ. ISBN: 0-13-110849-2

Harris CD (1954) The market as a factor in the localization of industry in the United States

Harrison MJ, McCabe BPM (1979) A test for heteroscedasticity based on ordinary least squares residuals. J Am Stat Assoc 74(366):494

Head K, Mayer T (2004) Market potential and the location of Japanese investment in the European Union. Rev Econ Stat 86(4):959–972

Heckman JJ (1979) Sample selection bias as a specification error. Econometrica 47(1):153

Holland D, Pain N (1998) The determinants and impact of foreign direct investment in the transition

ILO (2016) ILO database of labour statistics: mean nominal monthly earnings of employees. http://ilo.org/global/statistics-and-databases/lang–en/index.htm

ILOSTAT (2016) Database: mean nominal monthly earnings of employees. http://www.ilo.org/ilostat/faces/oracle/webcenter/portalapp/pagehierarchy/Page137.jspx?_afrLoop=552230679810060&clean=true#!%40%40%3F_afrLoop%3D552230679810060%26clean%3Dtrue%26_adf.ctrl-state%3Dpak6ybvwc_9

International Monetary Fund (2016) World Economic Outlook Database. http://www.imf.org/external/pubs/ft/weo/2016/02/weodata/index.aspx. Accessed 25 Nov 2016

Iwasaki I, Suganuma K (2009) EU enlargement and foreign direct investment into transition economies revisited. Transl Corp 18(3):27–57

Janssens S, Konings J (1996) How do Western companies respond to the opening of Central and East European economies? Survey evidence from a small open economy-Belgium. Katholieke Universiteit, Leuven

Kinoshita Y, Campos N (2003) Why does FDI go where it goes? New Evidence from the transition economies. IMF Working Papers. International Monetary Fund (03/228). http://EconPapers.repec.org/RePEc:imf:imfwpa:03/228

Kleibergen F, Paap R (2002) Priors, posteriors and bayes factors for a Bayesian analysis of cointegration. J Econ 111(2):223–249

Kleiber C, Zeileis A (2008) Applied econometrics with R. Springer, New York. ISBN: 978-0-387-77316-2. https://doi.org/10.1007/978-0-387-77318-6
Krkoska L (2001) Foreign direct investment financing of capital formation in Central and Eastern Europe. http://www.ebrd.com/downloads/research/economics/workingpapers/wp0067.pdf
Lankes H-P, Venables AJ (1996) Foreign direct investment in economic transition: the changing pattern of investments. Econ Transit 4(2):331–347
Lansbury M, Pain N, Šmídková K (1996) Foreign direct investment in Central Europe since 1990: an econometric study. Natl Inst Econ Rev 156(1)
Meyer K (1998) Direct investment in economies in transition. University, Dissertation – London. Elgar, Cheltenham. ISBN: 978 1 85898 736 1
Phillips PCB, Perron P (1988) Testing for a unit root in time series regression. Biometrika 75 (2):335–346
Puga D, Venables AJ (1997) Preferential trading arrangements and industrial location. J Int Econ 43 (3–4):347–368
Resmini L (2000) The Determinants of foreign direct investment in the CEECs: new evidence from sectoral patterns. Econ Transit 8(3):665–689
Roland G, Verdier T (2003) Law enforcement and transition. Eur Econ Rev 47(4):669–685
Rolfe RJ, Woodward DP (2004) Attracting foreign investment through privatization: the Zambian experience. J Afr Bus 5(1):5–27
Savary J (1997) The French firms motivations for investing in Eastern Europe countries. A study of investors and potential investors. In: Witkowska J, Wysokinska Z, Zofia (eds) Motivations of foreign direct investors and their propensity to exports in the context of European integration process. University of Lódz, Lódz, pp 43–76
Stern N (1997) The transition in Eastern Europe and the former Soviet Union: some strategic lessons from the experience of 25 countries over six years
Stock JH, Yogo M (2005) Testing for weak instruments in linear IV regression. In: Identification and inference for econometric models : essays in honor of Thomas Rothenberg. Cambridge University Press, Cambridge, pp 80–120
The World Bank (2016) National accounts: output and expenditure. http://econ.worldbank.org/WBSITE/EXTERNAL/DATASTATISTICS/0,print:Y~isCURL:Y~contentMDK:20451590~menuPK:64133152~pagePK:64133150~piPK:64133175~theSitePK:239419,00.html
Thursby JG (1982) Misspecification, heteroscedasticity, and the chow and Goldfeld-Quandt tests. Rev Econ Stat 64(2):314
UNCTAD (2003) World investment report: FDI policies for development: national and international perspectives. United Nations, New York. ISBN: 92-1-112580-4
UNCTAD (2004) World investment report: the shift towards services. United Nations, New York. ISBN: 92-1-112644-4
UNCTAD (2016c) UNCTADstat: Foreign direct investment: inward and outward flows and stock, annual, 1970–2015 Table summary. http://unctadstat.unctad.org/wds/TableViewer/tableView.aspx?ReportId=96740
UNCTAD (2016d) UNCTADstat: Gross domestic product: total and per capita, current and constant (2005) prices, annual, 1970–2015. http://unctadstat.unctad.org/wds/TableViewer/tableView.aspx?ReportId=96
Vernon R (1966) International investment and international trade in the product cycle. Q J Econ 80 (2):190–207
Wooldridge JM (2010) Econometric analysis of cross section and panel data. MIT Press, Cambridge, MA. ISBN: 9780262232586. http://search.ebscohost.com/login.aspx?direct=true&scope=site&db=nlebk&db=nlabk&AN=550663
Wooldridge JM (2012) Panel data models with heterogeneity and endogeneity: programme evaluation for policy analysis. https://www.ifs.org.uk/docs/wooldridge%20session%204.pdf
Wooldridge JM (2013) Introductory econometrics: a modern approach. South-Western Cengage Learning, Mason, OH. ISBN: 978-1-111-53104-1

Chapter 5
Summary and Conclusions

5.1 Summary of the Findings

After the fall of Communism in 1991, post-soviet countries started integrating dynamically into the world economy and the EU in particular. An important premise behind European economic integration was the belief that unification of European economies would allow international companies to access bigger markets. This would make these companies more efficient, and in turn, would allow them to reduce prices, raise quality and gain competitiveness in external markets.

Indeed, FDI has increased strongly over the last 25 years in the CEECs. As a whole, these countries have accumulated $6,8 trillion of FDI since 1990. Accession to the EU has stimulated investors' confidence, and contributed to those countries' economic development. However, integration aside, numerous other factors continue to influence FDI inflow in the CEECs. This is why it is difficult to assess whether integration is the most important determinant of a country's attractiveness.

This book has explored the principal economic and political determinants of FDI inflow in CEE for the period 1992–2015, focussing on the effects of integration on FDI.

In Chap. 2 we have shown that patterns of FDI inflow varied significantly among the studied countries during the selected period. Descriptive data indicates that FDI is higher in larger countries with improved political stability, and anticipated EU membership. The responsiveness of FDI on integration of CEE with the EU shows similarities to the integration effect on FDI in prior to accession countries.

However, it is difficult to identify the most important factors that influence the decision to invest in a particular country based only on observations of the main trends within the statistics. For this reason, in Sect. 2.3, we investigated the empirical literature on the subject. In general, empirical studies on FDI identified market size, labour costs, exchange rate and exchange rate volatility, regional integration, openness to trade, infrastructure, government stability, and privatisation progress as the main factors that affect FDI.

H. Makhavikova, *Determinants of FDI in Central and Eastern Europe*,
Contributions to Economics, https://doi.org/10.1007/978-3-319-91878-5_5

However, due to broad differences in perspectives, methodologies, sample selection, and analytical tools, the existing literature showed no consensus on the widely accepted sets of determinants of FDI inflow. Moreover, on different stages of transformation and integration, and for different countries, factors such as privatisation, labour cost, natural resources endowments and market size were either more or less significant. On the whole, the effects of regional economic integration on FDI inflow has received more empirical attention than theoretical analysis.

It is for this reason that we constructed a theoretical model in the **third chapter** that helps us to organise our thinking on the FDI determinants in CEE after closer integration into the EU. The theoretical framework highlights differences between two modes of entry—FDI and exports—connected with the fall of intra-regional trade barriers.

We started by considering the basic model offered by Neary (2002) which studies location choices in homogenous countries, and examined three scenarios: equal external and internal trade barriers, regional preferential trade agreements, and zero trading costs between member countries. Further, we implemented these three scenarios for heterogeneous countries with different market sizes, external tariffs, labour and installation costs and analysed how changed market characteristics influence the previous findings. Finally, we derived a FDI model.

In our model, FDI appears in two cases; when a firm avoids high external trade barriers, or when a firm installs an inside plant to supply the other members of the integration union.

The first case is called the *tariff-jumping* motive. It appears when a foreign firm decides to supply a host country from a local plant, rather than paying trade costs. In this case, protective trade barriers favour FDI over exporting.

The second case is the *export platform* motive. It appears once the internal tariffs fall, and a multinational is allowed to export to the other member-countries of the integration union at reduced internal tariffs. Thus, the integration reduces the tariff-jumping motive (to establish more than one plant in the union market), however, it increases the intent to establish an export-platform.

A final implication of this strategy is that the same firm engages in both exports and FDI, albeit not across the same frontier. Hence exports and FDI become complementary rather than substitutes for each other.

In the example with heterogeneous countries, we found that when a preferential or free-trade area is formed, firms from outside the region are motivated to move their production to the integrated bloc because the benefit of preferential market access is exclusive to inside firms. However, the impact is not equal across countries. Countries that have access to bigger markets are more likely to attract greater FDI inflow. Moreover, foreign investors are more likely to concentrate in countries with relatively low production and installation costs.

The results explain why we should observe a changing pattern of FDI inflow during integration.

The main finding of Chap. 3 is that our FDI model can be estimated empirically.

Thus, based on the formulation of a theoretical model in the third chapter, we presented the estimation strategy and explanation of empirical results in Chap. 4.

The main objective of the chapter was to empirically identify the factors that affected FDI location in CEE.

We employed panel data models to the CEE members and candidate countries of the EU during the period 1992–2015. The countries covered were Albania, Bosnia and Herzegovina, Bulgaria, Croatia, the Czech Republic, Estonia, Georgia, Hungary, Latvia, Lithuania, Moldova, Montenegro, Poland, Romania, Serbia, Slovakia, Slovenia, TFYR Macedonia, and Ukraine. There are 440 observations in unbalanced panel.

In our paper, we analyse and present consistent estimators for three basic models of panel data; the OLS model, the fixed effects model, and the random effects model. Relying on the Hausman test, the FE model is used to test various variable combinations. We accounted for heterogeneity and endogeneity by employing 2SLS and GMM estimators with FE.

Our empirical results are similar to those of the previous research. The estimation of the empirical equation suggests that international investments are mainly determined by host country characteristics such as market size, labour cost, agglomeration, and access to large markets. Our supplementary specifications also mark out GCF, GDP growth rates and integration dummies as important determinants of FDI.

The size of the domestic market is the most significant factor attracting FDI inflow to the new members of the EU and candidate countries. These results suggest that in future, countries such as Albania, Bosnia and Herzegovina and Moldova, which are relatively smaller than most CEECs may have problems in attracting foreign investment. This may be due to the small potential demand and the fact that their purchasing power is also low. Countries with such features may become less desirable for foreign investors interested in market-seeking FDI.

The empirical component of the book provides results that are in line with the theoretical model's predictions. A strong positive impact of the market-access variables on FDI indicates that improved market accessibility within an integrated region leads to an increase in multinationals' activities. This shows an implicit and rarely mentioned benefit of smaller countries (such as Albania, Bosnia and Herzegovina, and Moldova) joining regional agreements. The effect is however, highly asymmetric across integrated countries. Within an integrated region, countries with cheaper labour costs (Moldova, Georgia and Ukraine) will attract more multinationals because wages appear with a negative sign.

Thus, our empirical estimations confirm our assumptions.

Our supplementary specifications also identified the relative importance of institutional factors. We found that the announcement of EU membership had a positive impact on inward FDI. These dummy variables revealed the influence of EU rules on FDI patterns. They show the extent that the ensuing institutional commitment has driven foreign investors searching for political and institutional stability to establish domestic affiliates in CEE. From this perspective, countries implementing EU accession regulations enforced by market economy policies successfully acquire EU membership earlier, which further speeds up FDI and leads to more growth and development. On the other hand, countries implementing EU regulations poorly are further from prospective membership, which may discourage FDI inflows.

In our book, we also include estimations for four distinct sub-regions: Eight Central European countries, South-East European countries, the Western Balkans, and three former members of the Soviet Union (Ukraine, Moldova, and Georgia). It is an important supplementary test because, for instance, the factors driving FDI to the Western Balkans differ from those that drive FDI to Central Europe.

By distinguishing between different sub-samples, this study provides further evidence that the importance of diverse location factors is not significantly different across the four groups of countries, but crucially they differ between them.

5.2 Academic Contributions and Policy Implications

Some of the findings of this book can be viewed as significant academic contributions to the debate about FDI, regional integration, and the European Union.

The findings of Chap. 2 explain why previous empirical research failed to clarify the role of European integration in determining FDI inflows. The main limitation of previous studies was the absence of a full set of all stages of integration. Therefore, in this chapter we considered all existing integration agreements between the CEECs and the EU, taking into account the sequence and associated institutional changes.

In general, the literature review shows that the relationship between economic integration and FDI inflow has been scarcely theoretically explored thus far.

This is why our theoretical model presented in Chap. 3 can be viewed as a significant contribution to the understanding of the process of integration and its influence on FDI.

Using the theoretical model of Neary (2002), we contribute to these strands of literature by examining the interplay of country asymmetry. This is achieved by including the differences in external trade barriers and market size as well as set-up and wage costs in determining multinationals' location decisions. This model explains the motives of FDI in the integrating region. Our model provides theoretical evidence concerning the hypothesis that FDI location may be central not only to traditional FDI location determinants, but also to changes associated with the building of the integration union.

These findings convey an important message for host-country policy makers—that changes in investment or trade policies will affect the volume of foreign direct investment. For example, an increase in tariffs within the integrating region, in fact, stimulates FDI.

However, the most important contribution is that we derived a FDI model from our theoretical model with the heterogeneous countries, that can be estimated empirically. We found that characteristics both of a country and an integration union should be included into an empirical model to get reliable results. Thus, we include in our empirical model novel factors that measure the full market size of an integration region. The factors account for additional opportunities that arise when countries reduce intraregional trade barriers.

Chapter 4 reduces the inconclusiveness of the empirical evidence regarding the contribution of European integration to FDI inflow in the CEECs. This is achieved by covering all Central and Eastern European countries where a large discrepancy between economic development levels in attracting FDI exists. Indeed, former research findings do not cover all countries participating in European integration, thus, the former results obtained do not represent a full picture of the influence of integration upon FDI inflow.

Our empirical evidence is broadly consistent with the theoretical expectations. Large market size, low labour costs and access to large markets are the determinants of FDI.

The empirical analysis suggests that the results may have clear implications. The CEE region is known as a supplier of cheap labour, and may therefore be of some interest to a number of investment projects. Efforts should be focused on the implementation of structural reforms capable of generating the necessary conditions to resource-seeking FDI.

The results confirm the importance of improved market access and falling intra-regional trade costs for attracting export-platform FDI. Regional arrangements can give a small country a marginal advantage over other similar small countries in attracting direct investment, because they obtain marginally more favourable access to a large market than other non-participating small countries.

Higher restrictions on international trade may stimulate the appearance of "tariff-jumping" FDI. This also can be considered as a policy option.

The significant results regarding institutional variables can help policy makers to realise the importance of institutions to foreign investors, and therefore give institutional reform a higher priority when formulating their policy options for attracting FDI.

Thus, we grounded and identified key components of the success of the leading CEE countries in the mobilisation of FDI.

The successful experience of the balanced investment policy, and other measures that promoted the inflow and effective application of FDI in the leading CEE countries, may be used by other CEE countries in the development of their policies. This information can also be used to estimate the impact of the prospective additional Eastern expansion of the EU upon FDI inflow by the countries currently not within the EU. Thus, the results of the research may also be of interest to public and private organisations, and companies involved in investment cooperation with foreign partners, including the countries of Central and Eastern Europe.

5.3 Limitations of the Study

This book has addressed some major limitations of previous research in terms of the theoretical and empirical approaches used. An effort has been made to make the book systemic and scientific, however, there are still limitations within this study.

Firstly, there are some **limitations within our modelling**. In our model, we do not allow new firms to enter our economic system. There is only the supplier in this industry, thus, there is no competition between firms. This situation is quite unrealistic, because improved market conditions stimulate appearance of new firms and competition in well-performing industries.

Moreover, when there is competition between local and foreign firms, both have their own advantages. For instance, local firms are more familiar with local peculiarities of business management and law, whereas foreign firms have better access to foreign capital sources, high technologies and international standards of business.

In our model, we do not distinguish between tariffs on different goods. This is a significant limitation of our model because tariffs may differ wildly in different branches of the economy (in agriculture, manufacturing or service sectors). Moreover, integration agreements often allow free trade in limited sectors. An example is AAs which allow free trade in manufacturing but not in the agriculture sector. This assumption was made primarily because of a lack of data. We are not able to differentiate between the host sectors, thus, we are not able to determine which sectors attract more FDI during different stages of integration.

For the same reason, we do not consider the source of FDI inflow, and therefore cannot identify whether integration shifts FDI from the EU-15 to the associated countries, or attracts FDI from the rest of the World. We also do not distinguish between types of FDI—M&As or Greenfield—different types of investment might hold different attraction factors. Answering these questions would likely shed additional light on the empirical relationship between regional integration and FDI.

Finally, there are some **limitations to our data** which can lead to statistic bias.

The flow data in the publication of UNCTAD World Investment Reports is compiled from statistical sources from each country. Data provided for the CEECs are collected from central banks and from published and unpublished national official FDI data. For those economies for which data was not available from national official sources, or for those for which data were not available for the entire period, data is obtained from other sources (International Monetary Fund (IMF), the World Bank and the Organisation for Economic Co-operation and Development (OECD), etc.) (UNCTAD 2016).

For the most part, FDI inflow data is based on company surveys, however, Bulgaria provides data partially based on direct reporting. Moreover, some countries, for example, Hungary, introduced a methodological change in the recording and publishing of data on FDI flows and stock during the studied period (UNCTAD 2016).

Furthermore, the measurement of FDI inflow also differs between countries. FDI flows are measured in market value in Czech Republic, Latvia, but in book value in Romania. Lithuania uses market price for listed companies and book value for non-listed companies, whereas Moldova takes book value and market value for listed enterprises (UNCTAD 2016).

Hence, although the best data available, the differences in measurement of FDI flow results in the approximation of FDI data.

5.4 Areas for Further Research

There are many promising avenues for future research which should be explored. From the standpoint of theory, it is necessary to study more carefully the heterogeneity of countries. It might be useful to relax the assumption that there is no entry of additional firms, particularly in response to market growth, and to consider the effect of increasing the number of insiders and outsiders to study the competition effect.

It might also be interesting to investigate whether the location of FDI in CEE affects the exports of CEE to third countries and the EU. We can expect a production shift effect to arise, as production is relocated from countries with relative expensive production costs to countries with relative cheap production costs.

Further work is needed to explore other implications of regional integration on FDI that consider not only the fall of trade barriers between countries, but also changes in factor and installation costs.

Finally, the analysis should be embedded in general equilibrium to investigate the implications of trade liberalisation on income and factor costs in individual member countries, and also in the union as a whole, after firms' location decisions are made.

In carrying out the empirical analysis, a crucial problem consistently encountered was the lack of adequate data on a range of issues. The FDI data used in Chaps. 2 and 4 is not classified according to type, source and sector. As more data for the developing countries appears, future research could possibly gain new insight into the relationship between FDI and integration.

In summary, we hope we have been able to provide a coherent framework to present the wide body of literature on the subject of FDI determinants. We also hope that this book sheds some light on the influence of European integration upon the attractiveness of the CEECs for foreign investors. We note that there are still areas which are severely under-researched. To close this gap, a joint effort is necessary, involving theoretical analysis, new empirical studies and the development of databases.

References

Neary JP (2002) Foreign direct investment and the single market. Manchester School 70 (3):291–314 https://ideas.repec.org/a/bla/manchs/v70y2002i3p291-314.html

UNCTAD (2016) Methodological note: world investment report 2016. http://unctad.org/en/PublicationChapters/wir2016chMethodNote_en.pdf

The manufacturer's authorised representative in the EU is Springer Nature Customer Service Centre GmbH, Europaplatz 3, 69115 Heidelberg, Germany. If you have any concerns regarding our products, please contact ProductSafety@springernature.com

Printed and bound by CPI Group (UK) Ltd, Croydon, CR0 4YY

25/09/2026

02222855-0004